DATE DUE

FORCED TO BE GOOD

FORCED TO BE GOOD

Why Trade Agreements Boost Human Rights

EMILIE M. HAFNER-BURTON

Cornell University Press
Ithaca and London

First published 2009 by Cornell University Press

Printed in the United States of America

Library of Congress Cataloging-in-Publication Data

Hafner-Burton, Emilie.
  Forced to be good : why trade agreements boost human rights
/ Emilie M. Hafner-Burton.
      p. cm.
  Includes bibliographical references and index.
  ISBN 978-0-8014-4643-6 (cloth : alk. paper)
  1. Tariff preferences—Social aspects. 2. Commercial treaties—
Social aspects. 3. International trade—Social aspects. 4. Human
rights—Economic aspects. I. Title.

  HF1721.H24 2009
  323—dc22   2008040971

Cornell University Press strives to use environmentally responsible suppliers and materials to the fullest extent possible in the publishing of its books. Such materials include vegetable-based, low-VOC inks and acid-free papers that are recycled, totally chlorine-free, or partly composed of nonwood fibers. For further information, visit our website at www.cornellpress.cornell.edu.

Cloth printing   10 9 8 7 6 5 4 3 2 1

To Kris

CONTENTS

Acknowledgments ix

Abbreviations xi

Introduction 1

Chapter 1. Forced to Be Good 4

Chapter 2. A Path to Answers 23

Chapter 3. Preferences 48

Chapter 4. Institutions 84

Chapter 5. Power 115

Chapter 6. Effects 142

Chapter 7. The Future 165

Appendix 175

References 181

Index 211

ACKNOWLEDGMENTS

I am grateful to the many people and institutions that have helped me to write this book. Nuffield College at Oxford University, the Center for International Security and Cooperation at Stanford University, and the Woodrow Wilson School for Public and International Affairs and the Department of Politics at Princeton University provided me with invaluable support during the writing of this book. I would especially like to thank Helen Milner and the Center for Globalization and Governance at Princeton University, Lynn Eden and the Center for International Security and Cooperation at Stanford University, and Jennifer Widner and the Mamdouha S. Bobst Center for Peace and Justice at Princeton University for their generous support at various stages in this project.

My sincere thanks go out to everyone who helped me by reading, listening, and critiquing my arguments, and especially to Dan Drezner, Helen Milner, Miles Kahler, Robert Keohane, Edward Mansfield, Sophie Meunier, Andrew Moravcsik, Jon Pevehouse, and Mark Pollack, who sat in a room with me for seven hours and told me how to write a better book. Thanks also to my reviewers, who were tremendously helpful.

I also extend my sincere thanks to Susan Aaronson, Suzanne Berger, Lorand Bartels, Joanne Gowa, Pieter Jan Kuyper, Walter Mattli, Frederik Mayer, Barry O'Neill, Jack Snyder, George Tsebelis, and Erik Voeten, who took the time to read and share comments on various portions of the book, as well as the many others who came to my assistance—in particular, Candice Cusack, Kathy Goldgeier, Rose Holendez, Gabriel Leon, Alexander Montgomery, and Daniel Scher.

A good deal of what I have learned while writing this book I have learned from the people I interviewed during the process—policymakers, academics, and interest group advocates—and to whom I am incredibly grateful. I could not have written this book without their help. Although their names remain anonymous, their guidance is visible all the way through the book, and I thank each one of them.

Finally, I extend my gratitude to Roger Haydon, the editor of this book, who has been supportive from day one and has helped me to make this book a reality.

ABBREVIATIONS

ACP	African, Caribbean, and Pacific group of countries
AFL-CIO	American Federation of Labor and Congress of Industrial Organizations
ALDE	Alliance of Liberals and Democrats for Europe
ANZUS	Security Treaty between Australia, New Zealand, and the United States
ASEAN	Association of Southeast Asian Nations
CAFTA	Central American Free Trade Agreement
COMESA	Common Market for Eastern and Southern Africa
CSCE	Commission on Security and Cooperation in Europe
EC	European Community
ECJ	European Court of Justice
EEA	European Economic Area
EEC	European Economic Community
EDF	European Development Fund
EFTA	European Free Trade Area
EP	European Parliament
EPP-ED	Group of the European People's Party and European Democrats
ETUC	European Trade Union Confederation
EU	European Union
FTAA	Free Trade Area of the Americas
GATT	General Agreement on Tariffs and Trade
GSP	Generalized System of Preferences
HRA	Human Rights Agreement
ICC	International Criminal Court

ICFTU	International Confederation of Free Trade Unions
ILO	International Labor Organization
IO	International Organization
ITO	International Trade Organization
MEP	Member of the European Parliament
MERCOSUR	Southern Common Market
MFN	Most favored nation
NAALC	North American Agreement on Labor Cooperation
NAFTA	North American Free Trade Agreement
NFTC	National Foreign Trade Council
NGO	Nongovernmental organization
OAS	Organization of American States
OECD	Organization for Economic Cooperation and Development
PTA	Preferential trade agreement
SEA	Single European Act
TEU	Treaty on the European Union
TPA	Trade Promotion Authority
UDHR	United Nations Universal Declaration on Human Rights
UNICE	Union of Industrial and Employers' Confederations of Europe
USCIB	United States Council for International Business
USITC	United States International Trade Commission
USTR	United States Trade Representative
WTO	World Trade Organization

FORCED TO BE GOOD

INTRODUCTION

Something is happening to global trade regulation. In the 1980s, the United States negotiated and signed what would become the first of several free trade agreements. These agreements, with Israel (1985) and Canada (1988), aimed to eliminate all duties and virtually all other restrictions on trade in goods between the countries. Neither agreement mentioned protecting people's well-being or their right to human dignity—the United States mentioned human rights only in one-way programs that gave other countries access to its market.

Decades later, the United States negotiated and signed free trade agreements with Chile (2003), Singapore (2003), Australia (2004), Morocco (2004), and Bahrain (2004). These agreements again sought to remove tariffs and quotas on goods. But they also obliged governments to protect workers' and children's human rights in domestic law. Under the agreements, all members, even the United States, could now be fined for violating these human rights.

This regulatory shift is not a uniquely American experience. Across the Atlantic, in 1975, the nine member states of the European Community (EC) signed the first trade-regulating Lomé Convention with nearly fifty African, Caribbean, and Pacific countries (ACP), most of them former Belgian, British, Dutch, or French colonies. For countries such as Chad, Liberia, and the Solomon Islands, the agreement established trade preferences for many exports to Europe and provided for European aid and investment. Many ACP governments beat, tortured, or murdered their citizens, but the agreement never said a word about protecting human rights. Neither did Europe's subsequent trade agreements with Algeria (1976) or Syria (1977).

More than two decades later, the fifteen member states of the EC and almost eighty ACP countries signed the Cotonou Convention, an agreement that provided a new framework for trade cooperation and development aid. This time, respect for human rights, democratic principles, and the rule of law were essential elements of the trade partnership. Violators could be fined or cut off entirely. New trade and cooperation agreements with Kazakhstan (1999), Bangladesh (2000), and South Africa (2004) did the same. A similar agreement with Iraq is under negotiation in 2008.

What happened to make possible these so-called fair trade regulations that protect human rights? Many policymakers, businesses, and activists have reviled the new standards of conduct protecting human rights, calling them either too strong or too weak. So why did Americans and Europeans, each in their own way, come to sign mutually binding trade agreements that safeguard people's rights and even impose penalties for violations? If human rights are indivisible and universal, why do American trade agreements focus exclusively on protecting human rights for workers and children, whereas European agreements center mostly on protecting human rights for voters and citizens? Most countries shy away from agreements that meddle in their domestic affairs. So why do other governments, especially the repressive ones, sign these regulations even though the restrictions ostensibly run counter to their leaders' interests and may very well be bad economics? The effects such agreements have on human rights practices are also unknown. Do these trade agreements regulating human rights matter at all for the politics of repression?

Different people offer different answers. One answer is government protection, driven by policymakers working inside the United States and Europe who want to appease domestic interest groups seeking to squelch international competition and soften the blows from globalization. In this view, policymakers use the human rights idiom as cover to satisfy labor unions and their supporters. Another answer is the power of global-norm advocates. In this view, activist nongovernmental organizations (NGOs) and citizens prompt policymakers to embrace, or at least acknowledge, universal human rights norms about the appropriate way to conduct business. Still another is that certain American and European trade partners and their leaders or interest groups, searching for ways to strengthen democracy and human rights at home, use these trade policies to make credible commitments to protect human rights.

This book examines how and why global norms for social justice, such as human rights, become international regulations linked to seemingly unrelated issues, such as trade. It is not a conventional account. Norms and their embrace by NGO advocates do not explain why American and European governments are choosing to employ preferential trade agreements to protect human rights of people. Most of these regulations protecting human rights correspond with global moral principles and laws when they serve policymakers' interests in accumulating power or resources or solving other problems. Otherwise, demands by moral advocates are tossed aside. Labor unions' demands have shaped the policy process, but these demands also do not fully explain the way policymakers design trade regulations. Countries do make credible commitments to policy, but such promises are rare when it comes to human rights. Most governments that sign on to these trade regulations totally oppose them and have no intention of putting the regulations into practice.

These shortcomings typically result from one of three scenarios: policymakers are not always convinced by what labor unions or NGOs want; when they are convinced, they may not have the ability to translate their convictions into policy at home; and when they have the ability, their government may not succeed in convincing others to sign on. This is because the rules of trade (which this book aims to explain) are influenced not only by the problems these policymakers face, which influence their preferences for a solution (the subject of chapter 3), but also by the rules that guide their collective choices (chapter 4's theme) and the capabilities of other countries with which they seek cooperation (examined in chapter 5). Thus, the trade policies that are put into place often depart in considerable ways from what interest groups want, even when it seems that NGO or labor union demands have led obviously to regulation. Nonetheless, preferential trade agreements that commit members to protect human rights can prevent some abuses or encourage incremental reforms that help to safeguard people's lives and rights, even though this was not the intent of the agreements (the subject of chapter 6).

What follows is an account of this extraordinary political conversion in the way governments manage trade—one that should spur new ways of thinking about how norms for social justice, such as protecting human rights, become woven into international regulation in seemingly unrelated policy areas, such as the economy, and whether it matters that they do.

CHAPTER 1

FORCED TO BE GOOD

By making trade conditional on respect for human beings' right to dignity, a few economically powerful countries are changing the politics of trade and also the politics of repression. They are pushing their human rights agenda one country at a time through the use of preferential trade agreements (PTAs). To date, a considerable number of these agreements promise to defend human rights of one kind or another, and some provide ways to enforce these promises. Many more agreements are in the process of negotiation.[1] Commerce, on the face of it, has never looked so principled.[2]

Why are the United States and Europe, once opposed to the idea, now regulating the protection of human rights through PTAs? Why does the design of these "fair" trade regulations vary considerably between the United States and Europe? Why are so many other countries, especially the abusive ones, subscribing to these trade regulations that seem diametrically opposed to their interests? And is any of this rule making helping to protect people's rights?

The reasons for these new regulations do not paint a rosy picture of how the global human rights movement has succeeded in earning universal respect

1. Beginning in 1999, Europe put into effect a temporary moratorium on new bilateral and regional negotiations aimed at concluding free trade agreements. Known as the "Lamy Doctrine," this policy was put into place to support negotiations during the Doha Round of WTO talks.

2. For an overview of American politics on trade and human rights, see Destler and Balint (1999), Elliot and Freeman (2003a, 2003b), and Drezner (2006). For legal histories and analyses of the European Union's human rights protections, see Fierro (2001, 2003) and Bartels (2005). See Howse and Mutua (2000), Howse (2002), and Petersmann (2003, 2004) on human rights in the WTO, and Porter et. al (2002) on efficiency, equity, and legitimacy in the WTO. See Tsogas (2000) and Reinhardt (2005) on the Generalized System of Preferences (GSP).

for people by spreading norms of justice. Nor are fair trade regulations merely the outcome of labor union pressures for them. Labor unions and NGOs sometimes influence what policymakers think and vote for, but they do not influence the rules for making policy or the global power politics that shape how trade agreements are made. The result is that powerful countries adopt bilateral and regional trade agreements that regulate human rights mainly to solve problems that have little, directly, to do with the protection of human rights. In this story, the end of the cold war was a turning point, and with it, changing geopolitical and economic circumstances have profoundly affected the politics of international human rights regulation and globalization. The United States and Europe have elevated human rights in preferential trade because the new regulations increasingly serve the interests of policymakers who have the power to veto and who use human rights to compete for influence over trade policy. At the same time, experiences on either side of the Atlantic have been considerably different— America's fair preferential trade regulations look nothing like Europe's.

A skeptic might wonder if these trade regulations are effective against repression or if they are just bits of cheap talk that defy enforcement and are never implemented. After all, the main argument of this book is that policymakers responsible for creating fair preferential trade rules in the United States and Europe have made them mostly to suit their own needs and purposes, seldom intending to help abused people elsewhere or to strengthen global norms. Their focus has most often, although not always, been on local or personal issues rather than on global or collective concerns. Yet trade rules are not all empty promises. The assortment of political institutions that have contributed to these policymakers' decisions has shaped not only the politics of trade regulation but also the politics of repression, in ways many policymakers never anticipated and some would prefer to avoid. Some fair trade regulations do make a difference insofar as they motivate governments to better protect people and to punish those who break the rules, even though their piecemeal implementation may not be good for global economics and was seldom expected by the people who created them (Hafner-Burton 2005).

The Friendly Face of Trade

Preferential trade agreements of various types are growing in popularity— hundreds are currently in force, and more are on the way.[3] On almost every

3. Preferential trade agreements include a diverse assortment of bilateral and regional agreements. They include nonreciprocal agreements, which offer one-way access of a country

continent, governments are establishing them to regulate access to markets, and while there is substantial disagreement about whether they enhance countries' welfare (De Santis and Vicarelli 2006; Frankel, Stein, and Wei 1997; Ozden and Reinhardt 2005; Schott 2004a), many agreements do fulfill their promise to bring some economic or political gains to their members, especially in the developing world (Baier and Bergstrade 2005; Whalley 1996).[4]

When the International Bill of Human Rights[5] took effect in 1976, no PTAs said anything about protecting the rights of people or enforcing those rights through the suspension of agreements. Today, rules about human dignity have become a legitimate domain of commerce to be regulated through preferential trade agreements almost everywhere. PTAs govern various types of human rights in more than one hundred and fifty countries at present, supplying rhetoric and rules linking markets to standards protecting people's human rights.[6] These are standards continually dismissed by the World Trade Organization (WTO), which says little about protecting human beings.[7] The United States has signed free trade agreements promoting human rights for workers and children with almost two

---

or party to the negotiated market of another country or trading entity; free trade areas, which prohibit internal tariffs among members, although each member country keeps its own external tariff policies; customs unions, which are free trade areas with common external tariff policies on goods imported from countries outside the union; common markets, which are customs unions with removal of restrictions on the free flow of capital, labor, and technology among members; and even economic unions (Balassa 1961). In the European context, they include partnership and cooperation agreements, association agreements, trade and cooperation agreements, and stabilization and cooperation agreements, among many other sorts.

4. For instance, Baier and Bergstrade (2005) estimate that, on average, free trade agreements between two countries increase trade by 86 percent in the first fifteen years. For an opposing view, see Frankel, Stein, and Wei (1997).

5. The International Bill of Human Rights consists of the Universal Declaration of Human Rights, the International Covenant on Economic, Social and Cultural Rights, and the International Covenant on Civil and Political Rights and its two optional protocols.

6. On linkage, see Oye (1979) and Stein (1980).

7. Western liberal countries have long tried to raise fair trade issues during multilateral trade negotiations. Developing countries have almost universally resisted, worried that such standards would be used to disguise protectionism for developed markets. Since 1996, countries of the WTO have agreed that human rights regulations do not belong in the doctrine of multilateral trade and should be governed by their own parallel institutions. Paragraph 4 of the WTO First Ministerial Declaration, adopted in Singapore in December 1996, declares: "We renew our commitment to the observance of internationally recognized core labour standards. The International Labour Organisation (ILO) is the competent body to set and deal with these standards, and we affirm our support for its work in promoting them." Available from http://www.wto.org/english/thewto_e/minist_e/min96_e/wtodec_e.htm. The compromise was upheld in Seattle (1999), Doha (2001), and Cancun (2003). See Howse and Mutua (2000); Howse (2002); Bartels (2007). Article XX of the GATT agreement provides for exceptional treatment only in the case of goods manufactured by prisoners.

dozen countries, and several more agreements are being negotiated. Europe has signed trade agreements protecting fundamental human rights and freedoms with more than one hundred countries, and still more are under way. Many of these rules are enforceable through trade penalties.[8]

What do these regulations look like? The US free trade agreement with Singapore, which took effect in 2004, is one example. This agreement obliges parties to "strive to ensure" that human rights—in particular, the right of association; the right to organize and bargain collectively; labor protections for children; and acceptable minimum wages, hours of work, and safe health conditions—"are recognized and protected by domestic law" (Article 17.1). It requires that both the United States and Singapore effectively enforce these laws and promote public awareness of them (Articles 17.2, 17.3). To further advance common commitments to the protection of people's rights, the trade agreement establishes a Labor Cooperation Mechanism (Annex 17A), procedures for consultation, and a joint committee to oversee implementation (Article 17.4). Similar agreements are in force with Canada and Mexico (1994), Jordan (2001), Chile (2004), Australia (2005), Bahrain (2006), Morocco (2006), and Costa Rica, the Dominican Republic, El Salvador, Honduras, and Nicaragua (2006). These agreements all regulate the protection of workers' and children's human rights in some fashion. Agreements with Oman and Peru will soon enter into force, and negotiations have been concluded but are pending approval with Colombia, Panama, and the Republic of Korea. The United States is also negotiating agreements with Malaysia, Thailand, South Africa and Swaziland, the UAE, and others.

The United States is not alone. Europe's Cotonou Convention with the African, Caribbean, and Pacific group of countries (ACP), which took effect in 2003, is another example.[9] The trade agreement commits "Parties [to] undertake to promote and protect all fundamental freedoms and human rights" (Articles 9, 13, 26). These principles are supported through a political dialogue designed to share information, to cultivate mutual understanding, and to facilitate the formation of shared priorities, including those concerning respect for human rights (Article 8). Obligations are binding on all participants. They are supported by a review mechanism established in the consultation procedures (Article 96), which requires reg-

8. For a discussion of how PTAs enforce human rights and which ones do so, see Hafner-Burton (2005) and Miller (2004) and chapter 6 of this book.

9. As this book goes to print, the Cotonou waiver from the WTO is about to expire. The European Union and the African, Caribbean, and Pacific Countries (ACP) have agreed to put in place new economic partnership agreements that aim at progressively removing barriers to trade and enhancing cooperation in all areas related to trade.

ular assessments of national developments concerning human rights. Alongside the agreement are conditional financial protocols allocating resources available to eligible countries through the European Development Fund. When members are perceived to have violated agreement terms, a variety of actions can be taken to influence behavior. These include the threat or act of withdrawal of membership or financial protocols, as well as the enforcement of economic or political sanctions. European regulations protecting human rights, with various standards for implementation, are in force in PTAs with Argentina (1990), Paraguay (1992), Macao (1992), Bulgaria (1993), Morocco (1995), Vietnam (1995), Israel (1995), Kazakhstan (1999), and the former Yugoslav Republic of Macedonia (2001), among many other agreements. More are being negotiated.

Fair Trade Is News

Human rights have long been an aim of foreign policy for Western countries (Forsythe 2000; Mertus 2004; Sikkink 2004). Not so long ago, though, human rights were purposely excluded from most international commercial agreements made by the United States or Europe.[10] When they were invoked, standards for protecting human rights were typically linked to unilateral trade preference programs, such as the Generalized System of Preferences (GSP) offered by the United States or Europe, or to national or subnational laws (Aaronson and Zimmerman 2007), which place no obligations on either the United States or Europe to protect human rights at all. Most fair trade PTAs, by contrast, now go both ways, creating shared obligations between countries to protect human rights. In these agreements, standards of conduct for protecting human rights have only recently been incorporated—gradually since 1994 in the United States and almost universally here since 2002; gradually in Europe since 1990 and almost universally there since 1995.

Most agreements also offer market and political incentives. Although PTAs have limited economic consequences for the United States and Europe, offering mainly opportunities for political influence abroad, they promise most other member countries considerable benefits. Preferential access to American and European markets may strengthen these countries' security assurances and boost their bargaining power in multilateral trade

10. Although their approach to reciprocal PTAs is new, both the United States and Europe have histories of unilaterally linking social justice issues to matters of trade, aid, and development, discussed in chapter 3.

negotiations (US Congressional Budget Office 2003; Whalley 1996). They may also provide economic benefits. Carla Hills, the former US trade representative under President George H. W. Bush, makes a convincing case:

> [E]ven on the small agreements like [the] Jordan [Free Trade Agreement], there are benefits, because Jordan is much more likely to adopt reforms as a result of that agreement, to move their reforms forward. Their liberalization is locked in, and they move forward. They've opened up their economy, and as a result, they have created some 40,000 jobs. And their exports have gone up. So there is something positive. Put it in . . . on the ledger sheet as things political instead of economic, but it's economic to that country. (Hills 2005)

Twenty years ago, preferential trade agreements with enforceable regulations protecting human rights were virtually unthinkable—only a few unilateral schemes said anything about human rights. Today, alongside the WTO, these regulations are a growing feature of global trade, for better or worse.

Four Questions

This book asks four questions about the rise of PTAs that regulate human rights. The first is why powerful governments wanted to change the face of market integration in the first place. The United States and Europe were once opposed to linking human rights to their preferential trade agreements, especially the mutually binding ones. Why did they eventually decide to create and promote new regulations protecting human rights in their PTAs? Why did they make these regulations a matter of binding law, ensuring that future agreements, with any country, would include some protections for people's human rights? In the United States, the now-expired Trade Act of 2002 required that all future trade agreements negotiated under the act include human rights protections, whereas in Europe, similar requirements were made in 1995 and are still in force today.[11] Were the United States and Europe motivated by labor unions or NGOs? Did they

11. Some American and European unilateral preference schemes also include human rights protections. For instance, the United States adopted the GSP Renewal Act of 1984, which included a clause linking a country's benefits status to the protections of workers' human rights. See Compa and Vogt (2005). In Europe, since 1995, a special unilateral incentives program has also been made available to reward compliance with ILO Conventions 87 (the freedom of association), 98 (the right to organize and to bargain collectively), and 138

do it out of moral principle? Did other countries convince them to do it? And why didn't they use institutions already designed explicitly to govern human rights, such as the International Labor Organization (ILO) or the United Nations (UN)? Why didn't they use the WTO?

The second question is why powerful liberal governments have approached this process so differently. PTA regulations emerged around the same time in the United States and Europe, but the United States and Europe designed rules that are vastly different. Why? In particular, why have the Americans taken up preferential trade protections of human rights for children and workers to the exclusion of other kinds of protections, such as standards of conduct outlawing murder or torture? Why have the Europeans designed their PTAs to protect mainly the human rights of voters and citizens but said less about workers until recently, mostly regulating standards of conduct for the protection of workers' rights through unilateral trade schemes instead?[12] And why do some PTAs create strong penalties for violating the human rights provisions while others hardly put them in force?

(child labor). Unlike PTAs, neither program places any conditions or restrictions on American or European human rights behavior.

12. Some have argued that workers' human rights are implicit in the broader category of "human rights" adopted by the European Community, citing the UN Vienna Declaration and Program of Action (1993), which acknowledges that "all human rights are universal, indivisible and interdependent and interrelated." This argument is not convincing. The European Union explicitly recognizes and regulates workers' human rights in its unilateral GSP, establishing precedent for use of the term "labor" in conjunction with human rights standards in trade relations. The use of the term in the GSP agreement but not in other PTAs is thus peculiar and certainly not accidental. Quite a few of my interview sources inside the European Commission, Council, and Parliament have confirmed that negotiations over whether or not to include explicit labor language in the European Union's human rights trade clause have long been taking place and are contentious, with considerable disagreement among member states over whether labor should be regulated through PTAs, the WTO, the ILO or the European Union (Interview record #37 2004; Interview record #50 2004). Although this link to protecting workers' human rights should be explicit according to some decision makers in the European Union, it is effectively part of a gray policy area and has not been at the forefront of the political agenda (Interview record #43 2004). The strongest links today have been made in DG trade rather than in external relations or development, advocated particularly by Commissioner Lamy after the 1999 Seattle riots protesting against the WTO. A 2001 Communication on Social Governance committed the European Union to the promotion of labor standards through the ILO rather than through PTAs. See European Commission (2001). Today a few European trade agreements do offer explicit protections for workers' rights, requiring their trade partners to enforce the core standards of the ILO. See Aaronson and Zimmerman (2007). Most, however, still say nothing in particular about workers, focusing instead on fundamental human rights and freedoms, with an emphasis on enforcement for core civil and political rights. For an analysis of the GSP system in Europe, see Bartels (2003).

The third question ponders the motivations of the other countries. Given that many governments in the world openly condemn the very idea of making trade agreements that regulate human rights and disagree over whether to protect workers or people more generally, why have so many repressive and otherwise resistant governments joined PTAs that are expressly designed to punish them? Why do other democracies that already protect human rights resist making these regulations? And why do governments that openly reject human rights regulations in the WTO accept these standards in bilateral or regional trade agreements with the United States or Europe?

The final question is whether any of this lawmaking has any effect on the politics of repression or on the lives of people. In the face of widespread opposition from policymakers and businesses, especially in the United States but also in Europe, as well as from governments all over the world, do these agreements ever help to protect people? Do they stop or prevent human rights violations? Or are they all just cheap talk?

Obvious Answers?

Readers might be surprised that fair preferential trade regulations protecting human rights are being made at all. By many accounts, human rights standards of conduct, enforced through PTAs, are not in the world's economic interest, and trade protectionism does more harm than good to global economic welfare. Trade policies benefit people most when they are global and nondiscriminatory, when countries are free from too many political limitations imposed by regulators (Ricardo [1817] 1996). Standard economic treatments continue to show that protectionism is costly, often putting policies in place that support inefficient firms and their highly unionized labor forces (Bhagwati 1988, 1991; Hufbauer, Berliner, and Elliot 1986). From this vantage point, the fact that governments use issues such as human rights or environmental protections to regulate markets is perceived at its most benign as a distraction and at its most insidious as a new form of regulatory hazard (Destler and Balint 1999).

This book does not argue about the global economics of fair PTA regulations; rather, it aims to explain why these regulations aimed at protecting human rights, perhaps harmful to global trade, have emerged and spread anyway. The most common and intuitive accounts emphasize policymakers' preferences. Trade policies are often explained mainly by what influential interest groups want, which is shaped by whether these groups stand to gain or lose from the policies in question (Frieden 1992). Trade protection

is an area where interest groups have been especially visible, lobbying policymakers, who sell protectionist trade regulations to interest groups that
can afford to buy them with campaign contributions, public displays of
conviction, or information (Grossman and Helpman 1994, 1995). Here the
explanation lies with labor unions and protesters seeking personal cover for
the ills they associate with globalization; these interest groups are changing how policymakers manage the global economy by spurring PTAs that
regulate issues such as human rights as a way to protect their own interests
(Aaronson and Zimmerman 2007).

Another answer credits the rise and spread of moral norms and activism with the potential for a global revolution in markets. Here the rise
and spread of the human rights regime explains why the Americans and
Europeans are increasingly linking human justice and dignity to market
access and assistance (Meyer et al. 1997; Thomas et al. 1987). Countries,
even the powerful ones, are being acculturated, socialized, or taught to
want and do certain things by the international society in which they
operate, one that is increasingly defined as much by the principled idea of
human rights as by trade liberalization (Finnemore 1996; Goodman and
Jinks 2003a).

A related answer draws attention to norm entrepreneurs—usually
NGOs—and their vital role in shaping countries' and policymakers' actions, beliefs, and interests. Moral entrepreneurs are people with strong
ideas about appropriate behavior in a community; it is hard to talk about
their motivations without reference to "empathy," "altruism," and "ide-
ational commitment" (Finnemore and Sikkink 1998, 898; Boli and Thomas
1999; Sikkink and Smith 2002). Here the growth and success of Western
human rights NGOs explains why the Americans and Europeans are now
linking human rights to trade in ways that affect policy outcomes. Western
NGOs—motivated by principled ideas and global norms—are encouraging powerful countries and their leaders to recognize the dangers of globalization and to make protecting human beings a policy priority, not because there is money to be made but because it is the right thing to do.

Still another explanation is that governments or interest groups in other
parts of the world are the cause. Perhaps the Americans and Europeans
made human rights a trade priority because NGOs in other countries
sought help from the international community to bring pressure from outside, launching international action that would lead to internal human
rights reforms (Keck and Sikkink 1998). Or perhaps leaders in the West
chose to promote human rights regulations because trade partners in the
developing world asked them to create international laws to lock in political
reforms in countries where uncertainty about the future of social justice,

the protection of human rights, and democracy is high (Moravcsik 2000; Pevehouse 2005).

These answers all seem persuasive, and all have merit. Interest groups, norms, and political uncertainty are all factors in policymakers' decisions about regulating markets, and all are features of the plot offered here. But these factors are not definitive explanations, and the answers are less obvious than they first appear. Policymakers' preferences for fair preferential trade regulations come from many sources, and preferences do not paint a full picture of the rise, spread, and results of a new kind of trade regulation. The story about how norms of social justice become matters for economic regulation inevitably leads to institutions and power.

Institutions and Power

The development of fair preferential trade regulations has its roots in the design and change of institutions, where contenders struggle for power and influence over policy. It begins with policymakers' incentives to solve cooperation problems within specific institutional settings and their power to shape policy relative to their partners in cooperation, both at home and abroad (Drezner 2007; Gilpin 1987; Gowa 1994; Grieco 1997; Haggard and Simmons 1987; Hirschman [1945] 1980; Ikenberry 2001; Keohane 1984, 1989; Krasner 1983; Milner 1997).

Yet the rules of trade (*policy outcomes*) are influenced not only by the problems these policymakers face and their resulting preferences for a solution (*preferences*) but also by the rules that guide their collective choices (*institutions*) and the capabilities of other countries with whom they seek cooperation (*power*). Thus, the policies that are put into place often depart in considerable ways from the preferences of policymakers choosing the rules, even when it seems that labor union or NGO demands for policy lead obviously to policy results.

Certainly, economic interest groups and moral entrepreneurs have shaped this process in crucial ways, but what they ask for does not account directly for what has happened or for why these regulations every now and then seem to work. Nor do their demands always make clear why the United States and Europe, which both welcome unions and human rights advocates, focus their regulations on different types of rights. The United States concentrates on a fairly narrow set of human rights for workers, while Europe has until recently focused its attention mostly on human rights to be free from coups and massacres. A world culture shaped by ever-stronger human rights norms, and championed by NGOs, hardly presents a better answer to the questions posed here; instead it is a context in which policymakers work.

These answers are all preference-driven explanations, and they can each break down at any of three stages in the policy process. Despite what interest groups, NGOs, or other leaders want, policymakers can fail to be convinced of an issue, allowing their own interests to trump those of their constituents or pressure groups. Even when policymakers become convinced of an issue, they may not have the capacity to effectively translate those preferences into policy outcomes, either because they lack veto power in their own institution or because they face influential competitors who want something else. And even when policymakers become convinced and do have the capacity to shape policy at the national level, their government may not possess the power or will to impose those policies on other countries that resist them during international negotiations.

Does this mean that the trade policy process is random or unpredictable (Cohen, March, and Olsen 1972)? No. Policies result, in fairly predictable ways, from the interaction of policymakers' various preferences, their capacities given the political institutions in which they operate, and countries' relative power in relation to their partners in trade cooperation. Policy consequences, however, are not always a direct result of the intentions of the individual policymakers championing those policies.

Four Arguments

This book makes four arguments with this framework in mind. First and foremost, fair trade regulations protecting human rights coincide with global justice norms and laws only when they serve the interests of the relevant policymakers. When those policymakers do not have such an interest, they blatantly contradict or avoid such regulations and toss norms aside. This is akin to a Prohibition-era tale of bootleggers and Baptists. The metaphor was inspired by American states' attempts to create blue laws outlawing the sale of liquor on Sundays (Yandle 1983). Baptists endorsed the policy on moral grounds, while bootleggers, for their own economic reasons, were happy to ally with moral advocates and endorse the regulations because they limited competition and thereby increased the bootleggers' profits. A similar dynamic is often at work here. Well-intentioned policymakers who advocate human-rights-protecting trade agreements favor protections when they stand to make considerable gains from the adoption of such guidelines—winning or preserving political power, influence, or wealth—*and* when they can publicly rationalize these gains through popular appeal to collective moral principles, whether they care deeply about the principles or not.

Second, the structure of domestic policymaking in the United States and Europe has greatly influenced the content of each agreement (Milner 1997). Voting rules, opportunities for amendments, and the size of the voting pool influence the policies that are adopted. It is often easier for members of the executive branch of government, such as the US president, to set the policies they want when their legislature votes by majority rather than unanimity and cannot make amendments, and when there are fewer active veto players that can block the executive will. When legislatures vote by unanimity or can amend trade proposals, executives are often less able to get what they want in domestic negotiations over trade. This disadvantage can also be exacerbated by a greater number of veto players with different policy preferences (Tsebelis 2002). The nature of the decision-making process, in terms of voting rules and number of veto players, thus determines which policymakers inside governments—working across political parties or political institutions—are apt to have the most leverage over regulations at which point in the policymaking process. These factors also help to explain why policymakers often settle for compromised outcomes that rarely reflect any single interest group's or policymaker's wishes, and why American and European trade practices, and not simply their policymakers' ideas about regulation, look so different.

Third, most other governments that commit to fair preferential trade regulations protecting human rights have not done so because they support human rights principles or because they seek help enforcing international laws protecting people. Rather, most have signed on only because the United States or Europe bullied them, making human rights a condition for access to their markets. Here, the end of the cold war has shaped the politics of international human rights regulation in significant ways, as great powers have shifted their own emphasis away from the military and toward markets. A few countries, especially the more advanced and industrial economies with big or valuable markets, have successfully resisted the fair trade ultimatum, rejecting a PTA with the United States or Europe or negotiating more agreeable human rights standards of conduct with weaker enforcement provisions. But most countries in the developing world have taken what they could get and signed on to trade regulations protecting human rights—even though they never wanted such protections and almost certainly did not intend to enforce them. Institutions matter here too. Once the United States and Europe passed legislation requiring human rights standards to be put into place, all countries lost their room to maneuver and either had to sign on or walk away.

Fourth, PTAs that create standards of conduct that commit members to the protection of human rights can sometimes make a difference, preventing abuses or encouraging incremental reforms by raising the costs of violations and the benefits of improvement. In this way they change the incentives for some leaders to shape up. This potential capability to affect human rights practices has paradoxically not been the main driver for the creation of these rules, as the previous arguments make clear. Instead, groups of American and European policymakers have created such rules for their own political benefits and have gone to considerable lengths to avoid enforcing them afterward when the rules conflict with their interests; PTAs protecting human rights are often more about fixing perceptions at home than fixing problems in other countries. Yet, by their very design, many still have the potential to influence the politics of repression when they trigger political mobilization inside a country or when the United States or Europe has the will to enforce them, which they sometimes do despite the potentially unfavorable effects on global trade.[13]

A Powerful Focus

While trade agreements exist around the world, not all are relevant to this story. The United States and Europe have largely motivated the rise of fair trade standards of conduct protecting human rights.[14] Together they account for almost all agreements that matter for the politics of repression, with some capacity for implementation. Thus the focus of this story is PTAs negotiated with other governments by the US government or by the European Community (EC)[15] and its member states. In some cases, these

13. As chapter 6 explains, the process of influence is very different in American and European trade agreements, mainly for institutional reasons. American PTAs largely encourage ex ante reforms from their trade partners, which take place before the agreement is even passed into law. European PTAs mostly encourage ex post reforms, where violations can be pursued after an agreement has taken effect.

14. The United States and European Union enjoy the world's largest aggregate market shares, with trade in global merchandise more than twice that of any other government, including Japan. Combined, their markets dominate and account for roughly half of global output and input and the vast majority of foreign direct investment as well as mergers and acquisitions. See Drezner (2007) and Quinlan (2003).

15. The focus here is on the external human rights policy of the EC, with an emphasis on EC law and related statements by EC institutions (the Commission, Council, Parliament, and Court of Justice). It is the EC and not the European Union proper that concludes and is party to a trade agreement. For simplicity, references here are to the European Union or simply to Europe as the common actor, and to the Community or the EC when a clear distinction is required.

PTAs defend voters' and citizens' human rights, and in other cases they single out the human rights of workers and children. This focus on American and European-sponsored PTAs reflects the fact that not all countries are of equal importance in this regulatory process. The agreements that do not involve the United States or Europe but do include some form of human rights regulation are mainly being formed between developing countries without tools for implementation. They are being made for other reasons, shaped by the low costs of creating human rights standards that are rarely adhered to, and thus they are not a major focus here.[16]

At the same time, from a practical standpoint the United States and Europe are similar systems with comparable features of politics, though they have starkly different approaches to policy (Lijphart 1971; Przeworski and Teune 1970). Both are world leaders in the effort to protect human rights around the globe. Both recognize and have made commitments to many international human rights laws, and both strongly support the existence of human rights advocates and labor unions. Although the European Union is not a nation-state like the United States, the two do share some decision-making features that make comparison possible. Both are democracies characterized by delegation to executive, legislative, and judicial institutions that adopt binding foreign policy to spread standards of conduct abroad (Hix 1999; Pollack 2005).[17] In the area of trade, for instance, the European Commission—the executive body—enjoys power to negotiate trade agreements, many of which are the exclusive competence of the European Community and not the member states.

Yet, despite their many similarities, the United States and Europe also show remarkable variation in their approaches to the design and implementation of trade regulations that protect human rights, and these variations raise important questions about the causes of the process at the core of this narrative. I choose to examine here particular agreements that feature these variations—not only geographically and over time but also across the design of agreements and across the types of countries making them. Inside the United States and Europe, I look at the historical processes leading

16. Although most fair preferential trade regulations that protect human rights are made by the United States or Europe, there are a growing number of these regulations now being made by other governments, including those of developing countries. Most are cheap talk, but some do offer procedures for implementation. These agreements will become an especially important subject worthy of research in their own right.

17. On matters of regulation of globalization, the European Union can be treated as a single foreign policy actor and is usefully compared with the United States. See Drezner (2007) and Meunier (2005).

up to two particular policy moments: the passage of the US Trade Act in 2002, now expired, which required that all PTAs negotiated under the act include jointly binding regulations protecting human rights for workers and children; and the passage of the 1995 Commission Communication and subsequent Community legislation requiring that standards of conduct be met in respect for human rights in Europe's future trade agreements.[18] Both of these historical events are summarized in time lines in the appendix.

However, the focus here on US and European preferential trade agreements does not exclude of the rest of the world. The United States and Europe have made PTAs with governments of all types—with rich and poor, repressive and rights-protecting, democratic and autocratic countries around the world. This book investigates agreements with countries in Africa, greater Europe, Asia, the Middle East, and Latin America, and the implications of this research are global.

Methods of Analysis

The core approach here to analyzing these PTAs is to trace their development through case studies that map out, step by step, the policymaking processes inside the United States and European Union. The PTAs' impact on human rights practices is examined through cases and, where appropriate, statistical data.

The historical analyses are supported by an array of primary source materials supplied by the US government and the European Union, as well as by secondary materials written by scholars, lawyers, policymakers, and NGOs and a large selection of archival documents. Many insights evolved from scores of interviews with government and bureaucratic officials involved in the policymaking process, nongovernmental policy advocates involved in lobbying governments on the issue, and academics and lawyers active in studying the process.

Interviewees in the United States were mostly individuals in the government who were currently working or, at various times and in various ca-

18. While renegotiations over the 2002 Trade Act are currently under way in the United States, Europe has made many advances on human rights since 1995. Although they are beyond the immediate focus of this book—which concentrates on explaining the process of regulating human rights as it developed into the crucial policies of 1995, which are still in force and central to the regulatory process—a great deal of scholarship explores these developments. See, for example, Kuyper (1993), King (1997), Brandtner and Rosas (1999), Fierro (2003), and Bartels (2005).

pacities, have worked in the State Department, the Office of the United States Trade Representative, Congress, and with foreign governments' ministries in charge of trade negotiations, as well as key negotiators of specific trade agreements. In Europe, interviewees worked at the Commission in external relations, development, and trade Directorates-General, among others, as well as in the Community's two legislative branches—the Council and Parliament. Members of the Economic and Social Committee and staff from the legal services unit and from information services also were interviewed. Among policy advocates, individuals from global human rights organizations and labor unions that were active in the policy area contributed their insight. Among academics, interviewees included scholars around the world in economics, law, and political science.

Overview

This book investigates the breadth of the American and European political processes that regulate human rights through preferential trade agreements.[19] Chapter 2 begins by building an analytical foundation, presenting a simple framework and implications for thinking about policy design focused on policymakers' preferences, the policymaking institutions through which they make choices, and the power dynamics of intercountry bargaining. It also proposes a way to examine the politics of implementation. The final section of chapter 2 places this analysis in the context of several other explanations for why governments are signing on to the fair preferential trade movement protecting human rights. It considers these insightful explanations as they apply to the central questions of this book and explains why they are not used as the core framework for analysis, although each plays a role.

The next several chapters address how and why human rights standards have been made and put into PTAs, applying insights from the framework set forth in chapter 2 to explore the core issues of the book empirically. The analyses are historical and comparative, tracing the policy process in discrete stages. I look first at what policymakers want and how they articulate their interests for making standards of human rights conduct. I then explore how these preferences were aggregated through various political institutions into national policy outcomes. Finally, I examine how these national policy outcomes have shaped international negotiations over agreements.

19. For an account of the rise of corporate social responsibility, see Vogel (2005).

Chapter 3 considers policymakers' preferences and asks why and how some policymakers began to articulate interests in making fair PTA standards of conduct, given that both the United States and Europe for years opposed regulating human rights through their trade agreements and only reluctantly began to do so through unilateral schemes they could control. It considers what types of human rights trade regulations NGOs, consumers, businesses, and labor unions on both sides of the Atlantic have promoted and how those interests relate to the preferences trade policymakers articulate. Most policymakers in the United States and Europe express an interest in regulating human rights when the regulations serve them politically. In the United States, that has sometimes meant a desire to win support from bootlegging labor unions at decisive political moments such as an election year. In Europe, that has also meant a desire to win more political influence, sometimes in Europe and other times with former colonies, and to solve other pressing security problems. Some policymakers—though not all—are clearly committed to human rights standards for principled as well as political reasons. A few are even human rights activists. Regardless of personal conviction, though, the moral discourse has increasingly become an important political tool, as policymakers of all stripes have come to publicize their views on the regulations in the language of ethics. Here, morality helps sell trade policy that is otherwise unpopular. Yet the argument here is that despite this moral rhetoric, policymakers have mainly represented the norm-laden message, shaped and spread by so many human rights advocates, when doing so solves other pressing problems or pays political rents to influential bootleggers; norms and the concerns of NGOs have been largely tossed aside otherwise.

Given this interest among some policymakers in creating fair preferential trade regulations protecting human rights, chapter 4 considers the next stage, looking at policymaking institutions to explain how policymakers' preferences, once in place, became national policies and why the regulations look so different in the United States and Europe and also over time. The answer is not simply that American and European interest groups and human rights advocates wanted different things or were subject to different norms, or that trade partners asked for different rules. These features of the political process have been relatively comparable. Rather, part of the answer lies in the different processes of collective decision making, such as who votes and how legislation is amended and passed.

Given that the United States and Europe eventually passed laws making certain human rights mandatory elements for regulation in all future preferential trade agreements—the United States in 2002 and the European Union in 1995—chapter 5 then considers the power politics of negotiations with other countries and explains why so many other governments that did not want human rights regulated through PTAs nonetheless agreed to these standards. Trade partners of the United States and Europe have, for the most part, taken on these regulations against their better interests, agreeing to various human rights conditions as tradeoffs for improved access to big markets. And the market supremacy of the United States and Europe has given both substantial leeway to place all kinds of issues on their preferential trade agendas—human rights, the environment, corruption, and security. These are issues they have been largely unsuccessful in raising through the WTO, where developing countries time and again organize against them and have the veto power to do so. By forcing protections for human rights into preferential trade negotiations and making legislative threats to reject further integration of markets if the protections are not accepted, the Americans and Europeans created incentives for other governments to accept human rights rules they never wanted and probably would never have taken up otherwise. Even so, other governments with the will or market power to do so have watered down the rules. Some have even walked away rather than sign on to the regulations.

Chapter 6 then explores the policies' effects, weighing the broad importance of these human rights protections in PTAs given that so many trade agreements say little about human rights and, of those that do, few are equipped to put in force the standards they preach. This chapter provides evidence to show that some PTAs have come to play a significant role in governing compliance with human rights. When they offer enforceable standards that tie material benefits of integration to conformity with human rights principles, trade agreements can be reasonably effective in changing behaviors of some perpetrators and helping out reformers. Despite their limitations, these agreements often are more effective in making a difference than are global human rights laws, which seem to work best for democratizing countries. It is these trade standards, which are changing the landscape of policy options for how countries carry out their human rights business, that are the focus of this book.

On the other hand, plenty of PTAs offer unenforceable standards of conduct that draw attention to human rights principles but then provide no avenues to put them into effect. These types of trade regulations are fair in name only; they are pervasive and hollow, doing little to change perpetrators' incentives for reform or to help local advocates. Because they matter little in the worlds of human rights or globalization, they do not play a central role in this narrative, even though they are common. Countries create them because they are low-cost tokens of support for human rights without the obligation to take action. Chapter 7 concludes with thoughts about what this evolution in human rights protections means for the world's trade institutions, the human rights regime, and global governance more generally.

This book is a uniquely political perspective on an international regulatory process playing out in the political economy. It emphasizes the power and institutional contexts in which policymakers work and discourages explanations for the linkage of human rights to trade that rely mostly on the preferences of NGOs or labor unions. Getting human rights into the trade process has not been an easy, uniform effort, and the success we see today does not represent a clear victory of NGOs or labor unions over states or norms over interests.

Something novel is taking place in the governance of the international political economy. New regulatory standards are emerging that reflect powerful countries' attempts to evolve with the changing structure of international relations, especially in the post–cold war period. They reveal a clever political manipulation of both moral norms and market institutions for mainly political ends. Policymakers in the United States and Europe have been strategically and often reactively solving emerging problems at home by designing PTAs that govern moral politics abroad, regardless of the economic consequences, which are still unclear. In the process, and not entirely by intention, the relationship between markets and people's human rights is being effectively transformed, bit by bit, and the face of globalization will probably never again look the same.

CHAPTER 2

A PATH TO ANSWERS

Fair preferential trade regulations protecting human rights should never have been created. They are costly: abusive governments run the risk of getting caught and losing considerable benefits, while enforcers hazard expensive implementation procedures that jeopardize market access (Baehr and Castermans-Holleman 2004). They are bad diplomacy: governments charged with human rights violations are quick to view accusations as meddling in their private affairs (Hoffman 1981). They are protectionist: they jeopardize a core principle of the global trade regime—nondiscrimination— intended to defend governments from measures to protect domestic markets, perhaps compromising global trade gains (Bhagwati 1988, 2000). And they are unpopular: since the days of the International Trade Organization (ITO),[1] most countries have doggedly rejected the protection of human rights as a trade concern, and today this rebuff has become a core principle of the WTO regime.[2]

Why then are these regulations spreading? Given the abundance of existing instruments to control repression and mountains of evidence that protectionist trade measures are bad economics, why are the United States

1. The draft of the 1948 Havana Charter establishing the ITO (which never came into force) stated: "The members recognize that unfair labor conditions, particularly in production for export, create difficulties in international trade and, accordingly, each member shall take whatever action may be feasible and appropriate to eliminate such conditions within its territory." The General Agreement on Tariffs and Trade (GATT), which took the place of the ITO, does not include rules governing human rights of any kind. Today, the WTO correspondingly says nothing directly about human rights, although Article XX does provide for exceptional treatment for prison-made goods.

2. For an excellent overview on the challenges of protecting human rights in the WTO, see Howse and Mututa (2000).

and Europe increasingly adopting PTAs that create standards of conduct for human rights, protecting voters and citizens as well as workers and children? Why are the rules inconsistent, with the United States focused on workers and Europe focused on voters? Why, when these regulations are costly and controversial, do countries all over the world accept them? And do these regulations ever stop human rights violations or improve peoples' lives?

Scholars have posited a variety of explanations, none of which is entirely convincing. Instead, I use insights from each approach to develop an accurate explanation of this important political phenomenon that is taking place all over the world.

A Framework for Explanation

The argument here is that trade policy outcomes reflect policymakers' preferences, but they also reflect the institutions through which they compete for decision-making influence and countries' relative market power. Another argument is that PTA regulations protecting human rights affect the human rights behavior of countries mainly when they provide the instruments and resources to change actors' incentives to take on reforms that would not otherwise be implemented.

Trade policymakers are most apt to develop and articulate preferences for including human rights standards of conduct in their PTAs when they personally stand to gain politically from the adoption of the regulation, either because the policy pays direct dividends to core constituencies that support them, such as bootlegging interest groups, or because the policy serves vital national security or economic purposes that are also in their interests. It helps, however, when policymakers can justify the regulation through popular appeal to widely accepted social values. Normative appeals for fair trade policy are rarely convincing alone but, increasingly, interest-based motivations benefit from morally persuasive overtones.

At the same time, domestic politics matter enormously. Changing trade rules is usually a combative process, and not every policymaker shares the same degree of satisfaction with or influence over the results. Democracy complicates the process. When democracies choose the trade policies they want to pursue with other governments, their own policymakers compete for influence. And which policymakers are the most successful in pushing their interests for regulation depends on the rules by which they make choices. Different domestic policymaking rules can lead countries to pursue different international regulations in fairly predictable ways. In particular, who votes, who makes amendments, and how policy passes into law shape the content of regulations.

Power politics matter too. Countries sometimes sign on to new trade rules even when they would prefer that the rules did not exist, and not all countries support regulatory standards based on protecting human rights. Powerful countries with big markets, including the United States or the countries of Europe, often force into discussions a regulatory issue that less powerful countries do not want to talk about. Sometimes the powerful countries make approval of the contentious issue a condition for cooperation, often at the insistence of their legislatures. In those cases, other countries must decide whether to approve the regulation even though they don't want it or to risk losing cooperation. The more other countries need trade cooperation, because their markets are small or their industries are dependent on exports, the harder it will be for them to reject the issue out of hand; many developing countries are thus particularly at a disadvantage in this process.

The surprising aspect of all this is that even though fair trade agreements are generally created to benefit certain American and European policymakers rather than explicitly to protect human rights in other countries, preferential trade regulations that create standards of conduct for human rights have nonetheless changed the politics of repression in some places. By providing governments, especially the abusive ones, with promises of trade and cooperation gains if they clean up their behavior, PTAs can give some perpetrators incentives to take on human rights reforms they would otherwise reject.

Preferences

It is easy to see human dignity as uniquely pressing and personal and therefore separate from other international issues, but human rights are in many ways no different from other issues subject to international regulation. Policymakers' preferences for new trade regulations protecting people have come about, and continue to spread, when policymakers stand to make considerable political gains from such regulations. It helps when they can justify their actions by appealing to widely accepted global norms espoused by human rights advocates, usually NGOs, dedicated to making the world a better place. The Baptists—in this case, hard-working NGOs and advocates—call for human rights to be taken seriously in foreign policies and laws for moral reasons. But even well-intentioned policymakers are most likely to take up the cause when they have something political to achieve, such as solving a tough political problem or gaining the support of influential interest groups—the bootleggers—who stand to benefit if the human rights regulation is enacted. To get regulation on human rights, Baptists need policymakers to have political interests in the success of the cause; without these interests, Baptists have less hope of influence. And since the end of the cold war, as human rights norms and advocates spread, politicians, still driven by the search for power and influence, have been more likely to push for human rights regulations, especially in contentious areas such as trade, when they can latch on to moral idioms and stake their profits on liberal global values.

Thus, the mere fact that policymakers pass laws or articulate preferences for a regulation that appears to satisfy NGOs or moral advocates does not mean that these advocates have influenced the regulation or the policymakers who created it. Policymakers don't need moral conviction to advocate or create what appear to be morally appropriate regulations, but they do need to benefit in some way. Therefore, human rights advocates, whether NGOs or international organizations (IOs), are most likely to be represented in the policymaking process when their moral message coincides with policymakers' interests for political gains, regardless of the policymakers' own personal commitment to the greater moral cause. When interests align, the moral advocates' influence can be substantial.[3] When they do not, advocates' demands are often left by the wayside. Chapter 3 explores these arguments with evidence from the trade experiences of the United States and Europe.

Institutions

Although the bootlegger-and-Baptist theory provides a powerful clue about the rise and spread of preferences for human rights trade regulations, the preferences of policymakers alone cannot fully explain why countries sign on to the particular trade laws they do, or why rules vary so much across the United States and Europe. Domestic politics—the rules by which policymakers operate to turn their preferences into policy outcomes—also play a role. At the most basic level, three kinds of domestic politics are involved: agenda setting, negotiating, and voting (Milner 1997).

Policymakers with agenda-setting power control a country's position on preferential trade regulations by providing guidelines for cooperation—a power usually held by legislatures such as the US Congress or the European Council. Policymakers with negotiating power influence regulations by bargaining over and drafting the text of a trade agreement with

---

3. See Keck and Sikkink (1998).

other countries—a power regularly held by executives such as the US president or the European Commission. To make new trade rules, it is best if an executive gets permission from the legislature to negotiate under the most agreeable terms. Once permission is given, the executive is mostly free, consistent with the legislature's directives for the negotiations, to recommend any policy that may or may not address human rights protections. However, the legislature retains the ability to pass into law, amend, or veto the executive's policy recommendation. This means that a strategic executive will anticipate the legislature's mood as he or she negotiates trade regulations that protect human rights; so too will the other countries at the bargaining table (Putnam 1998; Tsebelis 2002).

A simple scenario helps illustrate the way in which policymaking institutions matter. Suppose a country faces a problem that current policies cannot solve—workers in the cotton industry believe their wages are being undercut by competition from global competitors that use child labor to produce cotton more cheaply. The country's executive, a free trader in this example, wants a new trade agreement that promotes trade and does not protect children working in cotton fields—Policy A. But the cotton workers' labor union protests, worried that such free trade will adversely affect them. The legislature, whose members want to curry favor with domestic cotton workers who give them campaign contributions, prefers a trade policy more in line with constituents' needs: something that restricts the use of child labor, on the grounds that it violates basic human rights—Policy D. Place these two alternatives at opposite ends of a spectrum, and consider where the likely policy outcome lies. The executive stands to gain most from, and so wants, Policy A, but he or she will accept a slightly more restrictive pact too—Policy B. If there is no other choice, the executive might also accept an agreement with fewer restrictions on child labor—Policy C. Suppose he or she will not, however, go any further than that and will reject Policy D no matter what. The legislature, meanwhile, stands to gain most from, and so wants, Policy D but will accept a slightly less restrictive agreement if it has to—Policy C—and, absent other options, will agree to an even less restrictive pact—Policy B. It will reject anything less stringent, such as Policy A. Given the preference limitations in this example, is the executive or the legislature more likely to prevail on the matter of regulating human rights for children?

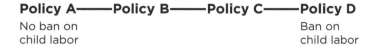

Policy A——**Policy B**——**Policy C**——**Policy D**
No ban on   Ban on
child labor   child labor

The answer depends on several factors. The first is power sharing in the government. If the country is a dictatorship and the executive has the sole authority to set foreign policy, the government will probably pursue what the leader wants regardless of complaints from citizens or legislatures. Our mock country will go into international negotiations advocating something close to a national Policy A in this example. But if the executive shares power with a legislature that can constrain the agenda and veto or amend proposals, the government will almost certainly pursue a different strategy. This strategy depends on the legislature's power to amend and constrain (Tsebelis 2000).

Consider the power to amend. Suppose the legislature can pass or veto an executive's trade proposal but not amend it. The executive will most likely first propose the policy he or she likes best that falls within the "win set"—the range of policies both the executive and the legislature are willing to consider (Putnam 1998). In this example, he or she will propose something close to Policy B, with modest child labor regulations. Unable to amend the proposal and willing to accept Policy B rather than nothing, the legislature will probably pass the executive's policy, which will become the country's mandate for international negotiations. But suppose the legislature can amend the proposal. In that case, a strategic executive will probably now propose a policy of greater compromise that is more attractive to the legislature—Policy C, with more protections for child labor. This is still better than no policy. Thus the power to amend gives the legislature leverage to curb the executive, since it is able to force the executive to compromise or tie up the policy deal in protracted negotiations.

Also, consider the legislature's power to constrain the agenda by setting directives for negotiation. Suppose the legislature has passed a law allowing the executive to negotiate a trade agreement. When this law does not set regulatory conditions on negotiations, a strategic executive will negotiate and propose the policy he or she likes most that falls within that win set—in this example, something as close as possible to Policy A that can win legislative approval. When the law does set conditions on negotiations—requiring the executive to include protections for children's human rights, for example—the legislature has used the law to reduce the win set of possible policy outcomes from which the executive may choose. The executive now must negotiate a trade agreement that meets the legislature's stated conditions—for example, nothing to the left of Policy B—because he or she knows that any proposed agreement outside the legislature's set of conditions will be rejected. Even so, the executive in this example will still pursue something akin to Policy B, which, though it is not ideal in the executive's mind, is still better than the alternative.

The real world is not so simple. But this logic demonstrates in a basic way that domestic politics play an important role in the spread of fair preferential trade standards protecting human rights; the preferences of policymakers and those they represent do not suffice to explain which laws come to pass. Indeed, because executives are often the negotiators of trade agreements, they generally have the last stage advantage in setting regulatory standards—recommending policies they most want within the range of options their legislatures will likely accept.

Although this model is useful to illustrate why policymaking institutions matter, it is simplistic to view the legislature as a single decision maker. So imagine now that a country's legislature has three decision makers representing different political parties—the first party favors Policy D, the second and third want Policy C—and each will accept a policy one move to the left on the policy spectrum in this example. Now, which actors have the most influence on policy depends on the way in which collective choices are made in the legislature (Golub 1999; Jupille 1999; Krehbiel 1998; Meunier 2000; Shepsle and Weingast 1981).

Suppose the legislature can pass policy by a majority—two out of three parties. The legislature cannot amend, and the executive must agree on the policy.[4] Policy change is possible only when the executive and at least two parties can agree. Within this majority win set, a strategic executive will still propose the policy he or she most wants—in this illustration, Policy B. Suppose instead the legislature must pass all policy unanimously. In this case, the only law that all policymakers can agree on is Policy C.[5] This scenario is also a simplified representation of a more complex decision-making process, but the patterns of behavior it suggests should play out empirically as we examine trade policy regulations.[6]

4. Much has been written about collective choice in multidimensional policy spaces, and it has been shown that without some restrictions on the configuration of ideal points or institutions that confine the sequence of proposals—see Shepsle and Weingast (1981)—majority rule decision-making processes are chaotic—see McKelvey (1986) and Cox (1987). Collective choice under majority rule is stable in a multidimensional context when issues are voted on one at a time and preferences are separable (the expected level of one issue has no influence on the ideal points of other issues). See Kramer (1972). See Hinich and Munger (1997) for a detailed discussion.

5. There is a rich and helpful debate taking place over how much the legal rules on policymaking procedures and voting matter and how much of the political decision-making process takes place informally in prevote bargaining. See Thomson et al. (2006) for a useful overview.

6. A great deal of literature usefully engages this type of argument and its various nuances in greater depth than this book allows. See Krehbiel (1998, 2004), Thomson et al. (2006), and Tsebelis (1995, 2000, 2002) for just a few examples.

First, what policymakers want does not single-handedly explain the rise or spread of fair trade regulations protecting human rights because the system in which these policymakers function is also crucial and is not influenced by the same forces. It should thus be common to observe big gaps between the goals of policymakers and interest groups, whether Baptists or bootleggers, and the policies that are actually made.

Second, executives will usually try to negotiate the policy most in their perceived favor, given the win set of policies the legislature is willing to consider. Thus different policymakers have influence at different stages in the policymaking process, and this sequence shapes the policies made.

Third, the legislature's voting rules affect its ability to curb executive opportunism.[7] The potential for new regulations, such as those protecting human rights, is always equal or greater when the legislature votes by majority rather than unanimity and when there are fewer veto players involved.[8] And having the power to amend is often an advantage for a legislature, constraining the executive's ability to win what he or she favors as ideal policy outcomes.[9]

Fourth, executives should be most apt to get what they want for trade regulations when faced with fewer veto players and a legislature that votes by majority and cannot amend. Alternatively, executives should be least apt to achieve what they consider an ideal agreement when faced with many veto players and a legislature that can amend agreements and votes by unanimity. Chapter 4 explores these arguments historically with evidence from the trade experiences of the United States and Europe.

Power

Once a country's executive is armed with a national policy position for trade cooperation, he or she negotiates with other countries over the rules, and bargaining takes place internationally (Garrett 1992; Moravcsik 1998; Tsebelis and Garrett 2001). We must now explore the same myriad outcomes on an international level: which laws will countries choose, and who will be most satisfied with the agreements that are reached?

7. A country whose legislature votes by majority rather than unanimity, for example, is not inevitably more likely to take on trade regulations protecting human rights. It is the distribution of preferences among policymakers that determines how voting rules shape trade policies; this distribution can prevail over the institutional determinants of policy (Garrett and Tsebelis 1996; Moravcsik 1991, 1993). I thank George Tsebelis for raising this point.

8. This assumes, of course, that preferences are constant.

9. Legislative amendments also come with costs, especially when policymakers will continue to negotiate other policies in the future and so will need to keep goodwill.

One of the most crucial insights from international relations is that power politics shape which countries have influence over policy outcomes; this is as true for markets as it is for militaries (Gilpin 1987; Gowa 1994; Grieco 1988; Waltz 1979). Negotiations over multiple issues, such as trade preferences and human rights protections, offer special opportunities for influence, often by creating disparities in issue salience—how much countries value their satisfaction on one issue versus another.[10] These disparities can reflect market-power inequalities. A country may care more about getting what it wants on one policy issue than another—for example, promoting trade may be more highly valued than avoiding human rights regulations. This usually happens when a country cannot get what it wants in another trade forum or when it is more vulnerable to, or dependent on, market access than its trade partner. These differences benefit other, more powerful countries by giving them room to force issues, such as human rights, into trade negotiations (Drezner 2007; Gilpin 1981; Hirschman [1945] 1980, 1970). Poor and developing countries are most often caught in this trap.

Consider another scenario in which two countries negotiate over trade policy. Assume that policymakers in Country 1 have already negotiated domestically and have concluded that they prefer Policy A, would take Policy B over Policy C, and will reject anything to the right of Policy C. Country 2 has done the same and prefers Policy D, would accept Policy C over Policy B, and will reject anything to the left of Policy B. When both countries place equal priority on promoting trade and protecting human rights, they will probably compromise and agree to something between Policies B and C. But now suppose Country 2 becomes poorer and more than ever needs the market access. This disparity almost certainly puts that country at a new disadvantage. Knowing the possibility for compromise is shrinking, Country 2 now views its second-favorite option, Policy B, as better than nothing. While Country 2 might not have adopted Policy B before, it might now accept the policy because promoting trade is more important than avoiding human rights protections. Knowing this, Country 1 might push for its position even harder. In short, market inequality has provided one richer country with incentives to push for more regulation and the other poorer country with incentives to take on human rights protections it doesn't want in order to gain on trade (Gruber 2000).

---

10. Issue salience does not mean that a country wants more of one policy than another; it refers to a country's willingness to accept unsatisfactory outcomes on one issue rather than another.

Yet market power does not tell the whole story; institutions also matter at this stage. This is because a country's ability to get what it wants during international negotiations is also shaped by the actions of other countries' legislatures—how they vote and constrain the agenda (Mayer 1992; Meunier 2000, 2005; Milner and Rosendorff 1997; Putnam 1998; Schelling 1960). Domestic ratification constraints can give a negotiator a bargaining advantage over other countries (Schelling 1960)[11] because legislatures can force certain issues into or out of international negotiations and compel other countries (and their own negotiators, as the previous section argues) to compromise, regardless of their market power. For example, when the legislatures of the United States or Europe pass laws that make regulating human rights compulsory in a trade agreement, other countries, even the rich ones, lose their ability to get a trade agreement without adopting standards of conduct to protect people.

Thus international power politics also help explain fair trade agreements and offer further empirical implications that should be evident in the policy process, but they are also shaped by domestic politics. Preferential trade partners of the United States and Europe should be most able to influence trade regulations protecting human rights when they have big or valuable markets of their own. Advanced industrial economies can often afford to turn down an agreement. This advantage is even bigger when these countries face no requirements on protecting human rights made by US or European legislatures. Trade partners should be least able to influence the regulations when they have relatively small or insignificant markets—poor and developing economies—and US and European legislatures make regulation of human rights compulsory. Thus, relative economic power determines which countries have the most say over trade policy regulation on human rights, while the legislative processes of the United States and Europe determine how much that power matters when it comes to the international bargaining process. Chapter 5 explores these arguments with evidence from the trade experiences of the United States and Europe with countries in Africa, Asia, Latin America, and the Middle East.

Effect

In the area of human rights reform, "hard" laws that create binding obligations through precise rules and that delegate enforcement (Abbott and Snidal 2001) are essential because change in repressive behavior almost al-

---

11. By contrast, Milner (1997) argues that divided government makes international cooperation less likely, but when it does occur it will favor the preferences of the legislature.

ways requires legally binding and enforceable obligations.[12] With these features, preferential trade regulations protecting human rights can improve human rights practices sometimes, despite the self-interest rather than altruism with which they are created.

The challenge in combating human rights repression is that many governments disregard the principled ideas spread internationally through global laws and networks of advocates. These governments purposely reject global rules because they stand to gain from practices that mistreat citizens. Violations of human rights—especially the worst violations—can rarely be explained by bureaucratic failure. Human rights laws are clear in their prohibitions on torture and indiscriminate killing. Difficult social or economic changes take place inside countries that do not repress their citizens. And human rights violations, whether they involve torture, child labor, or restrictions on free speech, are largely calculated acts taken by people who expect some form of gain from repression. Once in motion, they may be hard to stop, but they are rarely committed by accident.

It is clear, however, that many international human rights laws and organizations do not supply adequate enforcement or motivation to reform, especially for the worst abusers (Hafner-Burton and Tsutsui 2005; Hathaway 2002; Neumayer 2005). But some American and European PTAs, with hard standards that can be enforced, have considerable potential to influence countries' behavior toward their citizens. In particular, PTAs with enforceable standards can deliver "the threat or act by a sender government or governments to disrupt economic exchange with the target country, unless the target acquiesces to the articulated demand" (Drezner 2003, 643). This coercion can be more effective than persuasion alone or "the active, often strategic, inculcation of norms" (Goodman and Jinks 2003b, 10).

There are several reasons to expect coercion to provide stronger incentives against repression than persuasion can alone, and for coercion and persuasion applied together to effectively influence human rights. Coercion is likely to be more effective than persuasion alone because it does not require changing abusers' preferences for repression. Instead, it increases

12. See Abbott and Snidal (2000) on "hard" and "soft" law. This view is explained in detail in Hafner-Burton (2005), from which this section of the chapter is taken, and stands in sharp contrast to the belief that coercion is unnecessary or counterproductive: that governments often conform to global human rights laws out of concern for legitimacy, even when laws are powerless to enforce compliance, and that coercion necessarily produces adverse consequences on the enjoyment of human rights. See Goodman and Jinks (2003a, 2003b), Johnston (2001), Payne (2001), Price (1998), Helfer and Slaughter (1997), Finnemore (1996), Koh (1996–97), Franck (1990), and Henkin (1979). For an exception, see Martin and Sikkink (1993).

the costs of using repression and also boosts the gains from adopting better human rights practices. A coerced actor can simultaneously want to abuse human rights and choose not to in exchange for other gains from international cooperation. The actor is likely to make that choice when the gains are more valuable than the benefits of repression. Reforms can be a side payment to get something else in return.

Coercion can take place much more quickly than persuasion. If an institution supplies valuable goods under the condition that targeted repressors make human rights policy changes now or in the near future, repressors are more likely to react in the short term to adopt new practices. Imminent sanctions on valuable goods provide strong incentives for reforms in the present rather than repressive behavior into the future.

Coercion can also change perpetrators' behavior when they value the gains of cooperation more than the gains of repression. In fact, any opponent of human rights who yearns for the goods achieved through international cooperation can be coerced into supporting otherwise unappealing human rights reforms.[13] Moreover, coercive instruments that successfully institutionalize new benefits can influence the preferences of future leaders who would otherwise choose repression. This happens when institutionalization of the coercive instrument has led to new gains, now perceived as valuable by an incoming government and thus trumping existing incentives to use repression.[14] Direct and repeated access to target repressors is not necessary for bullying to succeed. The only requirement is that target actors see the coercion trade-off and that they value the benefits of international cooperation more than they value the gains from repression.

Coercion can influence human rights behaviors short of implementation, so effective cases of bullying are often likely to end with a threat of punishment rather than with the implementation of punishment (Drezner 2003; Eaton and Engers 1999).[15] Fair preferential trade regulations in this category improve members' human rights in some instances by supplying the instruments and resources to change repressive actors' incentives to promote policy reforms that would not otherwise be implemented.

13. Also see Moravscik (2000) for a similar argument in the European context.
14. For a discussion of hand tying through credible commitment, see Martin (1998, 2000), Abbot and Snidal (2001), and Kahler and Lake (2003).
15. The Organization for Economic Cooperation and Development (OECD) concludes, for example, that the Generalized System of Preferences review process creates an independent and strong incentive for improving workers' human rights conditioned by the agreement, short of the imposition of sanctions. Recipient states have an economic stake in receiving a positive review, to avoid sanctions but also to encourage potential investment. See OECD (1996), Cleveland (2001a, 2001b).

However, trade regulations that protect human rights are not a cure-all for repression even when they are enforceable. They can generate economic costs associated with protectionism (Bhagwati, Krishna, and Panagariya 1999). Reforms are likely to be small and incremental, not radical. Not all regulations are likely to be enforced because enforcers will not always muster the will to put them into effect. And they are likely to be much less effective in influencing armed opposition groups or governments under insurrection, where opponents have no preference for economic liberalization. Nor are all leaders likely to be influenced by all agreements. Severely repressive elites who reap extensive benefits from repression and value those more than integration are apt to defect from trade agreements that offer only small gains or require large-scale political upheaval. And countries that are not dependent on American or European markets or can afford to lose them—because they are wealthy, perhaps from an abundance of natural resources, or they have trade ties to other rich nations willing to overlook human rights violations, such as China—are unlikely to be affected by human rights trade conditions.

These factors imply that US and European PTAs with enforceable human rights standards should sometimes lessen repression, especially in poor countries that rely heavily on access to their markets, even though many trade agreements were not created with this purpose in mind and the reforms are prone to be small or incremental. They also suggest that these trade agreements may be more useful than many human rights agreements (HRAs) in encouraging reforms because the HRAs often do a fine job of establishing principles but mostly lack the capacity to implement them (Hafner-Burton and Tsutsui 2007; Hathaway 2002, 2005). Chapter 6 explores these arguments with evidence from the trade experiences of the United States and Europe.

TABLE 1. TEN IMPLICATIONS FOR TRADE POLICY

PREFERENCES
1. Moral advocates are not necessarily the primary influence on policymakers when human rights regulations are being considered.
2. Policymakers can regulate moral issues without holding moral convictions on the issues.
3. Human rights advocates are most successful in shaping policy when the regulations they promote on moral grounds also serve to advance political or economic interests of policymakers.

INSTITUTIONS

4. Often, a policymaker's initial intent is only faintly reflected in the agreement that is eventually approved.

5. A strategic executive will propose the policy that best achieves her own goals within the set of options she thinks her legislature will accept.

6. A government's executive is more likely to get the policy she wants when her legislature has few veto players, votes by majority, and cannot amend proposals; she is less likely to get this policy when her legislature has many veto players, votes by unanimity, and can adopt amendments.

POWER

7. When American and European trade negotiators have no legal requirements for human rights regulations, their trade partners, especially those with strong markets, have considerable influence on an agreement's human rights provisions.

8. When American and European trade negotiators are bound by law to include human rights regulations in agreements, trade partners, especially those with weaker markets, have less influence on the agreement's human rights provisions.

EFFECT

9. American and European PTAs with enforceable human rights standards of conduct encourage reforms the most in poor countries where perpetrators rely heavily on access to Western markets.

10. These PTA regulations can be more successful in encouraging reforms than are many human rights agreements.

Other Explanations

PTAs are created for all kinds of reasons (Mansfield and Milner 1997)—for example, to improve their members' economic welfare (Krugman 1991, 1993), security (Kupchan 1997), or bargaining power in multilateral institutions (Whalley 1996). Existing theories in economics, law, politics, and sociology do offer substantial insights into the process of how and why these regulations are being made, even though they fall short of generating a full account of this phenomenon.

Protectionism

One of the most compelling and pervasive explanations for the rise and spread of fair trade regulations suggests that governments use human rights standards of conduct to disguise trade protectionism, seeking to raise barriers to market access (Dowlah 2004). This view is expressed in countless statements by governments, particularly in the developing world, that "reject the use of labour standards for protectionist purposes, and agree that the comparative advantage of countries, particularly low-wage developing countries, must in no way be put into question" (World Trade Organization 1996).

The theory is simple and powerful and suggests that governments design PTAs to internalize "externalities" that cross country borders (Mattli 1999). Scholars of economic institutions (North 1990; Rutherford 1994; Williamson 1975) and the environment (DeSombre 2000; Koorney and Krause 1997) are familiar with this reasoning. An externality exists whenever one actor's behavior affects the welfare of another actor who did not have a choice in the matter and whose interests were not considered. The problem is characterized by interdependence between countries, and the best solution is cooperation.[16]

When it comes to economic globalization, market interdependence among countries creates many externalities, including some involving human rights. They include the risks that market actors confront in their opportunistic dealings with foreign governments and firms. Because externalities can be negative and costly—perhaps created by lax standards of conduct that violate workers' human rights or by refugee crises that result from civil wars or conflicts—government leaders facing them in the global marketplace have incentives to design PTAs that will ease the problem, thereby decreasing production of the harmful product or behavior (Haas 1958; Nye 1968). This is especially the case in democracies.

Why? Because democratic governments are responsive to their interest groups (Moravcsik 1991, 1997; Peltzman 1976; Stigler 1971), forging economic policies in general and protectionist policies specifically in response to demands by persuasive special interests seeking to get their way (Frieden 1992; Helfand 2000; Mansfield and Milner 1997; Milner 1988; Rogowski

---

16. A classic example is environmental contamination. A city emitting heavy industrial pollutants situated upwind from a village that suffers the harmful effects of resulting air contamination creates a negative externality harmful to the welfare of the villagers. Such externalities undermine the efficient performance of the market endeavoring to maximize total utility of the society being affected. Actors producing the externality of air pollution have no incentives to factor in the costs of their actions to those affected, so the market equilibrium price of the good involved will not reflect a portion of the actual costs.

1989). Governments rarely aim to enhance general economic efficiency but to redistribute wealth in their favor (Thorbecke 1997). For elected policymakers, such as representatives in the European Parliament or US Congress, "it's constituent interests first and foremost" (Hufbauer 2007). Thus preferential trade agreements and their associated regulations can be seen as objects for sale to the highest bidders, motivated by desires for personal profit (Grossman and Helpman 1994). Many believe that labor unions are among the most influential of those special interests, pushing for human rights standards of conduct to prevent what they perceive as unfair competition from developing countries with cheap labor exploited through rights abuses (Aaronson 2001; Aaronson and Zimmerman 2007; Hansson 1983; Mazur 1999).

This forceful theory suggests that fair trade regulations protecting human rights should develop and spread when labor unions and other groups whose own interests are threatened by free trade mobilize to defend their jobs. They lobby their policymakers for standards of fair trade conduct. This should be most likely when big economic interests are at stake in an agreement. The theory also suggests that fair trade regulations are likely to focus on protecting human rights of workers and children, whose labor contributes to the comparative trade advantage, but not the rights of voters and citizens or other groups more broadly. It also points to what should be favorable reactions from labor unions to fair trade regulations created to reflect their needs in the first place. And if governments do create fair trade standards to protect workers' human rights in selected industries, they should be likely, at least some of the time, to use the new regulations to limit imports of specific goods facing competition and to protect the workers being harmed.

This theory has much to offer. Governments may want to shield their inefficient domestic industries—especially those at risk of suffering from international competition. As we shall see later, protectionist motivations occupy an important place in this story—particularly in the development of standards protecting workers' and children's human rights in the United States. Bootlegging labor unions matter enormously here, and politicians are often very tuned in to their needs. Yet the influence of protectionist interest groups, though significant, cannot alone explain what has happened with trade agreements.

Labor unions rarely called for fair trade standards of conduct to protect workers' and children's human rights. Instead, they generally opposed trade agreements altogether and asked their policymakers to do the same. Only recently have trade unions come to argue for the creation of regulations protecting human rights, often invoking standards of conduct as a way to oppose trade agreements more than as a way to help correct agreements' shortcomings. Many unions call for more regulations backed by more effective enforcement remedies and penalties on the same footing as those available for violations of commercial provisions. But in the United States, most labor unions continue to ask for a moratorium on any lesser agreement that does not live up to those ideals (AFL-CIO 2006a, 2006b). So far that includes all agreements, despite substantial improvements toward crafting regulations that protect workers' and children's human rights. And in Europe, most labor unions continue to call for more attention to "economic and social" rights, by which they mean human rights for workers and children too. Yet labor unions' specific interests in preventing market access are not very well represented in the new preferential trade agreements policymakers are putting together, either in the United States or in Europe. Moreover, both the United States and Europe continue to make trade deals, with countries such as Jordan and Kazakhstan, that have very little economic effect on their workers one way or the other; the labor unions are nevertheless opposed.

In the United States, PTAs aim to protect workers' and children's human rights, but they ignore broader human rights. In contrast, most European PTAs say little or nothing about workers or children. They focus instead on "fundamental" human rights, which in principle include the rights of all people but in practice are profoundly focused on protections for voters' and citizens' human rights, especially in the implementation stage. Human rights for workers and children, which could affect comparative economic advantage, are a core principle of Europe's unilateral trade system, the GSP, but they have for the most part been passed over or sidelined in most preferential trade agreements, despite what Europe's largest labor unions want or have asked for. This has only recently begun to change.

On the whole, labor unions have rarely supported the new human rights standards of conduct that are placed in PTAs. And today, among the many trade agreements in effect, few actually protect domestic industries by using trade standards of conduct to protect human rights (Elliot and Freeman 2003a). In part, that is because international trade accounts for only a small share of growing income inequality and labor-market displacement in the United States (Lawrence 2008). Governments employ human rights trade regulations with varying degrees of success to protect people; these regulations, however, are almost never targeted at specific goods or industries (Alston, Bustelo, and Heenan 1999; Fierro 2003; Hafner-Burton 2005). Moreover, if the goal of fair preferential trade regulations is to provide a tool for policymakers to help American and European workers save their jobs and keep their wages high, most economists will explain that there are almost certainly better ways to achieve that objective.

Even when labor unions, rightly worried about members' wages and jobs, manage to convince policymakers to protect them from the ills associated with free trade—and they certainly have some of the time—the gaps are considerable between what labor unions articulate they want and which regulations are enacted. This interest-based motivation is a valuable starting point to explain what has happened, but it is incomplete without a corresponding account of institutions—which determine whose interests are best represented in policymaking at home and abroad—and of power, which shapes other countries' influence over regulatory outcomes. Moreover, interest groups in general, including labor unions seeking protections, have no ability to shape either the institutional or the power features of the process.

Human Rights Norms and Advocates

Another valuable explanation for policymakers' attitudes toward human rights trade regulations is that the worldwide human rights movement has had enormous success in putting forward high standards of conduct for countries and societies to follow, encouraging policymakers to act in new and appropriate ways. The normative explanation is very different from the economic one, asserting that the approach to policymaking is principled rather than driven by the desire for material power and influence. On matters of human rights, global norms have been spreading in a legalized and pervasive way since the mid-1980s, when they reached a tipping point at which so many countries had signed on to protect human rights that the spread of these norms could be described as contagious (Risse, Ropp, and Sikkink 1999; Tsutsui and Min Wotipka 2004). Since then, these norms have assumed a near taken-for-granted status, influencing the activities of people, countries, and organizations around the world who relate and act more and more as members of an international community bound by respect for basic human dignity (Finnemore and Sikkink 1998). Now countries that violate human rights are being judged against a new yardstick for what constitutes acceptable behavior.

There are variations on how norms and their advocates are believed to shape international laws and markets. One view holds that advocacy networks made up of human rights entrepreneurs, usually NGOs, mobilize around international norms for the purpose of shaping public opinion, informing policymakers, and diffusing international principles of human rights to countries (Forsythe 2000; Weiss and Gordenker 1996). These entrepreneurs have "strong notions about appropriate or desirable behavior in their community" (Finnemore and Sikkink 1998, 896), often motivated by principled ideas or values rather than by money or natural resources alone (Keck and Sikkink 1998). To be effective, they must win the support of policymakers willing to endorse their norms and able to influence policy outcomes, and they aim to change minds by framing political debates in innovative ways, pressuring targets, and convincing policymakers that something seen as natural or appropriate is actually wrong or inappropriate (Brysk 1993; Finnemore and Sikkink 1998). Under the right circumstances, the global norms they plant become internalized and implemented in domestic policy, first for instrumental reasons but later because policymakers have been socialized to want them (Risse, Ropp, and Sikkink 1999).

Another variation of this theory emphasizes the role of IOs, calling attention to the ways in which they and international laws have become focal points for the affirmation of community norms (Franck 1990; Slaughter 1995). International organizations can actively teach and socialize governments to acknowledge and assume new political goals and values with lasting impacts on important issues like war and human rights (Pevehouse 2005). These new goals and values not only constrain countries' actions but also can alter what countries and their policymakers want (Finnemore 1996).

Still another variation emphasizes acculturation—the general practice of assuming the attitudes and behaviors common to the surrounding culture (Meyer et al. 1997; Powell and DiMaggio 1991). Countries participate in world cultural models that spell out the nature of politics and the purposes of action (Swindler 1986). These cultural forces play an important role in determining countries' regulatory actions (Thomas et al. 1987), orienting policymakers and providing social identities and roles by which they organize to pursue their interests and gain legitimacy (Meyer et al. 1997). Because global regulatory models are available to all countries, the policy result is often "isomorphism"—actors everywhere define themselves in similar ways and engage in similar politics by similar methods (Boli and Thomas 1999). Thus, nations that are under these cultural pressures to assimilate with other countries in the international system may adopt human rights standards of conduct to conform with accepted global norms of behavior spelled out in existing laws and conventions (Goodman and Jinks 2003a, 2003b).

These explanations suggest where else we can look for evidence of the motivations behind human rights regulations in PTAs and what to expect to find. One variation suggests that networks of human rights NGOs are crucial actors, successfully lobbying policymakers to take on their cause. It also suggests that, as a consequence, NGOs should be fairly contented with, or at least not opposed to, the new trade regulations being passed, since they were created partially to respond to their demands. Moreover, it suggests that human rights for all people, not just workers and children, should be taken up by policymakers in this quest to regulate preferential trade markets. Some policymakers who do take up the fair trade plight to protect human rights for instrumental reasons should, over time, come to believe in the rightness of the policies. The second variation suggests that human rights IOs may also play a role in convincing countries to promote human rights through PTAs, changing policymakers' interests. And the final variation suggests a general tendency toward convergence in institutional regulatory design and not much resistance from trade partners, as more and more countries come to see the value of promoting human rights in all affairs, even commerce.

The importance of NGOs and IOs in pressuring governments to adopt trade reforms is carefully considered throughout the following pages. Certainly NGOs have helped force the human rights issue onto political agendas and raise awareness, sometimes even changing policymakers' incentives by making the costs of avoiding the issue more damaging. They have been particularly helpful when it comes to enforcement. Nonetheless, the influence of global norms and their advocates, while growing and at times important, does not explain why the United States and Europe are changing the rules of preferential trade to protect human rights or why most other countries are joining them.

There are several reasons for this. Human rights NGOs and advocates are crucial in explaining what has happened, not so much for their persuasion but for their definition of the problem. They provide the normative discourse used by policymakers with political interests in promoting fair PTA regulations to convince the broader public to support their policy choices—whether the policymakers believe the discourse or not.

In addition, most human rights NGOs, like trade unions, were late to the game of making fair trade standards of conduct, having long argued against preferential trade agreements altogether rather than for agreements with standards protecting human rights. Now savvy NGOs such as Human Rights Watch and Amnesty International are generally on board with the regulatory mission, arguing that more and better trade regulations protecting people are needed (Amnesty International 2005). Few, though, are particularly happy with the policies being made, and many are openly disparaging of them, calling for a major renovation in the way trade agreements regulate human rights and still rejecting most agreements outright on that basis (Human Rights Watch 2004; Interview record #81 2007).

Another shortcoming of this explanation is that American PTAs say nothing about voters' and citizens' human rights at all, despite repeated calls by prominent NGOs and activists. And that is not accidental. Most congressional policymakers in the United States who support human rights for workers and children as part of trade negotiations do not support or advocate human rights for citizens more broadly; rather, most candidly reject them as unacceptable infringements on national sovereignty.

Similarly, international human rights organizations, such as the United Nations or the ILO, have played almost no role in this process of spurring passage of regulations protecting human rights.[17] What is more, many policymakers and governments have signed on to these rules in spite of, or in reaction to the failures of, the global human rights regime, not as a direct result of persuasion by its most important organizations. And some of the human rights trade standards that have been put into practice are in direct conflict with the principles of these organizations.

As should now be clear, policy convergence in no way accurately describes the human rights regulations being made. True, the United States and Europe have both created and spread preferential trade regulations protecting people's human rights, mostly since the end of the cold war. The profound variations between their approaches to law, however, make clear that imitation is not a satisfying explanation for the regulatory trend and that isomorphism is hardly the best way to characterize the institutional outcome or the resulting effects on human rights.

Last, even when human rights norms and advocates, operating on moral principles rather than economic interests, do persuade trade policymakers to do the right thing—to protect people, despite the economic costs—this achievement does not alone explain the specific regulations being made, spread, and implemented. And this explanation for policy preferences is no better than the protectionist account at taking either institutions or power into consideration. Like the labor unions, no NGOs seeking to make a difference and persuade policymakers to act on moral conviction have the capacity to shape either institutions or power.

Credible Commitment

Demand for fair trade standards of conduct can also emerge not from Western human rights bootleggers in search of ways to protect their inter-

---

17. The ILO, however, has been quite helpful and active in advising policymakers on how to implement, as well as monitor, progress in putting America's human rights regulations into practice abroad (Interview Record #72 2006).

ests or from Western human rights Baptists in search of conformity with global norms but from some of the very countries that will be affected by the regulations: democratizing countries in search of better human rights at home.

Why would a country in the developing world with human rights problems want to sign on to PTAs with human rights standards that place conditions on market access to its trading partners? Scholars have considered a similar question about the European Convention for the Protection of Human Rights (Moravcsik 2000). Andrew Moravcsik makes a persuasive case that government leaders who want human rights protected, when confronting substantial domestic political uncertainty, have strong incentives to commit to international institutions as a way to lock in human rights policies at home for the future. Newly minted and transitioning democracies, he argues, are the most likely candidates. Moreover, studies show that the strongest support for binding human rights laws and treaties is likely to develop in recently established and potentially unstable democracies, precisely because countries often turn to IOs to make their own commitments to democratization credible in the eyes of their domestic audiences (Hafner-Burton, Mansfield, and Pevehouse 2008).

Jon Pevehouse (2002, 2005) makes a related argument about regional organizations, which have proven to be a potent force for instilling and protecting democracy throughout the world. Certain types of regional IOs provide strong policy guarantees to key groups inside countries, including leaders, business elites, and the military. They help to assuage fears and persuade these governments to support political liberalization, reassuring elites that their interests will be protected on the issues they value.

This view suggests that many other countries could want and may even initiate the creation of fair PTA standards of conduct protecting people. This should happen especially when human rights are not effectively secured at home but groups of politicians, businesses, or military want to secure human rights at home. It also suggests that democratic and autocratic countries characterized by greater political stability are both likely to resist making human rights trade regulations of any kind.

It is entirely reasonable to think that policymakers from countries other than the United States and those in Europe might come to the preferential trade negotiating table with human rights in mind. And this credible-commitment account usefully draws attention to the role that troubled countries with inspired leaders or domestic groups play in designing trade agreement regulations; most of all, it encourages a perspective that emphasizes these countries' agency, interests, and capacity to shape markets through international laws.

While we will see later that this account is not wrong—in a few instances, governments have approached the West and requested trade regulations protecting human rights—a deeper look at the international bargaining process reveals that these instances are exceptions. Most governments have passionately challenged the American and European push for fair PTA regulations protecting human rights from start to finish, even those on a path to democracy. Many countries in the preferential trade process are hardly democratic or transitional; some are outright authoritarians with no intention of protecting people's rights, but they sign on anyway. Like protectionism and norms, which help explain the origin of policymakers' preferences, this description of the policy process cannot account for either institutions or power and so remains an incomplete explanation. Table 2 reviews the expectations that follow from these alternative arguments—in the pages to come, only a few will be supported by evidence.

TABLE 2. IMPLICATIONS FROM THREE ALTERNATIVE ACCOUNTS

PROTECTIONISM
1. Policymakers create fair PTA standards of human rights conduct because labor unions, seeking protection from international competition, demand them. (RARELY)
2. Fair PTA standards protecting human rights regulate workers' and children's human rights but not broader voters' and citizens' human rights. (ONLY IN THE UNITED STATES)
3. Labor unions do not oppose fair PTA standards of conduct designed to help them. (WRONG)
4. Policymakers who create trade regulations protecting human rights also seek to use them to limit imports of specific goods facing competition. (RARELY)

NORMS AND MORAL ADVOCATES
5. Policymakers create fair PTA standards of human rights conduct because NGOs, for moral reasons, demand them. (RARELY)
6. Human rights NGOs do not oppose fair PTA standards of conduct designed to help them. (WRONG)
7. Fair PTA regulations protect human rights for all people, not just workers and children. (ONLY IN EUROPE)
8. Some policymakers who advocate fair trade regulations for political reasons also over time become moral advocates. (RARELY)

9. Human rights IOs convince countries to create fair PTA regulations by lobbying to change policymakers' interests. (NEVER)
10. Fair PTA regulations in the United States and Europe converge, looking more alike. (NO)
11. Trade partners show little resistance to accepting fair PTA regulations protecting human rights. (WRONG)

COMMITMENT

12. Countries transitioning to democracy and suffering from political instability want fair PTA regulations protecting human rights. (RARELY)
13. Democratic and autocratic countries characterized by political stability resist including any human rights standards of conduct in trade agreements. (OFTEN)

People are worried about globalization. Protectionist motivations, driven by domestic economic interests, are clearly present and do shape policy. Yet the following chapters will show that the policymakers who have most strongly advocated for PTA regulations protecting human rights have seldom faithfully represented the position of most labor unions or globalization critics, which have been and remain quite critical of the regulations. Rather, some policymakers who advocate for fair trade standards of conduct have sought to take the edge off labor unions' hostility toward trade agreements by offering regulations that fall quite short of the policy most unions really favor—no trade at all. This is especially true in the United States. Other policymakers aim to make PTA regulations that protect human rights for reasons entirely unrelated to what labor unions are asking for, aiming instead to solve bureaucratic and security problems. This is especially true in Europe. Thus the gap between what labor unions want and which policies get made is massive.

Much the same can be said for norms. The story to come will show that global human rights norms do exist, and dedicated advocates champion them, but trade regulations protecting human rights are also out of sync with what most activists want or are asking for. What is more, advocates have been most represented in the trade policymaking process when their arguments have served the political needs of politicians or of bootleggers—in this case, interest groups that stand to profit from the rules. They have had very little sway over the regulations otherwise and are often ignored. Even so, their work has become crucial for implementation of the regulations. Commitment theories also fall short because most countries oppose trade standards of conduct protecting human rights and sign on for regulations only as a concession to win market access or political connection to the West. There are a few exceptions.

Most important of all, none of the three other accounts— protectionism, norms, and uncertainty—considers in any systematic way how institutions and power shape these policies, or how these policies affect the behavior of perpetrators.

The spread of fair trade standards of conduct is the result of a major and unprecedented series of policy changes. It has been and remains a contentious process. It has been driven through trial and error and institutional precedent by smart American and European policymakers responding to their political environments and using their policymaking capacity to advocate for their interests, often against the wishes of other policymakers and countries. And, despite policymakers' main intentions, which only sometimes include forcing perpetrators in other countries to protect the lives and rights of their people, these regulations can make a difference in the lives of some people. These first two chapters have set the stage for understanding the process. The remainder of this book tells the story as it happened.

CHAPTER 3

PREFERENCES

We turn back now to our original question: Why did some policymakers in the United States and Europe advocate for regulations protecting human rights within preferential trade agreements? Chapter 2 described the conditions under which this advocacy develops. Policymakers want human rights protections when those regulations help them to solve other political problems or to win the support of bootlegger interest groups that can help them amass more money, power, or influence and when they can use moral language to sell the policy, regardless of whether they share the moral convictions about the value of protecting people's human rights. Therefore, moral advocates such as NGOs or IOs that champion human rights trade regulations on principled grounds mostly have their goals represented when moral convictions and political interests overlap. Otherwise they are likely to be sidelined or ignored.[1]

This chapter provides historical evidence for those scenarios, at the same time dispelling ideas that policymakers want to make fair PTA regulations protecting human rights because NGOs or IOs demand them; that labor unions have been successful in swaying policymakers to do what they want; and that policymakers swayed by moral advocates favor human rights protections for all people, not just for certain sectors or groups.[2] The truth is that moral arguments are often put aside; labor unions have persuaded some policymakers but not others; and policymakers commonly advocate for regulations on some human rights but not others. In the process, fair

1. These arguments are summarized in table 1 of chapter 2.
2. These alternative arguments are summarized in table 2 of chapter 2.

trade regulations have developed in richly different ways in the United States and Europe.

What follows is a more in-depth look at policymakers' views on whether to include human rights standards of conduct in PTAs, which human rights to regulate, and whether and how to enforce them.

Changing Regulations

Between 1947, when the GATT was signed, and 1994, when the WTO was created, countries made hundreds of PTAs.[3] In 1947, none of them said a word about protecting human rights, though European and American governments were already advocating for human rights around the world through various other foreign policies.

The US government has a long history of trying to influence human rights abroad, and national legislation restricting trade and financial or other assistance to repressive governments has been common (Hufbauer, Schott, and Elliott 1990). In the late 1800s, the McKinley Tariff Act prohibited the import of goods produced by prison labor. That provision was expanded in the 1930 Smoot-Hawley Tariff Act (19 U.S.C. § 1307) to include a prohibition on the importation of goods produced by forced, convict, or indentured labor, which is still in force today.[4] The Jackson-Vanik Amendment (1974) to the Trade Act explicitly linked human rights to US unilateral trade preferences for the first time, conditioning the Soviet Union's trade status on its willingness to accept Jewish immigrants. The Trade Act also instructed US negotiators to seek fair labor standards in the GATT, although such standards were never adopted.[5] The Harking Amendment (1975) to the US International Development and Food Assistance Act prohibited aid to governments repressing human rights unless that aid would directly benefit those most in need (Kumado 1993). In 1984, Congress passed the GSP, unilaterally granting duty-free access to less-developed

3. GATT/WTO members participating in preferential trade agreements are required to meet a set of preferential trading conditions defined in the text of GATT Article XXIV, and its updates that include the 1994 Understanding on the Interpretation of Article XXIV of the General Agreement on Tariffs and Trade, as well as the text of GATT Article V. Note that many agreements are not notified to the WTO.

4. In May 2005, Senator Thomas Harkin (D-IA) introduced a bill to amend the Tariff Act of 1930 to eliminate the consumptive demand exception relating to the importation of goods made with forced labor.

5. In 1950, the US House of Representatives passed a bill (HR 7797) requiring that trade agreements with less-developed countries establish fair labor standards on wages and working conditions. The bill never became law. See Charnovitz (1987).

countries' exports, subject to protection of certain human rights for workers—although it did not accept the ILO's definition of which human rights were essential (Elliot and Freeman 2003a).[6] Similar laws have followed. By the time the WTO came into being, the US government had more than one hundred such laws on the books, and American states and local municipalities had passed their own legislation to censure governments that abuse human rights (US International Trade Commission 1998).

Although the United States was quick to embrace human rights in matters of foreign policy, it was relatively slow to welcome bilateral and regional trade integration. In 1985 the United States and Israel signed a free trade agreement—the US government's first such PTA. It was designed to eliminate within a decade all tariff barriers on industrial products (Rosen 2004) and was enacted mainly to assert US support for Israel (Fergusson and Sek 2005).[7] Four years later the United States entered into a similar agreement with Canada. Neither agreement mentioned protections for people at all. Grave violations of human rights committed by the Israeli government against Palestinian, Syrian, and Lebanese civilians were ignored, playing no role in the negotiation of the free trade agreement with Israel despite substantial public outcry (Abraham et al. 1988; Amnesty International 1983). Lawmakers argued that bilateral market agreements were not the place to combat repression because other policies were available to do the job.

Europe's experience has been quite different, as the practice of using European foreign policy to influence human rights has been limited by the pace at which Europe became a union. During the cold war, policies designed to promote human rights in other countries were mostly left to the discretion of the member states of the European Community (1957).[8] As signatories to the European Convention on Human Rights (1950), many member states pursued aid and trade policies by themselves designed to force repressive governments around the world to reform (Gillies 1996). But from the perspective of the EC, human rights did not become a focus

6. The United States did not accept the ILO norm against discrimination in the workplace but included rules protecting minimum wages and hours. See the Trade and Tariff Act of 1984 (P.L. 98-573). Six laws have since authorized GSP packages (most recently P.L. 107-210).

7. The agreement was amended in 1996 to include the West Bank and Gaza Strip and qualifying industrial zones between Israel and Jordan and Israel and Egypt.

8. The Treaty of Rome founded the European Economic Community in 1957. In 1992, the European Community became the first of three pillars of the European Union by the Maastricht Treaty, and today it is the primary legal entity representing the European Union in external relations.

of external relations until the late 1980s, when the use of sanctions tools was first coordinated within the framework of European Political Co-operation (EPC) (Brandtner and Rosas 1998; Hazelzet 2001).[9]

While slow to formulate supranational policies on human rights, the EC began to create PTAs almost immediately after its formation, signing successive trade agreements, known as the Lomé conventions, with African, Caribbean, and Pacific countries (ACP) that would, years later, become the trade agreement known as the Cotonou Convention, and finally, economic partnership agreements.[10] Trade agreements with Iceland and Norway (1973), Algeria (1976), and Syria (1977), among many others, were made; and Europe formalized trade cooperation with more than one hundred nations by the following decade. Nonetheless, protections for human rights were intentionally kept out of the trade agreements for years, and rights violations were rarely acted upon, despite requests from the European Parliament (EP) and activist groups. Many times, grave abuses by Europe's trade partners were rejected as reasons for suspending agreements.[11] Back then, human rights was not a legitimate issue for European PTA regulations and was rejected explicitly and repeatedly (Bartels 2005).

Then regulatory change came by storm. Europe began first, creating one of its earliest fair PTAs protecting human rights in 1990: the Lomé IV Convention made market access for ACP countries conditional upon fundamental human rights, as did a trade agreement with Argentina.[12] In 1991, the European Commission expanded these protections of human rights

9. Nonetheless, human rights did appear in some European Political Co-operation statements between 1970 and 1989, although no significant actions were taken. See Stavridis (1991). In 1986, the EPC produced a Declaration on Human Rights signaling the first public and comprehensive statement by the then twelve EC member states recognizing human rights as a cornerstone of European cooperation but offering no guidelines for how to promote human rights abroad. See King (1999).

10. The successive Lomé conventions established a system of trade preferences designed to ensure that manufactured and agricultural products entering Europe would not compete with products covered by Europe's Common Agricultural Policy and would not be subject to duties or quantitative restrictions.

11. In 1982, Surinam's government executed fifteen opposition leaders, prompting the Netherlands to immediately suspend its development cooperation treaty. The European Commission refused to do the same (Fierro 2003; Smits 1980), just as it had refused the request of the EP to suspend cooperation with the Central African Republic for severe human rights violations a few years earlier (European Parliament 1978b). It also chose not to suspend an agreement with Zaire for brutal violations of human rights, instead affirming the Community's commitment to trade under the PTA, Lomé I (European Parliament 1980d).

12. One of the first mentions of human rights in the body of a trade agreement was in Article 5 of the fourth Lomé Convention, concluded in December 1989. Article 5, however, did not create a transparent legal basis to suspend agreements in the event of serious human rights violations. See the European Commission (1995). In an earlier agreement with several Central American countries (1985), support for human rights was mentioned in the

to all Community-level PTAs with developing countries. Four years later, the Commission issued another communication, followed by a resolution from the European Parliament and a decision by the European Council, to make protections for human rights a standard feature of trade agreements. These decisions meant that all preferential trade agreements, although not sectoral trade agreements, now required as "essential elements" suspension mechanisms to enforce human rights and democracy. This 1995 legislation remains the cornerstone of European regulatory policy on trade standards protecting human rights.[13] Around the same time, Europe reformed its unilateral GSP to protect workers' human rights.

The United States, which had already begun the process of linking human rights to development aid under President Jimmy Carter, would soon follow Europe's lead in incorporating human rights protections in PTAs, although via a different course. The United States created its first free trade agreement protecting workers' human rights in 1994: the North American Agreement on Labor Cooperation (NAALC), which was a side agreement to NAFTA. That was followed by an even stronger commitment to protect the human rights of workers. The United States signed the US-Jordan Free Trade Agreement in 2000 and in 2002 made PTA protection of workers' and children's human rights national law, requiring that all future free trade agreements negotiated within the time frame of this law include the protection.[14] By the time the WTO was up and running, human rights of various kinds were being regulated by preferential trade agreements all over the world, and more of these rules were on their way.

Actors Vying for Influence

What happened in this short time to make policymakers want more trade regulation to protect human rights? Who wanted human rights standards of conduct? Which kinds of human rights did they want to protect? And with whose interests were they likely to align? A variety of actors and

---

preamble, although it was not lawfully enforceable. See the Council of the European Union (1986).

13. There have been many additional developments since 1995; some are summarized in the timeline in the appendix.

14. Unlike the 1995 European Council decision, which is binding without term limit, the 2002 US Trade Act expired in July 2007. It granted the president trade promotion authority on the condition that protection for workers' and children's human rights were a core element of trade agreements.

interest groups were vying to influence policymakers to get what they wanted.

Norms and IOs

Human rights norms were on the rise throughout the twentieth century, and laws and organizations supporting them have long been spreading.[15] Between the creation of the GATT and the WTO, more and more global human rights laws were adopted. This international norm regime is now championed by a growing number of treaties and instruments designed to protect identifiable groups, such as women and children, as well as to protect all people against particular government behaviors, such as torture. At the heart of this regime are the 1945 UN Charter (Article 55), the Universal Declaration on Human Rights, seven international agreements that define a set of global regulations—the first created in 1965—and a host of regional instruments.[16] In addition, the 1919 ILO is home to several global conventions dating back to 1930 that protect workers[17] and today provide instruments to protect four core human rights—freedom of association, elimination of forced or compulsory labor, abolition of child labor, and elimination of employment discrimination—among many other rights.[18]

Almost all countries in the world have ratified one or more of these instruments. The United States and Europe, however, have approached support of the regime differently and today acknowledge different interna-

15. Before World War II, international law protecting human rights was meager, as countries limited their international legal obligations to declarations of intent and to a small number of developing treaties and conventions. Examples include the formal prohibition of the slave trade by the Treaty of Vienna (1815) and the General Act of Brussels (1890).

16. These include the International Convention on the Elimination of All Forms of Racial Discrimination (1965); International Convention on Economic, Social and Cultural Rights (1966); International Convention on Civil and Political Rights (1966); Convention on the Elimination of All Forms of Discrimination Against Women (1979); Convention Against Torture and Other Cruel, Inhuman or Degrading Treatment or Punishment (1989); Convention on the Rights of the Child (1989); and the International Convention on the Protection of the Rights of All Migrant Workers and Members of Their Families (2003).

17. These include No. 29, Forced Labor Convention (1930); No. 87, Freedom of Association and Protection of the Right to Organize Convention (1948); No. 98, Right to Organize and Collective Bargaining Convention (1949); No. 100, Equal Remuneration Convention (1951); No. 105, Abolition of Forced Labor Convention (1957); No. 111, Discrimination (Employment and Occupation) Convention (1958); No. 138, Minimum Age Convention, (1973); and No. 182, Convention Concerning the Prohibition and Immediate Action for the Elimination of the Worst Forms of Child Labor (1999).

18. These core human rights standards are articulated in the 1998 ILO Declaration on Fundamental Principles and Rights at Work.

tional norms and laws. The US government has ratified only two ILO conventions—banning forced labor and child labor—and only three human rights treaties—protecting civil and political rights and protecting against racial discrimination and torture.[19] Europe, by contrast, has a more involved track record, with member states signing on to most human rights laws and labor conventions.

NGOs

Since the era of mass mobilization against the Vietnam War, NGOs have worked especially hard to rouse and channel popular concern for human rights into American and European foreign policies, drawing upon the development of global norms and laws (Dorsey 2000).[20] In their fight to change minds and shape policies, NGOs of all shapes and sizes have set out to collect accurate information about abuses, report to the public, push for accountability, and win support from liberal governments willing to do something about the problem of human rights violations (Keck and Sikkink 1998; Khagram, Riker, and Sikkink 2002; Tarrow 2005). Ever since the end of the cold war, as advancements in communications technology have made global networks increasingly sophisticated, these networks have focused much of their activism on the dangers of globalization. These networks include NGOs representing worldwide campaigns for internationally recognized human rights. Among them are Amnesty International, with more than two million members in more than 150 countries; Human Rights Watch, the largest human rights organization based in America; and the Network of European World Shops, representing thousands of shops that offer fair trade products. These groups also work alongside locally based advocacy organizations committed to the same cause.

On the whole, human rights NGOs are concerned that PTAs undermine human rights among the most vulnerable sectors of the population and that efforts to create new trade deals prompt violence and repression against challengers (Amnesty International 2006). They have argued that trading with perpetrators violates global norms against torture, discrimination against women, and protection of civil and political rights, as well as the fundamental human rights of workers. And although their policy recommendations vary—some oppose making trade agreements altogether,

19. The United States ratified the Convention Against Torture with reservations and has ratified two optional protocols to the Convention on the Rights of the Child, although not the convention itself.

20. Amnesty International was an early human rights organization, created in 1961 to help secure the release of political prisoners.

while others take no position on trade per se—hundreds of NGOs in the United States and Europe are organizing, lobbying, and sometimes demonstrating in favor of human rights. The NGOs say, if trade agreements must be made, they should include protections for people.

Human Rights Watch, for instance, has argued that measures to protect human rights "should be built into trade agreements to ensure that globalization does not come at the expense of human rights" (Human Rights Watch 2006b), especially those internationally recognized by law (Human Rights Watch 2002; Human Rights Watch 2005; Interview record #81, 2007). Amnesty International, meanwhile, has frequently called for governments to carry out human rights impact assessments before concluding any new trade and investment agreements, as well as after the adoption of any such agreements. The group believes these steps are critical to evaluate the full range of governments' human rights obligations spelled out in the United Nations Charter and treaties—protections for workers and children but also civil and political rights, rights for women and migrants, and freedom from torture (Amnesty International 2006). Both NGOs and other human rights groups have continually pressured American and European policymakers to place a broad collection of human rights standards of conduct into preferential trade agreements, criticizing agreements such as NAFTA or Europe's agreements with Latin America and Caribbean countries for not going far enough to effectively protect people, especially those who are most defenseless (Amnesty International 2006).

Voters

While NGOs have been vocal in their concerns, many voters don't share their worry about whether or how the government protects human rights abroad. Beginning in the 1970s, the Chicago Council on Foreign Relations undertook a survey of foreign policy attitudes in the United States. In 1978, 1982, 1986, 1990, and 1994, survey respondents were asked how important they thought "promoting and defending human rights in other countries" was as a foreign policy goal. Human rights never emerged as a top priority. About one in three respondents thought the issue was "very important" in 1978; this number rose to one in two right after the fall of the Berlin Wall, but even then, human rights ranked behind the long-time goal of protecting American workers,[21] as well as protecting the interests of American firms abroad, securing energy supplies, and defending American allies.

21. For an excellent overview of the issue in the United States, see Elliot and Freeman (2003b).

And that support declined rapidly: in 1994 only one in three respondents thought human rights was a very important goal.[22] A 1993 Times Mirror survey put that number at 28 percent. Surveys gauging American leaders' opinion on human rights in foreign policy show even less support (Holsti 2000).[23]

Public support for human rights among European consumers has also been weak. Before the creation of the EU, few Europeans believed that the issue of human rights was sufficiently important "to do something about." A 1987 survey found that one in two French respondents thought human rights merited attention, while fewer than one in three British respondents and about one in ten German respondents agreed (Eurobarometer 1987).[24] Surveys after the creation of the European Union showed that only one in three respondents believed the European Parliament, directly elected by the people, should pay particular attention to "human rights throughout the world" (Eurobarometer 1995a; Eurobarometer 1995b). Meanwhile, a European election study in 1994 revealed that protection of workers' human rights was not a major European election issue that year, with fewer than one in twenty respondents citing workers' human rights as the issue with the most influence on their vote (European Election Study Group 1996); a Eurobarometer study a few years later showed that one in three French and German respondents and one in seven British respondents identified the "fight for workers' rights" as the issue that would most influence their vote in the next general election (Eurobarometer 1996). Certainly, many American and European voters care deeply about human rights and want to see them protected, but when it comes to the issues people vote for, protecting human rights in other countries has never been a top priority.

22. The general public showed even less support for a related survey question on "helping to bring a democratic form of government to other countries" as a foreign policy goal. See Holsti (2000).

23. Three surveys gauge public opinion on human rights among American leaders—the Chicago Council on Foreign Relations panels and the Times Mirror survey (both discussed above), and the Foreign Policy Leadership Project, run in 1980, 1984, 1988, 1992, and 1996. All show that when asked to rank "promoting and defending human rights in other countries" as an American foreign policy goal, leaders are even less apt than the general public to categorize them as "very important."

24. Respondents were asked: "Which of the ideas or causes in the following list are sufficiently important for you to do something about, even if this might involve giving up other things?" Sexual equality. Protection of environment. World peace. Struggle against poverty. (Your country's) defenses. Religious faith. The unification of Europe. Freedom of the individual. Human rights. The revolution. Help to the third world. Multiple answers were possible.

Labor Unions

The United States and Europe are also home to some of the world's most influential labor unions, organized to persuade policymakers to represent workers' interests.[25] Among these organizations, the American Federation of Labor and Congress of Industrial Organizations (AFL-CIO), founded in 1955, is a coalition made up of fifty-four national and international labor unions that represents some ten million workers. The International Confederation of Free Trade Unions (ICFTU), formed a few years earlier, now has hundreds of affiliated organizations in more than one hundred countries around the world, representing 155 million people. The European Trade Union Confederation (ETUC), established in 1973, represents workers' needs within EC institutions. Its members include more than eighty National Trade Union Confederations from thirty-six European countries. Together, these organizations and others like them aim to promote and protect workers' well-being and security. Since the end of the cold war, these groups have increasingly lobbied for regulations to shield workers—though not other victims—from the perceived ills brought on by globalization.

In the United States, labor unions are largely opposed to most free trade agreements, perceiving them as counterproductive to their members' economic interests.[26] The AFL-CIO has argued that US trade policies "have utterly failed to ensure that American producers and workers are able to compete successfully in the global economy" (AFL-CIO 2007b). It believes that NAFTA has been a "disaster" for workers (AFL-CIO 2002; AFL-CIO 2007c), hastening American job losses and lowering standards of living by intensifying wage-based competition with countries that exploit their

25. Europe has recently experienced an extensive decline of labor union support. Presently, the European Union's four largest countries have fairly small levels of unionization among their employed workers, with Italy at 30 percent; the UK, 29 percent;, Germany, 27 percent; and France, 9 percent. Consequently, three out of four European workers do not belong to a labor union. See the Federation of European Employers (2007). In the last three decades, union membership as a percentage of the US workforce has also progressively declined, from 23 percent in 1977 to only 13 percent in 2003, as the total number of union members decreased by four million. See Hufbauer and Schott (2002). On the effect of trade on deunionization in the United States between 1977 and 1997, see Baldwin (2003).

26. In addition to lobbying Congress, labor groups have long advised the administration on matters of trade. The Trade Act of 1974 established a trade advisory committee system to advise the US administration on trade policy, and it is run in cooperation with five federal agencies, including the US Trade Representative's Office, the Departments of Commerce, Agriculture, and Labor, and the Environmental Protection Agency. Advisory groups are made up of more than 750 advisers representing business, labor, agriculture, environmental groups, consumers, local governments, and academic and other experts.

workers to their own comparative advantage. It fears other similar trade agreements such as the DR-CAFTA or accords with Colombia, Oman, or South Korea will deliver more bad news for American workers: job losses and wage reductions (AFL-CIO 2006a; AFL-CIO 2007a).

To protect American wages and jobs, labor unions have allied with human rights groups, embracing their principled concerns for workers in other countries and arguing that future trade agreements should include enforceable protection for workers' fundamental human rights, as recognized by the ILO (AFL-CIO 2006b; International Confederation of Free Trade Unions 2004). Citing horrible cases of brutality against workers and union leaders around the world and appealing to principles of international law, American labor unions have increasingly made their economic case against free trade into a moral case. They have demanded a moratorium on new trade agreements until those agreements protect and advance workers' interests everywhere. Unions hope such protections will save Americans from bad working conditions and foreigners from brutality associated with their working conditions (AFL-CIO 2006b; International Confederation of Free Trade Unions 2004).

European labor unions have mainly taken a similar, although less critical, position on preferential trade agreements. The ETUC has stressed that it is "not opposed to the development of bilateral or inter-regional agreements." However, the secretary-general of the confederation has also made clear that "Europe's trade policy must integrate basic principles, such as the promotion of decent work, social protection and core labour standards in all its negotiations," and has criticized Europe's choice of trade partners, such as Korea and India, which are "ignoring international obligations on workers' rights" (EurActiv 2006). Like their American counterparts, many European labor unions have allied with human rights advocates to promote their cause, calling for "the development and enforcement of fair rules on international trade and investment that are in conformity with human rights standards, including core labour rights" (European Trade Union Confederation 2004). They have been vocal about including these regulations in trade agreements with the ACP countries (European Trade Union Confederation 2004a, 2004b, 2004c), Turkey (European Trade Union Confederation 2005a), and the WTO (European Trade Union Confederation 2005b), among many others.

Economist Bruce Yandle neatly summarized the matter nearly three decades ago:

What do industry and labor want from the regulators? They want protection from competition, from technological change, and from losses that threaten profits and jobs. A carefully constructed regulation can accomplish all kinds of anticompetitive goals of this sort, while giving the citizenry the impression that the only goal is to serve the public interest. (1983, 13)

Businesses

Businesses are certainly among the largest political donors to policymakers involved in crafting trade policies and as such have been extremely influential. The US Chamber of Commerce, set up in 1912, today represents more than three million businesses, from large Fortune 500 companies to small firms, including hundreds of associations and thousands of local chambers. The National Foreign Trade Council (NFTC), created a few years later by a group of American companies that supported an open world trading system, now serves more than three hundred member companies. The US Council for International Business (USCIB), founded in 1945 to promote free trade, has an active membership of more than three hundred multinational companies, law firms, and business associations. Meanwhile, the Confederation of European Business (UNICE), with thirty-nine members from thirty-three countries, speaks for the European institutions. For the past fifty years, UNICE has worked to implement reforms for growth and jobs, integrate the European market, fight national protectionism, and take advantage of the opportunities of enlargement.

Some businesses, especially in export manufacturing industries, want trade protections, but these large business associations and many others like them support free trade because they are eager to access foreign markets.[27] In the United States during the last two decades, they have come out strongly in favor of trade agreements, including NAFTA and agreements with Jordan, Chile, Singapore, Morocco, and South Korea, as well as legislation for trade promotion authority (TPA). As the next chapter explains, this allows the president to negotiate trade agreements under special rules (National Foreign Trade Council 2001; US Chamber of Commerce 2000; US Chamber of Commerce 2004; US Council for International Business 2001). In Europe, there are also businesses that want protection against cheap imports, but many large business associations have also keenly supported multilateral trade negotiations through the GATT and WTO for decades, recognizing that PTAs with countries that receive high volumes

27. One exception is the US Business and Industry Council (USBIC), an organization representing the interests of American firms in the manufacturing, processing, and fabricating industries since 1933. One of the few of its kind among national business associations, the USBIC has time after time opposed free trade agreements, even before NAFTA.

of European exports, such as India, are essential to stimulate competition and growth in Europe (Confederation of European Business 2006; Confederation of European Business 2007; EurActiv 2006).

Because many of the largest business associations want more free trade, they also oppose protectionist regulations, such as trade standards of conduct for protecting human rights, whether for workers or other victims of abuses. Still, like the labor unions, they have often employed a moral discourse on human rights to justify their economic interests. In the United States, for instance, the USCIB "recognizes the importance of improving worker rights in the global economy and shares concerns that countries be held accountable in cases of abusive labor practices." It has argued, however, that the "most effective way to do this is to strengthen the capacity of the International Labor Organization to effectively address violations of fundamental worker rights." It has also resisted the use of regulations to enforce human rights for workers through preferential trade agreements on that basis (US Council for International Business 2007). The US Chamber of Commerce and NFTC have done the same.

Nonetheless, all three organizations have supported the passage of American trade agreements, such as the one with Jordan, or laws, such as the 2002 Trade Promotion Authority, that establish trade regulations protecting workers' and children's human rights, despite their general opposition to protectionist measures (National Foreign Trade Council 2002; US Chamber of Commerce 2000). They have done so not because they want the human rights regulations but because they want the trade and would prefer agreements with human rights regulations to no agreements at all. Many have been silent on the issue of labor during national debates over TPA to avoid undermining progress on the issue they care about most: gaining more market access.[28] In Europe, the UNICE has done much the same, supporting the creation of new trade agreements, even those that include human rights protections, but arguing that "non-tariff barriers should be effectively tackled" and that "negotiations should be clearly labeled as trade agreements and not be linked to parallel political cooperation accords" (Confederation of European Business 2006). Few large business associations have supported suspending PTAs to enforce human rights regulatory conditions on trade partners, but most have been eager to see more trade deals made.

---

28. American business associations, including the USCIB and others, were vocal about the possible extension of TPA past the July 1, 2007, deadline, coming out in opposition to Democrats' proposals on labor. These groups said they would prefer to see the trade agenda fold rather than accept those demands. See Vaughan (2007).

Policymakers' Preferences

It is very hard to read the minds of people in power to understand why they make the decisions they do, and asking them to explain their motivations is not always illuminating either. Nonetheless, it is clear that interest groups and moral advocates shape policymakers' views, but so do other political problems as well as decisive political events beyond the control of most interest groups and human rights advocates.

The story of why PTAs came to protect human rights starts not with NGOs or labor unions but with policymakers in powerful countries searching for ways to solve troubling economic and security problems that arose as a result of the cold war and its end. In both the United States and Europe, executive branches of government sought new preferential trading relationships with countries around the world—many of them repressive and undemocratic—to make political or economic gains. This desire to forge new market ties, alongside decisive political events such as elections and genocides, created windows of opportunity for other policymakers to place human rights on the trade agenda. They did so by offering their support for trade in exchange for regulations protecting people. The issue of human rights was thus progressively taken up in debates over preferential trade policy as a way to fight for political influence, in the United States mostly at home and in Europe both at home and abroad.

The following section considers some of the policymakers who came to play a role in shaping the regulations and what they hoped to achieve in the area of trade and human rights for voters and citizens, workers and children.

The United States

The movement toward fair preferential trade agreements mainly took off in the United States with the changing geopolitics of markets and political loyalties that followed the end of the cold war. Cooperation problems during the Uruguay Trade Round—the multilateral negotiations that would eventually lead to the creation of the WTO—motivated Republican president Ronald Reagan's administration to pursue other paths to secure US trade interests (Schott 2004a). At the heart of the problem were disagreements over agricultural policy. The US administration wanted the elimination of European export subsidies and trade-distorting policies among GATT members, and multilateral trade negotiations teetered on the brink of failure over the issue for nearly a decade. At the same time, Mexico was pulling out of an economic recession and began a process of liberal reform, seeking GATT membership (1986) and a Framework Understanding on Trade and Investment with the

United States (1987). These initiatives were bolstered by the election in 1988 of Mexican president Salinas de Gortari, who came to office with an agenda of market liberalization. In 1990, as Communism collapsed, President Salinas and Mexican secretary of trade Jaime Serra proposed a free trade agreement with the United States and Canada, which would eventually become NAFTA. Motivated by faltering GATT negotiations and Mexico's improvements, the US administration agreed (Hufbauer and Goodrich 2004; Ruggiero 2004). Discussions would take the better part of the next few years (Cameron and Tomlin 2000; Drydan 1995; Mayer 1998).

NAFTA opened the door to labor protections. President Ronald Reagan, true to his Republican Party's commitment to free trade, consistently opposed trade regulations to protect human rights of any kind. The trade agreements he negotiated with Israel and Canada during his tenure said nothing about protecting people. Under his watch, though, the 1984 GSP Renewal Act did impose unilateral standards, requiring other countries to take steps in support of workers' human rights as a condition for GSP benefits. Reagan himself opposed the regulations. He was concerned that even though the regulations were vague and weak, they would diminish his administration's flexibility to offer trade preferences or suspend benefits, and more specifically that they would harm American relations with oil-producing allies where discrimination against women and non-Muslims was common (Compa and Vogt 2005).

During NAFTA negotiations the administration of President George H. W. Bush was similarly uninterested in including human rights protections in the trade agreement, especially since the standards would now be applied to the United States as well. Bush's administration was sympathetic to big business interests and the Republican Party's platform against protectionism and thus opposed fair trade regulations of any kind. United States Trade Representative (USTR) Carla Hills negotiated NAFTA accordingly. The presidential election in 1992, however, would complicate matters because NAFTA would have to pass through Congress during the next administration in order to become law.

Democrats had long been divided on the issue of linking trade and worker protections. Particularly troublesome was the question of whether the United States should join trade accords that imposed mutual obligations on all partners, including the American government. Unilateral obligations on other countries were easier to agree on because they could not be used against the United States.[29] When Ross Perot announced his

---

29. In 1984, Congress passed the GSP Renewal Act, which allowed the United States to link unilateral trade preferences to another country's protections for labor rights; the

intention to run for president as a third-party candidate, he decried NAFTA as a fiasco that would create a "giant sucking sound" as American jobs left the country (Perot 1992). Fueled by Perot's campaign against outsourcing jobs, political disputes over whether and how to protect human rights for workers and children gained new momentum among Democratic contenders for their party's presidential nomination.[30]

Paul Tsongas, the former senator from Massachusetts, came out strongly in favor of NAFTA. Jerry Brown, the former California governor and a favorite of the labor unions, opposed NAFTA, saying he would support a trade agreement negotiated by representatives of working people but not one ordered by US corporations that wanted to move their plants to Mexico (Orme 1996). The Reverend Jesse Jackson, who would come to play a major role in the party's effort to register and mobilize minority voters, also opposed NAFTA. Meanwhile, Bill Clinton, then governor of Arkansas, was between a rock and a hard place, having previously declared his support for NAFTA but now facing mounting opposition from his own party base. Core Democratic voters were concerned about NAFTA's effects on workers and the environment, despite evidence that the agreement would probably create net gains for most sectors in the United States. After much deliberation, Clinton eventually took the middle road, announcing late in 1992 that he would support NAFTA but assuring American workers they would be supported through adjustment assistance programs. He also called for additional negotiations with Mexico and Canada to manage the agreement's shortcomings on worker-rights protections.

Sensitive both to labor constituents who opposed NAFTA and to business leaders who supported it, Clinton's stance on labor regulation reflected an attempt to distance himself from his competitors' extreme views—both in the Democratic primaries and then in the general election. He found his middle ground with the advice of many influential Democrats in Congress, including Senator Daniel Patrick Moynihan (D-NY) and Senator Bill Bradley (D-NJ), who helped him find his strategic position on the labor

---

act, however, made no such requirements of the American government, making it less controversial.

30. Concerns over labor standards in the United States certainly did not begin with NAFTA. Throughout the nineteenth century, "pauper labor" arguments had been part of tariff debates, and throughout the twentieth century delegation to trade institutions for protections of workers' human rights has been repeatedly discussed. The 1984 GSP linked human rights to unilateral trade preferences. The novelty during NAFTA negotiations was the fierceness of the opposition mobilized by the US labor movement, prompted by fears of a race to the bottom resulting from an agreement with a developing neighbor and by Ross Perot's campaign opposition to the agreement. Resistance had never before been so well mobilized. See Hufbauer and Schott (2002).

issue for the election (Tapper 1999; Mayer 1998).[31] According to one Senate staff member at the time, Clinton's early NAFTA strategy on regulations to protect workers' human rights was judiciously crafted "to give cover to the Democrats" and win him the election; it was intended to appease labor leaders who opposed free trade but to stop short of their goal of killing the trade agreement (Interview record #60, 2007). Once in office, Clinton and his team of advisers, many of whom were personally opposed to NAFTA, "scrambled together a package that would win more support" (Mayer 1998, 6).[32]

During the eight years of his presidency, Clinton strove for authority to create more agreements. But as he had promised, he also supported trade regulations to protect workers' and children's human rights, despite rising opposition from labor unions that were furious about NAFTA's weak rules protecting workers. He appointed Mickey Kantor to be his first USTR and Robert Reich to be labor secretary—both of whom were fairly responsive to labor's concerns (Interview record #55, 2006; Interview record #60, 2007). In his foreign policy stance more generally, Clinton spoke openly in favor of protecting human rights, advocating international criminal prosecutions of war criminals and supporting universal rights at the convention in Vienna, for both moral and political reasons (Forsythe 2000). Yet his broader political interests limited his posture on human rights. In 1994, for instance, he separated human rights issues from consideration of China's most favored nation (MFN) trading status (Auger 1995), which drew harsh criticism from labor unions and NGOs but earned praise from much of the business community.

Since the United States' first free trade agreement—in 1985 with Israel—took effect, Clinton has been the president most supportive of protecting workers' and children's human rights in preferential trade agreements. During his two terms, he repeatedly sold his message to the American public on moral as well as national-interest grounds. "For decades, we have preached and preached and preached greater democracy, greater respect for human rights, and more open markets to Latin America. NAFTA

31. One internal communication from a Democratic senator advising Clinton argues that "Governor Clinton has been losing on NAFTA, both by appearing indecisive and by allowing Bush to control the agenda. I don't think he can continue to put off taking some position on the issue. His best option is to come out in support of NAFTA, with a strong statement concerning the package of economic policies that need to accompany it. This strategy is most likely to shift the public discussion away from 'free trade' versus 'protection,' and bring it back to Bush's failures on the economy and his own plans for the economy" (Personal communication to Clinton 1992).

32. For careful and detailed analyses of the NAFTA process, see Mayer (1998) and also Cameron and Tomlin (2000).

finally offers them the opportunity to reap the benefits of this" (US Office of the Press Secretary 1993). His views on the issue, however, never fit neatly into what labor unions, NGOs, or businesses wanted; rather, they appeared to represent a delicate balance of personal conviction and appeasement of special interests, crafted during a tough election campaign and evolving throughout his presidency.

In 2000, George W. Bush was elected president, and in 2001 he arrived in office eager to promote market integration. In an outline of his legislative agenda for international trade, Bush informed Congress he would seek approval to negotiate market access; his intention was to negotiate a new WTO round, a Free Trade Area of the Americas, and dozens of regional and bilateral PTAs all over the world (Schott 2004b). Like his father, along with many business lobbies and most Republicans in Congress, Bush opposed regulating markets through human rights standards, even those protecting workers and children. However, as we shall see in the chapter to come, Congress would eventually force his hand. Thanks to Clinton, by the time Bush took office, protections for workers' rights were already legal precedent in two free trade agreements, NAFTA and the agreement with Jordan,[33] and during Clinton's eight years in office, Democrats had mobilized considerable congressional attention to the issue. The relevant question for Bush became not whether human rights should be included in free trade agreements—they already were—but whether they should be enforced, and this his administration resisted time after time.

Throughout two terms in office, the Bush administration did much to water down trade regulations for internationally accepted human rights standards, particularly protections for workers (Aaronson and Zimmerman 2007; Interview record #80 2007; Koffler 2007; McGrane 2007), even when American negotiating partners were willing to accept more (Baucus 2004). At the same time, his administration justified these actions in terms of American values on human rights. He reminded the public

that open trade is in our nation's interest, and open trade helps us all adhere to values that we share—common values. Values that call for respect of human rights and values that believe in the worth of each individual, and values that hold democracy and freedom dear. . . . Oh, there's a lot of talk I hear about labor and environmental agreements. A prosperous nation is one more likely to take care of its workers. And a prosperous nation is one more likely, much more likely, to be able to afford the technology

33. The US agreement with Jordan was negotiated under Clinton but passed into law under George W. Bush.

necessary to protect the environment. And then, of course, trade creates the habits of freedom. . . . And the habits of freedom begin to create the expectations of democracy and demands for better democratic institutions. . . . And for those of us who care about values and believe in values—not just American values, but universal values that promote human dignity—trade is a good way to do that. (US Office of the Press Secretary 2002)

Presidents, however, do not pass trade agreements into law. Congress does. And the party divide over labor issues has nowhere been stronger than in the US Congress. Republicans, representing their business constituents and donors, vote mainly in favor of free trade and oppose regulations protecting human rights or the environment, including regulations protecting human rights in unilateral schemes such as the GSP and agreements that go both ways such as NAFTA. Democrats, with complex and often mixed loyalties to labor and business, and themselves split on the matter of trade, typically favor protections for American jobs and workers and increasingly articulate those interests with reference to human rights laws and principles. Some Democrats have been more enthusiastic than others, and there is a clear bootlegging pattern to their support, just as there is a clear bootlegging pattern to Republican opposition.

Before, during, and especially since NAFTA, several key Democrats in Congress have led the charge for enforceable regulations protecting workers' human rights in trade agreements. Sometimes they did so as a way to oppose trade agreements more generally, and always they acted in their own political interests, often to help their constituents. Since taking office in 1979, Senator Carl Levin (D-MI) has been at the forefront of the campaign to protect workers' human rights. He voted against NAFTA, concerned that the agreement would discriminate against some of the principal products made in his home state of Michigan and that Michigan workers would lose jobs as a result of increased imports from or plant relocations to Mexico or Canada. According to Levin, "We've lost too many manufacturing jobs because our trade policies have been so weak over the decades. . . . We should negotiate trade agreements to protect human rights as well as labor and environmental standards" (C. Levin 2002). In 2002, for much the same reason, he opposed a bill granting the president TPA and, shortly afterward, voted against DR-CAFTA, arguing that "[t]rade should not be a race to the bottom in which US workers must compete with countries that do not recognize core international labor standards and basic worker rights. . . . Writing labor and environmental standards into trade agreements is an important way to ensure that free trade is fair trade" (Levin 2005).

Senator Max Baucus (D-MT) took office in 1978 representing a state where export-oriented manufacturing accounts for only 5 percent of state GDP. He chaired the Senate Finance Committee during the negotiations on the 2002 TPA (US Bureau of Labor Statistics 2007b). Not surprisingly, he has been a longtime supporter of free trade but has also favored including some regulations protecting workers' human rights (Baucus 2004). In contrast to other Democrats such as Levin who have opposed PTAs without enforceable regulations for workers' and children's human rights, Baucus has taken a moderate approach to the issue—one more compatible with the business community's concerns about the potentially harmful consequences of regulating American trade by international laws and its opposition to enforcement through sanctions. Addressing the debate over TPA in 2002, which he voted to support, Baucus stated:

> Some have said that this legislation does not go far enough on labor and the environment. Many critics, I believe, will never be satisfied. They simply oppose trade. . . . It is not realistic to suggest that we can take our labor and environmental laws—impose them on developing countries—and slap sanctions on them if their laws don't live up to our standards. . . . That's not to say that we must wait a century for progress; labor and environmental standards are on the agenda now, and every trade agreement must recognize that reality. We can lock in positive changes that have already been achieved. And we can create positive incentives for countries to raise their standards. (Baucus 2002)

Former Senator Daniel Patrick Moynihan (D-NY), first elected to the Senate in 1976 and recognized for his commitment to free trade, was another key leader on the issue. For instance, he supported China's entry into the WTO. Yet Moynihan, who became chair of the Senate Finance Committee in 1993 and received substantial political support from labor unions throughout his Senate career, was also a strong supporter of labor issues, having served as assistant secretary of labor in the Kennedy and Johnson administrations. After much debate and substantial pressure from labor unions in his home state of New York, he voted against NAFTA, reportedly to "mollify organized labor" (Katzmann 1998, 171). He then argued for years in support of enforceable standards of trade conduct protecting international workers' human rights. Together with Senator Levin, he put forward an amendment to require the president to consider whether a country recognized basic human rights standards—defined by international law and including the rights of association, organizing, and collective bargaining and a minimum age for the employment of children—before granting sub-Saharan African countries unilateral trade preferences (Levin 1999). He explained his motivations:

> The impact of globalization on working conditions and, indeed, on workers' rights in general, has arisen as an important, and somewhat difficult, issue in the debate over the direction of America's trade policy. In 1997, I suggested to the Administration that they might look to the International Labor Organization for assistance in addressing this matter. After all, the ILO was established in 1919 for the express purpose of providing governments that wanted to do something to improve labor standards with a means of so doing—international conventions—that would not compromise their competitive advantages. (US Senate 1999)

By contrast, Senator Bill Bradley (D-NJ), who served from 1979 to 1997, was one of the Senate's foremost NAFTA proponents, convinced that NAFTA would be the most significant foreign policy issue of Clinton's first term (Tapper 1999). Bradley advised the Clinton administration on how to position itself on labor to sell the agreement to the American public.[34] Allegedly "respectful but not warm" toward labor unions, Bradley was an intellectual with strong ties to the business community who thought NAFTA was a crucial step forward (Interview record #60 2007). He believed that protecting workers' human rights was a good political idea and one that would help Mexico modernize (Interview #55, 2006). Although he would not remain in office long enough to vote on the US-Jordan PTA (2000) or on TPA legislation (2002), his influence on the Clinton administration had a lasting effect.

Meanwhile, the most contentious debate over human rights regulation has taken place in the US House of Representatives, where labor interests have been a rallying cry for several Democrats, particularly those with constituents in the Northeast and Midwest who want their jobs protected from foreign competition (Destler and Balint 1999). Before NAFTA, Congress in 1984 passed the GSP Renewal Act, imposing unilateral worker rights regulations on other countries as a condition for GSP benefits. At

---

34. Several personal communications in 1992 from Bradley to then Governor Clinton reveal that Bradley advised Clinton to strongly support NAFTA but to insist that the legislation implementing NAFTA correct some of the problems with the agreement negotiated by the George H. W. Bush administration, especially the effects of NAFTA on American workers and the environment. For any shortcomings that could not be addressed through implementing legislation, Bradley counseled Clinton to call for additional negotiations with Mexico and Canada to correct them, to be concluded in time to be considered as part of a package with the NAFTA implementing legislation.

that time, Representative Donald J. Pease (D-OH) was a high-ranking member of the Trade Subcommittee of the House Ways and Means Committee. Representing labor-strong Ohio, where manufacturing accounted for 20 percent of the state GDP, Pease made the protection of internationally recognized workers' human rights a personal cause. Pease's chief administrative assistant, William Goold, explained Pease's incentives: "Workers are being [pitted] against one another. . . . Capital is moving faster and faster, but workers stay in the same place. It can become a dog-eat-dog situation, or the working people can achieve a common interest. That is the only alternative." Without laws to "protect international labor rights, all the pressure will be to lower wages, forcing them down in a sinking spiral" (Targ 1987).

Former Representative Richard Gephardt (D-MO), House majority leader from 1989 to 1995 and minority leader from 1995 to 2003, was also a strong opponent of free trade. He, too, represented a state of manufacturers—their products accounted for about 15 percent of Missouri's GDP, and almost 95 percent of merchandise exports (US Bureau of Labor Statistics 2007a)—and was understandably worried about competition from globalization. Gephardt, who had long received substantial political contributions from labor unions, too, championed an amendment that would have imposed sanctions on countries that ran bilateral trade surpluses with the United States. He led the House in opposition to NAFTA, normalized trade relations with China, and, later, TPA. The US trade deficit, Gephardt argued, "is both an American crisis and a global tragedy." American multinational corporations are causing a global race to the bottom, he said, in which they "have thrown morality to the winds and sought out those countries where exploitation knows no bounds" (Griswold 2004). His views on human rights trade regulations are understandable in light of his political interests, which he expressed in an interview in 2002:

> The business community cares about intellectual property and so they insist on it being protected . . . but when it gets to labor rights and environmental concerns and human rights, the proponents of trade and many in the business community don't care. They don't think it should be part of trade negotiations because, frankly, they don't care about those things. I understand that, but I think it's inconsistent and I think it's wrong. What I wanted in NAFTA were enforceable provisions in the core of the treaty for [labor rights and environmental concerns and human rights], just as there were for intellectual property. [This would then] cause the better enforcement of national laws on labor rights, environmental concerns, and human rights. (PBS 2002)

Longtime Representatives Sander Levin (D-MI), chairman of the House Ways and Means Trade Subcommittee, and Charles Rangel (D-NY), chairman of the House Ways and Means Committee, have also played key roles in the regulation debate in the House over the years. Despite their ties to labor unions in their home states, both have voted fairly often against trade barriers, much to the dissatisfaction of labor unions in Missouri and New York. Levin came out in support of PTAs with Chile and Singapore, yet he voted against DR-CAFTA, apparently dissatisfied with the agreement's labor regulations, which require the participants to enforce only their own domestic labor standards of conduct rather than ILO laws.[35] Rangel, who supported PTAs with Chile, Morocco, and Singapore, came out against a trade agreement with Oman, citing a controversy over the country's labor standards. Like most Democrats in the House seeking to stall Republican enthusiasm for free trade, he voted against NAFTA and, a decade later, opposed granting TPA to Bush. He also voted against DR-CAFTA, arguing that the agreement's labor and environmental laws were inadequate on matters of enforcement (Currie 2006).

Over the years, Rangel and Levin have together led the House Democrats' call for enforceable regulations protecting workers' human rights, proposing several bills regulating standards of conduct in trade agreements. All these bills called for trade deals to include core labor rights protected by international law, specifically ILO protections for the rights to associate and to bargain collectively and prohibitions on child labor, discrimination, and forced labor (Goodman 2007).[36] The congressmen have argued in favor of global development as well as American protectionism, explaining that "[a]ddressing the labor market standards issue in international trade agreements will help countries develop. When workers can organize and bargain collectively, they will be able to press for decent working conditions and for better wages; they will be able to garner a larger share of the fruits of globalization" (S. Levin 2002).

Europe

When the United States began its push for preferential trade relations, Europe was already a decade ahead, having begun to pursue PTAs in the 1970s mainly for geopolitical reasons—to authorize assistance to poor

35. The agreements with Chile and Singapore have the same regulations.
36. Their proposed bill on TPA, which called for the enforcement of ILO guidelines, was rejected by the Ways and Means Committee by a vote of 26 to 12. Republicans were sympathetic to USTR Robert Zoellick's argument that such an agreement would leave little room for US maneuvering during trade negotiations.

countries otherwise thought to be susceptible to Communist influence and to allow the British, Dutch, and French to maintain special relations with their former colonies (Whiteman 1998). In 1973, Denmark, Ireland, and the United Kingdom joined the European Community. That year, mainly in response to British entry, African, Caribbean, and Pacific countries formed a group of countries, the ACP, which would forever change these countries' bargaining power with Europe. At the same time, this opened a door for the European Community to craft a global development policy. Negotiations between Europe and the ACP—then fewer than fifty countries[37]—began immediately, concluding eighteen months later with a pioneering trade and aid agreement signed in Lomé, Togo (1975). Later, the loss of Soviet control over Eastern Europe gave added momentum to this trade movement, creating European incentives to pursue more preferential integration to access new markets, to shore up regional security and economic growth, and to prepare the way to add new members to the European Union (Pinelli 2004).

As in the United States, the issue of incorporating human rights into preferential trade regulations is a politicized issue. But in contrast to the American experience, in which candidates in a polarized presidential election campaign after the end of the cold war successfully raised the profile of workers' human rights, the European process began with the worries of a few member states whose former colonies became extremely violent and an executive institution never directly elected by the people—the European Commission. The Commission was driven by its agenda for more European integration as well as its development agenda with Europe's former colonies, many of which were now run by brutal dictatorships responsible for mass murder and torture.

In this setting, one individual in the European Commission launched a sea change in thinking on European trade and development policy. Claude Cheysson was a French Socialist and European commissioner in the development unit in charge of the first and second Lomé negotiations during most of the 1970s.[38] He later served under European Commission president Jacques Delors as commissioner for Mediterranean policy and North-South relations (1985–89). Dubbed "Pompidou's gift to the British," Cheysson sketched out "the Fresco," a multifaceted vision of European foreign policy with agreements such as Lomé at the foundation, to be followed by a global system of PTAs that would eventually tie Asia, Latin America, and the Middle East into a sustainable framework of development (Whiteman 1998).

37. The ACP group now includes almost eighty countries.
38. Cheysson resigned in April 1981 to become France's minister of foreign affairs.

Enforceable human rights standards of conduct were not at first part of that vision,[39] and at the time, Lomé was valued for its political neutrality. Cheysson, like the Commission more broadly, was mostly unconcerned with the particular nature of regimes with which Europe would do business. His goal was development rather than political restructuring.

Thus human rights never officially made their way into Lomé I or II regulations, despite a vocal campaign from David Owen, then foreign secretary of the United Kingdom, who urged suspension of Lomé aid cooperation to Uganda in 1977 in response to atrocities carried out there under the Idi Amin regime.[40] According to press reports, Cheysson claimed that the many regional projects and export facilities involved in Lomé negotiations were politically more important than human rights considerations (European Parliament 1980b). Other sources suggest, however, that he personally would have welcomed making human rights part of the negotiating mandate for the new Lomé Convention (Bartels 2005; Fierro 2003).[41] Cheysson, in a 1981 interview, articulated his views on regulating human rights in Europe's foreign policy:

> For us the fundamental principles, the rights of man and the rights of the people will be our rule. It's difficult to stick to great principles, but we shall. . . . Take Poland. What is happening in Poland is fantastic. . . . Of course, we could go and stoke the fire and find that there are still people in jail who should immediately be liberated. What is happening in Poland on the whole is far more important. Yes, we will be inspired by human rights. But not in a kind of neurotic manner bearing on every individual. We are not Amnesty International. We are very pleased that there is in-

39. Cheysson was clear, however, that Europe's trade and cooperation agreements with the ACP carried out different political objectives than those with Europe's neighbors. The preambles of the latter often referred to the Community's basic values, which in principle should include human rights, though human rights was not explicitly mentioned. See Bartels (2005) for details.

40. Although cooperation with Uganda was never formally suspended under Lomé in reaction to violations of human rights, the EC did react informally, using a variety of other measures to postpone financial protocols and development assistance. Moreover, the Commission quickly adopted the Uganda Guidelines in 1978, formalizing a policy that would allow Europe, as the United States had already done, to hold unilateral aid allocations to countries committing human rights violations, although not to suspend their broader commitments under trade and cooperation agreements. See King (1997).

41. This statement was reported by Mr. Karl Habsburg-Lothringen, German MEP, who cites press reports as his source. The European Commission, in an answer to Mr. Habsburg's question, claimed "no knowledge of the press reports to which the Honorable Member refers," and contended that "no statement of this kind has ever been made by Mr. Cheysson or by any other Member of the Commission."

deed an Amnesty International, but we are not Amnesty International. (Cheysson 1981)

Although Cheysson himself did not include human rights protections in the enforceable provisions of the early Lomé agreements he negotiated, he did open the door for future trade regulations protecting human rights, while the atrocities committed in Uganda put the issue front and center for the Commission. Several more political events would eventually make regulations on human rights possible, directly affecting the interests of European policymakers. Among them, the European Parliament gained the right to veto certain PTAs, granted in 1986 under the Single European Act (SEA); the ACP slid throughout the 1980s and 1990s into more and more economic turmoil; the cold war ended; and severe human rights violations occurred during the war in Bosnia.

After the United Kingdom's appeal to curb aid to Uganda, a few members of the Commission became sympathetic to the idea of regulating (though not necessarily enforcing) human rights standards of conduct through preferential trade agreements to protect people from being massacred. In 1983, one commissioner, who remains unidentified, was even reported in the European press to have staged a fast in order to seek assurance that the negotiations of the future Lomé agreements "will reach agreement on a 'human rights' article as an integral part of the new Convention" (European Parliament 1984b). Most commissioners at the time, including Cheysson, had become sensitive to the issues raised by brutal violations of human rights taking place in the ACP, but they were not keen to enforce such standards of conduct through trade sanctions or to take on ACP resistance to the regulations, despite murmurs from some member states.

The next ten years were defined by the Commission presidency of French Socialist Jacques Delors, who ran the Commission for three consecutive terms, from 1985, before human rights were adopted as preferential trade standards of conduct, to 1995, when PTAs protecting human rights were made mandatory and enforceable, not just in the ACP but in every European trade agreement to come, except sectoral agreements. Delors' leadership and focus, along with Africa's economic downfall and growing brutality, help explain Europe's near silence on workers' human rights in their PTAs, with the emphasis instead on broad human rights for all people under the rubric of "fundamental" human rights.

Delors came to office inspired by the idea of a "new Social Europe" that would successfully combine social justice and a market economy. France's weak social-democratic culture fueled his desire to strengthen the role of social intermediaries such as labor unions (Drake 2000). He believed market competition and integration, which he strongly supported, must go hand in hand with social protections for working and living conditions in Europe and should be regulated Europe-wide as they already were in Sweden, Germany, the Netherlands, and Denmark. In many countries labor unions lauded his efforts. The ETUC launched the "Val Duchesse" process, whereby business and labor met to discuss social considerations, such as protections for workers, in the single European market (Trubek, Mosher, and Rothstein 2000). Under Delors' reign, protections for workers' human rights were debated mainly as matters for European regulation, not for global trade protection. This would change: labor issues took on greater importance in the late 1990s when European fears about deteriorating social protections sparked mass protests against integration and calls for labor protections in trade agreements.[42] In the meantime, the Commission began to regulate in trade agreements more broadly the types of human rights violations taking place in the ACP countries, mostly sidestepping workers' rights.

Another influential policymaker in the Commission was Manuel Marín, a member of the Spanish Socialist Party, who served first as commissioner in the cooperation and development unit beginning in 1989, and then as commissioner for external relations with Southern Mediterranean countries, the Middle East, Latin America, and Asia, until 1999. A labor supporter who was concerned about the effects of globalization, Marín led the Commission to propose that the EC suspend its trade agreement with Burma, which offered preferential tariffs for industrial exports to Europe, in response to evidence on the use of forced labor (Burma Headline News 1996). During his tenure, Marín also advocated protecting human rights in Europe's external relations more broadly, including PTAs. The end of the cold war especially appears to have moved him. In his words,

> In my ten-year experience within the European Commission, I have witnessed from a privileged position the irreversible globalization process of the world economy. The Union has been suddenly confronted with the problem of managing the interdependencies and the socio-economic imbalances, in the context which arose after the fall of the Berlin Wall. In this framework, the EU only recently realised the importance of its external relations. (Marín 1997)

---

42. In the mid-1990s, protections for workers' human rights would emerge as a core element of Europe's unilateral GSP scheme. In June 2001, the Commission agreed to redefine the GSP to include a system of tariff-based incentives to encourage developing country exporters to sign on for and follow core rights protections for workers.

Respect for human rights, would become "one of the prime objectives of European foreign policy" (Marín 1993).[43]

In 1991, the Delors Commission issued the first of several groundbreaking communications to the Council and Parliament on "Human Rights, Democracy and Development Cooperation Policy." The long-awaited initial document was vague on issues of enforcement, reflecting certain commissioners' doubts about implementation through sanctions or other punitive actions and setting the tone for the regulations still to come protecting human rights. It explained that civil and political rights were of particular concern. A statement by the Commission clarified its motivations for creating this document:

> The aim of this communication is to establish general lines of conduct for the Community and the Member Countries concerning the relationship between development cooperation policy on the one hand and the promotion and defense of human rights and support for the democratic process in all developing countries on the other. The need for this stems from the high profile these issues have been given by the significant developments which have taken place on the international scene and in many developing countries, and from the sensitivity of public opinion to them. It has therefore become vital that human rights and democracy figure more prominently in the guidelines for cooperation policy than has hitherto been the case. (European Commission 1991)

In the United States almost all policymakers supporting the creation of human rights trade regulations have been Democrats; in Europe, by contrast, many but not all have been Socialists. Senior Dutch politician Frans Andriessen, who served as European commissioner for external relations and trade from 1989 to 1993, and former Netherlands minister of foreign affairs Hans van den Broek, who held the same Commission position from 1993 to 1995,[44] were both members of the ruling Christian Democratic Party, which supported European integration and free markets but also endorsed some interventions on social issues such as human rights. For commissioners such as Andriessen and van den Broek who were not committed Socialists, PTA regulations protecting human rights would also come to serve their political interests, legitimizing trade agreements to an

---

43. In a 1999 investigation into the Santer Commission, Marín was cited for creating a Mediterranean program that he failed to monitor properly, waiting almost two years after indiscretions were alleged to take action. See James (1999).

44. He was then commissioner for external relations with Central and Eastern Europe under Jacques Santer.

increasingly skeptical European public—much as labor regulations would do for the American business community—and nurturing the region's security in the new world order. Inside the Commission, however, disagreements persisted over the matter of enforcement.

By the time the Berlin Wall fell in 1989, several commissioners and a few member states had already begun to call for the creation of PTA regulations protecting human rights, although there was no clear consensus among these various advocates as to how to implement them. And then crises hit. The 1991 coup in Haiti, followed by the genocide that took place during the Bosnian war from 1992 to 1995, had profound effects on both the Commission's and the Council's views on whether and how to implement human rights regulations in PTAs (Interview record #13, 2004). Bound to Haiti by Lomé and to Yugoslavia by a 1983 trade cooperation agreement, the EC found itself with no standard legal recourse to terminate its trade obligations to governments overthrown by force or that were massacring people. These crises changed the politics of European trade regulation forever. Although the European Community would suspend its trade concessions to Haiti and Yugoslavia anyway,[45] both crises made clear to policymakers that the EC needed to create a more consistent safety valve, providing Europe with a legally coherent procedure for suspending its trade commitments with partners embroiled in unforeseen political emergencies (Brandtner and Rosas 1998). The growing feeling among policymakers, liberal and conservative, was that trade regulations protecting human rights were going to be necessary to enhance regional security but also to legitimize further integration with countries, especially those in transition and those that could potentially join the European Union in the years to come.

However, in great contrast to the United States, where individual policymakers' preferences for trade protections never converged around a larger set of goals, policymakers in Europe at this time were in search of wider influence abroad. Those interested in human rights regulatory reform began to converge around PTAs as one potential tool, despite considerable disagreements over enforcement. Many of the same policymakers who were arguing over the form Europe's trade regulations should take also played a hand in forging other policies, among them, the Treaty on the European Union (TEU). The TEU took effect in 1993 and provided the

---

45. The Council formally enacted economic sanctions on November 11, 1991, and, following approval by the Parliament, suspended the trade agreement, along with an agreement on coal and steel and benefits derived under the GSP. See Decision 91/602/ECSC, OJ 1991 L 325/23; Regulation 3300/91, OJ 1991 L 315/1; Decision 91/588/ECSC, OJ 1991 L 315/49 and Decision 91/589/ECSC, OJ 1991 L 315/46, 50.

EC with a legal basis to expand its human rights trade regulations, although it said nothing about the form these regulations should take or whether and how they would be implemented.[46]

In January 1993, Hans van den Broek, then commissioner for external relations, wrote a letter to the Council, Parliament, and member states on behalf of the Commission, explaining the decision to adopt guidelines regulating human rights and instructing that negotiating directives for certain PTAs should include "a clause specifying that relations between the Community and the country concerned and all provisions of the relevant agreement are based on respect for the democratic principles and human rights which inspire the domestic and external policies of the Community" (European Commission 1995). As a commissioner, van den Broek himself cited the clause to justify forging new trade agreements with neighboring countries such as Uzbekistan, which was guilty of serious human rights violations. He emphasized that Europe could use the trade regulations to pressure such abusive governments for a political dialogue (European Parliament 1998). The clause would help to sell the agreement to a skeptical public.

As in the United States, though, the executive branch of government in Europe does not have the authority to make trade agreements into law; legislatures do. And in Europe there are two supranational legislative institutions that have been active in the trade lawmaking process.

One of these institutions is the European Council, made up of ministers of the member states. Its member states have held various views on human rights trade regulations, varying in some measure according to the ideological platform of the political party holding power in the country at the time—more conservative parties generally have not supported trade protections for workers' and children's human rights. The United Kingdom, for instance, opposed putting regulations protecting workers' human rights in Europe's multilateral trade agreements during the time that Conservative Party members Margaret Thatcher (1979–90) and John Major (1990–97) served as prime ministers. Yet just a few years earlier, under the leadership of Labor prime minister James Callaghan (1976–79), the United Kingdom had advocated for creating strong and legally enforceable Community trade regulations with the ACP that protected human rights (Baehr

46. Article 6 of the TEU is the key provision, stating that the "Union is founded on the principles of liberty, democracy, respect for human rights and fundamental freedoms and the rule of law, principles which are common to the Member Countries," and that the "Union shall provide itself the means necessary to attain its objectives and carry through its policies." The treaty also says the EC policy for development cooperation must contribute to these goals.

1996). It did so with the crisis of Uganda in mind, and it called for the creation of standardized human rights language with operational consequences that could allow for the partial or complete suspension of the Lomé Convention in the event of severe human rights violations.[47] The Netherlands also asked for human rights trade standards, with prime ministers Andreas van Agt (1977–82) and Ruud Lubbers (1982–94), both Christian Democrats, in power. Strong supporters of enforceable trade regulations protecting human rights (Miller 2004), the Dutch wanted the Lomé agreement to include an even stronger reference to human rights, accompanied by a protocol establishing procedures for suspension, which might be included in future agreements with other governments (Fierro 2003; Smits 1980).

On the other hand, Belgium and Germany also had Christian Democrats in power and shared the view that human rights were of growing concern but that regulation and enforcement through PTAs was not the best strategy. During initial negotiations with the ACP, both countries advocated a short and vague reference to human rights in the preamble of the new trade agreement, arguing that anything more would be unwarranted interference in the private affairs of sovereign nations (Fierro 2003; Kaminga 1989). They argued that enforcement mechanisms were unacceptable. Germany would also go on to oppose raising workers' rights in multilateral negotiations in the GATT for many years to come. France, meanwhile, with center-right president Valéry Giscard d'Estaing in office during the first Lomé negotiations, had no intention of allowing European trade or aid preferences to be suspended with political allies in the ACP. As Cheysson had done in the Commission, France claimed neutrality on the subject, arguing that the link between trade cooperation and human rights was premature and preferring discrete spheres of regulation for each issue (Garnick and Cosgrove Twichett 1979; Young-Anawaty 1980). Years later, under Socialist rule, France would advocate for workers' rights protections in the WTO and GSP.[48]

Over the years, member states' interests have changed some, mainly in reaction to shifting political circumstances. The end of the cold war created a massive shock to the system that gave "rise to a growing belief among EU member countries that bilateral agreements could be used as a lever to encourage good governance and the rule of law" (Gonzalez 1996). The crises in Haiti and Yugoslavia made enforcement more attractive. Moreover,

47. Yet, also concerned about relations with former colonies, Margaret Thatcher's Conservative government asked the Commission to make European aid to Ethiopia conditional on its efforts to end flagrant violations of human rights (European Parliament 1986) despite Thatcher's dislike of trade regulations protecting workers' human rights.

48. See Fierro (2003) for details.

shifting political coalitions in the member states, as well as expanding EU membership, have also undoubtedly affected the Council's views over time. By 1995, when the Council voted to extend human rights trade regulations to all future European PTAs, with modest enforcement provisions, France, Ireland, the Netherlands, and Portugal had Socialist or Labor parties in power, generally more favorable to market interventions for human rights protections than their more conservative predecessors and counterparts in the Council. That same year, Austria, Finland, and Sweden joined the European Union, all three with Social Democrats at the helm—Chancellor Franz Vranitzky, President Martti Ahtisaari, and Prime Minister Ingvar Carlsson, respectively—who were keen to place protections for European citizens into European law. Protections for workers' human rights were put inside the GSP, while protections for a broader set of human rights were put inside most European trade agreements.

The other supranational legislative institution is the European Parliament. Among European policymaking institutions, the EP has seen some of the strongest calls for human rights standards in trade agreements. The Parliament is the weakest among these institutions but is also the most directly accountable to the citizens of the member states. Dozens of members of Parliament (MEPs) have vocalized concerns about Europe's trade relations with brutal dictators since the very beginning of relations with the ACP. As in the Commission and Council, however, there has been a great range of views on the issues of preferential trade and human rights regulations among MEPs. These disagreements often correspond to party lines—with more leftist MEPs calling for interventions through markets and more conservative MEPs calling for more free trade—and sometimes correspond to member states' particular national interest in a given trade partner (European Parliament 1996).

Within the European Parliament, the Party of European Socialists (PES), created in 1953, has played a pivotal role. In the first general elections in 1979, the PES won 113 of 411 seats.[49] In 1994, the party emerged as the largest and also the most cohesive group, with strong connections to labor unions across Europe and a historically interventionist approach to trade policy, motivated by concerns about the effects of market integration on European workers. Its platform has long included the enforceable protection of human rights, and its members have for decades led demands for European sanctions against abusive regimes, as well as for the creation of fair trade and market access for the world's poorest countries.

---

49. Today there are more than seven hundred seats in the European Parliament.

A statistical review of all official questions that MEPs have directed to the Council, Commission, and foreign ministers since the Parliament's election in 1979 shows that Socialist MEPs have most often raised the issue of human rights trade standards.[50] For instance, in 1979, just before Lomé II came into effect, Ernest Glinne, MEP from Belgium, raised the question of whether Europe's commitment to human rights among member states would also affect violations outside the EC (European Parliament 1980a). During the early 1980s, Karl van Miert, another Belgian MEP who later became vice president of the International Socialist Party (1986–92), often raised questions on the nature of human rights in Lomé III as well as in South Korea. Richard Balfe, British Labor's longest-serving MEP (1979–2004), frequently raised the issue of human rights during his tenure. In 1993 he called attention to human rights protections in Europe's trade agreement with Israel (European Parliament 1993).[51] In the early 1990s, Henri Saby, MEP from France, also strongly favored the insertion of enforceable human rights protections in Europe's development policy (European Parliament 1992a; European Parliament 1992b).

The Alliance of Liberals and Democrats for Europe (ALDE), formed in 1952, is the third largest political group in the EP, bringing together MEPs representing Liberal and Democratic parties across Europe and holding the balance of power between the left and right. This group represents centrist views on Europe's market liberalization. "Promoting human rights throughout the world regardless of nationality has been and remains one of the top priorities for the Alliance of European Liberals and Democrats for Europe," and "issues concerning human rights, the protection of minorities and the promotion of democratic values in third countries" rank among the topics its foreign affairs committee permanently considers (ALDE 2007). Among the MEPs who have raised human rights questions over the years, several Liberal Democrats have been vocal on trade. Luxembourg MEP Colette Flesch, for instance, raised the issue of human rights in the context of Lomé II in 1980 (European Parliament 1980c). After taking office in 1984, Gijs M. de Vries, Dutch MEP and leader of ALDE (1994–98), was extremely active in bringing human rights issues to the Commission and Council for consideration, pressing for the suspension of Lomé III benefits to Ethiopia in light of human rights atrocities there (European Parliament 1986). Throughout the 1980s and 1990s, he called attention to

50. Data were collected by the author on all MEP questions since 1979 with the terms "human rights" in their title—in all, just over one thousand. These data are available upon request from the author.

51. In 2002, Mr. Balfe defected to the Conservative Party in protest against Labor's "growing arrogance and dishonesty" (BBC 2002).

repression in Sudan, Egypt, Turkey, Croatia, and Russia, among many other countries. Newton Dunn, a British MEP since 1979, also drew attention to human rights and trade agreements and to rights violations taking place in Romania in particular. ALDE's international trade committee has taken the position that the "Commission must insist on the respect of human rights and international labour law" (ALDE 2006).

The Group of the European People's Party (Christian Democrats) and European Democrats in the European Parliament (EPP-ED), which unites Christian Democrats, Conservatives, and other mainstream center-right parties across Europe, has also been a powerful influence in the European Parliament, holding more seats than other blocks since 1999. As strong supporters of free trade through the multilateral system, the party's members have been vocal on human rights as a moral imperative. Its MEPs have been active members of the Subcommittee on Human Rights of the European Parliament, which examines apparent breaches of international law and issues annual reports on human rights in and beyond Europe. Several members of the party have also actively raised questions about human rights to the Commission and Council over the years, a few concerning matters of trade in particular. For instance, in 1980 Karl Habsburg-Lothringen, MEP from Germany, raised the concern that Lomé II contained no human rights regulations, and he inquired about the Commission's motivations for excluding them and its future intentions on the issue (European Parliament 1980b). He remained active throughout the 1990s on human rights, co-initiating a Parliament resolution condemning China's indiscriminate use of the death penalty. By and large, however, the party's MEPs have been reluctant to enforce human rights through trade agreements, deeming enforceable human rights regulations to be unsuitable or, in one MEP's views, unhelpful to Europe's goals (Interview record #10, 2004). In addition to espousing Christian values and acceptance of fundamental democratic ideals, the EPP-ED now also identifies human rights as basic political values that Europe should work to spread worldwide. The group supports further trade liberalization and rejects the use of protectionist measures. Like President George W. Bush, the EPP-ED has an ideological commitment to weak enforcement of human rights trade measures, justified on moral grounds and expressed in its policy on Asia:

> The EU's priority in Asia, for strategic and security as well as moral reasons, is to foster democracy and human rights. This cannot be achieved by economic and political exclusion. Increased trade and cooperation makes a vital and positive contribution to political development. It must go hand in hand with intensified, political and diplomatic pressure for

democracy and human rights. To be successful, however, this can only be achieved by means of EU solidarity. (EPP-ED 1999)

This chapter introduces readers to the preferences articulated by many actors that have played a role in creating fair trade regulations protecting human rights. Policymakers advocate human rights protections when doing so guarantees political gain, by paying rents to bootleggers or solving other political problems, regardless of their own moral conviction on the issue, and they often use moral language to justify their views. Advocates that champion human rights trade regulations on principled grounds most often win over policymakers when moral conviction and political interest overlap. Otherwise, moral advocates are sidelined or ignored.

This apparent indifference of the political process to moral causes that conflict with political interests is perhaps best seen in the United States' apathy toward using PTAs to regulate brutal violations of human rights. American PTAs address only limited rights of workers and children. In spite of considerable political pressure by NGOs and human rights advocates to protect civil and political rights in preferential trade agreements and to create shared and binding obligations on all countries, no group of policymakers has taken up the call. Even Democrats who support standards of conduct in line with ILO provisions and make the case for labor regulations on principled grounds have demurred. Similarly, the labor unions, which might gain if human rights regulations were used as disguised protectionism, and which may care deeply about the treatment of workers living in other countries, are not calling for a broader understanding of rights. Here NGOs have made little headway.

In Europe, by contrast, the process has been quite different on this account. For years, civil and political rights were given more emphasis than workers' human rights in Europe's PTAs, both in the text of agreements and, to this day, in enforcement. Protections for labor rights came later and mainly unilaterally because member states to this day disagree on their implementation. Colonialism has also shaped this policy. Human rights were raised quite early because they served the political interests of certain member states seeking influence over their former colonies. After the end of the cold war, human rights protections served a variety of new political agendas for different actors, helping Europe shore up regional security and further European integration and helping policymakers gain political support and influence, both at home and abroad. But chance has also played a role, because the crises in Yugoslavia and Haiti influenced policymakers' views as well. Those events demonstrated to skeptical policymakers how human rights PTA regulations could serve as a safety valve for Europe by halting or reducing trade privileges when crises occur. Europe would later use those regulations to sell more trade agreements to the public and to push forward its own process of integration.

The formation of political coalitions around trade regulations has also played out differently in the United States and Europe. In the United States, policymakers, especially in Congress, want to regulate a narrow set of human rights to push for more influence over the political process at home. Since the end of the cold war, their views have become more polarized across parties. In Europe, since the end of the cold war, however, more policymakers in all branches of European government have come to see European integration and regional stability as dependent on some form of human rights protections. Despite policymakers' opposing views over enforcement of such regulations, they have learned to exploit various tools, including PTAs, to make the most of Europe's influence abroad, enshrining that authority in the TEU, which permits Europe eventually to make human rights a general trade cause.

To be sure, the moral discourse on human rights has evolved tremendously in the last several decades. So, too, have policymakers' ideas about trade policy and what should be regulated in preferential trade agreements. Yet it is clear that moral norms did not find a clear path to regulation. The same can be said for protectionism and the desires of labor unions. Policymakers on both sides of the Atlantic have taken up the human rights idiom to justify their own causes and advance their own various political interests—only sometimes did they respond to NGOs' and unions' demands. But as we shall see in the next chapter, fair PTA regulations protecting human rights were enacted in the United States and Europe only after decision makers struggled to embed their own political interests into law.

CHAPTER 4

INSTITUTIONS

Now that we have seen how the political interests of policymakers in the United States and Europe prompted their desire for preferential trade agreements that include human rights protections, we turn to the next step in the process: how these policymakers then succeeded in placing human rights standards of conduct into trade policies in the United States and Europe.

As we saw in chapter 2, institutional dynamics are central to the story. Policymakers' preferences are not always directly reflected in the eventual regulations that are adopted. Moreover, not all policymakers have equal influence at every stage of the regulatory process. Executive branches of government are usually well positioned to get what they want from negotiating trade regulations, but they act strategically to negotiate and recommend the kinds of policies they most want *within the range of options* the legislature will accept. Thus the legislature limits executive opportunism when it can by determining the range of policy options that are available to the executive, sometimes forcing new regulatory issues into or out of the executive's negotiations with other countries. This works especially well when the legislature has the right of amendment and votes by unanimity or some related form of strong consent, or when there are multiple veto players—for instance, multiple institutions that must agree to a policy.[1]

The following pages explore these characteristics of domestic policymaking institutions historically and comparatively across the United States and Europe. They draw on countries' experiences to further demonstrate themes raised in the previous chapters: that fair PTA regulations protecting

1. These expectations are summarized in table 1 of chapter 2.

human rights do not result directly from demands by human rights activists or labor unions that ask for them; that both NGOs and labor unions are therefore not always pleased with the regulations being made; and that fair trade PTAs do not often regulate all types of human rights but tend to deal with specific groups: workers and children or voters and citizens.[2]

These trends are best seen in the United States in the events leading to the passage of the 2002 Trade Act and in Europe in the decisions leading to the 1995 Commission Communication and Council Decision. Two time lines, offered in the appendix, place both policies into the broader historical context of policymaking in the United States and Europe. In the United States the 2002 Trade Act is the latest policy regulating placement of human rights standards of conduct in PTAs; it expired before the 2008 presidential election. In Europe, though there have been many developments since 1995, that year's regulations on protecting human rights in PTAs represent the most important turning point in the process.

This chapter explores the contentious nature of the institutional processes in the United States and Europe leading up to these pivotal moments of policymaking. It also illustrates the great variation in processes and results between the United States and Europe and over time.

The United States

Article I of the US Constitution (1789) gives Congress primary responsibility for governing foreign trade. Although the president enjoys constitutional authority to negotiate and enter agreements with other governments, he or she has no authority to impose duties unless Congress delegates this responsibility. Constitutionally, Congress has greater power to design and enter into trade agreements and thus enjoys substantial agenda-setting authority.

However, since the early twentieth century Congress has at times given specific trade authority to presidents to help conclude international trade deals, including PTAs and multilateral GATT trade rounds. This delegation has always come with a price: the president must consult with congressional committees in the process of negotiations (Destler 1995).[3] At times,

2. These alternative expectations are summarized in table 2 of chapter 2.
3. Delegation began in 1922 with the Fordney-McCumber Act empowering the president to manipulate tariffs to equalize production costs with foreign competitors. The Reciprocal Trade Agreements Act of 1934 was the first to delegate authority to the executive branch to link tariff setting to international negotiations. The Trade Act, giving the president new authority to negotiate agreements on nontariff trade distortions, followed this in

presidents have been given authority to negotiate trade agreements under "fast track" trade promotion procedures that were designed to augment their bargaining credibility abroad. Under fast track, Congress gives the president a set of negotiating directives that he or she must follow during international negotiations and over which the president has little say. In return, Congress agrees to consider a presidential proposal to implement a trade agreement within mandatory deadlines—without amendment and with limited debate—effectively reducing its ordinary legislative powers.[4] From 1974 to 1990, Congress granted this authority to American presidents almost continuously (Sek 2001; Smith 2006).

1974 to 1990

Before NAFTA, human rights never made it into the American government's free trade agreements—the issue only made it into unilateral programs in the 1980s. Through bipartisan coalitions, Congress repeatedly gave presidents fast-track authority to negotiate trade deals with little concern for human rights. The US government's first two PTAs, the United States-Israel Free Trade Agreement (1985) and the Canada-United States Free Trade Agreement (1989), say nothing about protecting human rights, and the US trade negotiators never publicly raised human rights issues during either negotiation.

The reason is simple: few policymakers during the early years wanted human rights protections in PTAs, so few demanded them. As chapter 3 explained, presidents Ronald Reagan and George H. W. Bush had no intention of negotiating protections for human rights in their trade deals with Israel and Canada or with any other country. At the same time, Republicans in Congress who supported the business lobby wanted more free trade and were keen to protect American sovereignty from outside intervention on matters such as human rights violations. They were especially eager to avoid criticism of American capital punishment (Interview record #20, 2004).

Despite protests from human rights NGOs and labor unions that opposed the agreements, most House and Senate Democrats had not yet come to articulate strong interests in protecting human rights through US PTAs. Instead, a few were focusing efforts on America's unilateral preferences schemes such as the GSP. Safeguards for workers' and children's

---

1974. For an excellent overview of US trade delegation history, as well as the policymaking process, see Destler (1986, 1995).

4. For detailed explanations of fast-track trade promotion authority, see Brainard and Shapiro (2001) and Smith (2006).

human rights had not yet become a hot-button political issue with the kind of national appeal it would soon develop.[5]

Between 1974 and 1990, Democrats and Republicans in Congress thus repeatedly granted presidents from both political parties fast-track authority to negotiate preferential trade agreements with little obvious concern for protecting workers' and children's rights through provisions in the agreements. This would soon change.

1991 to 1993

Regulatory change required a change in policymakers' preferences and in their ability to influence decisions. This meant that not only did more policymakers have to care about linking human rights protections to preferential trade agreements, but they had to have the veto power to make it happen. Chapter 3 explained how a unique window of opportunity opened with NAFTA, triggering a crucial change in some policymakers' preferences. This chapter addresses the next step: how those policymakers leveraged their influence to delay or shut down the passage of new trade legislation that did not conform to their liking.

In 1990, anticipating the next presidential election and facing stalled GATT negotiations, President George H. W. Bush notified the Senate Finance Committee and the House Ways and Means Committee of his intention to negotiate a preferential trade agreement with Mexico and to request a congressional extension of fast-track authority in order to do so. By law (the Trade and Tariff Act of 1974 and its 1984 amendment), each congressional committee had sixty legislative days to consider the president's request and set conditions for delegation. Democrats controlled both houses of Congress at that time and immediately voiced opposition to the president's request for trade delegation. Democrats were particularly wor-

---

5. In 1950, the House passed a bill (H.R. 7797) establishing that agreements could be forged with less-developed countries to promote trade and to establish fair labor standards for wages and working conditions. This bill never became law. See Charnovitz (1987). The 1974 Trade Act that authorized American negotiations during the Tokyo Round directed the president to ask for fair international labor standards, although the directive was largely symbolic. In 1984, Congress made that link real when it included unilateral labor conditions in the GSP. The labor regulations in the GSP were championed by the House's Democratic majority, including Representative Donald J. Pease (D-OH). In order to win the right to grant other countries unilateral preferences, President Ronald Reagan had no choice but to take on labor regulations sponsored by House Democrats. However, his administration wanted to cut from the original draft a clause that prohibited discrimination on the basis of race, sex, religion, or national origin and a clause providing for mandatory sanctions in the event of violations. The final legislation thus reflects a compromise: both the nondiscrimination and mandatory sanctions clauses were cut. See Compa and Vogt (2005).

ried about the concerns of labor unions that were increasingly vocal on the need to protect American workers from competition with cheaper labor elsewhere (Destler and Balint 1999). NAFTA struck a chord: many Americans feared that preferential trade with a developing country such as Mexico was especially threatening. They worried that despite the economic evidence, NAFTA would jeopardize Americans' wages and jobs, widening the gap between skilled and unskilled labor and weakening labor conditions (Hufbauer and Schott 2002).

In response to this pervasive concern, some members of the Democratic majority in Congress openly articulated their desire to protect workers' human rights and asked the president to address these rights during his negotiations of any new trade agreement (Cameron and Tomlin 2000). A Democratic Congress thus loosely forced President Bush's hand, and for the first time, congressional support for a preferential trade agreement depended on protecting human rights—but only for a single group of people: workers. Just enough Democrats, armed with veto power by virtue of their majority in Congress, forced the issue of workers' human rights. But this agenda was still vague and weak because ideas varied greatly, even among the Democrats, about the appropriate way to regulate these rights.

The president cared most about getting a trade agreement in place. So to avoid stalemate with Democrats but against his better judgment, he proposed a compromise in which he would address a limited number of provisions protecting a few human rights for workers during the negotiations. Although the plan was unclear on terms and totally lacking on enforcement, it won the support of a sufficient number of Democrats (including the chairs of the trade subcommittees of Finance and Ways and Means, as well as Majority Leader Richard Gephardt [D-MO]). A solid majority in both the Senate and House granted the president fast-track authority in May 1991. The new trade mandate, however, required very little in the way of concrete labor regulations with enforceable provisions. Bush, who never favored worker protections in the first place, negotiated and signed NAFTA in 1992 without binding language to protect human rights of any kind.

Meanwhile, fears about NAFTA's effects on American workers became a central theme of the 1992 presidential campaign, making trade policy a frequently debated topic. Millions of voters around the country watched as political candidates from both parties argued the merits of NAFTA on live television. Regardless of who would win the presidency, NAFTA would ultimately require bipartisan congressional support to become law. That meant a president from either party could win NAFTA's passage only by convincing enough Democrats to support it while still keeping an adequate number of Republicans on board.

Bill Clinton had campaigned in favor of a NAFTA that included protections for workers' human rights (*New York Times* 1992), and so as president-elect he vowed to delay ratification of the trade agreement his predecessor had negotiated until it was supplemented by rules protecting labor standards and the environment. At his request, discussions resumed with Canada and Mexico, and NAFTA finally passed into law in 1993 with a frail side agreement addressing workers' human rights, the North American Agreement on Labor Cooperation (NAALC). This was sufficient to convince enough Democrats with veto power to support NAFTA, while being weak enough to please most Republicans, who were eager for the new trade agreement but preferred that it not address human rights (Reich 1995).[6]

The process of creating regulations to protect human rights in US PTAs had a humble start. Although various Democrats had fought reasonably hard in favor of the regulations, the party was quite divided on the matter of whether to enforce the standards of conduct. Presidents from both parties took advantage of the situation to push for what they wanted. President George H. W. Bush negotiated a policy that was as close as possible to his own interests within the greater range of options he believed Congress would likely pass—rhetoric about but no real protection for workers.[7] President Clinton had a limited ability to include regulations protecting workers' human rights after international negotiations had concluded. He managed nevertheless to get the issue into the agreement—human rights for workers had to appear in the trade deal, but the issue was marginalized into a side agreement that Republicans would not veto. Broader human rights protections were never mentioned because no one, not even the Democrats, asked for them.

This shift in institutional balance affected the policymaking process. Under Clinton, congressional Republicans remained strongly opposed to enforceable protections for human rights. But a Democratic majority in Congress had forced Republicans to accept a plan that included minimal standards of conduct for workers in a trade agreement Republicans otherwise favored. The regulatory shift was minimal, but for the first time, the human rights regulations in NAFTA represented a political compromise

6. Sixty-one senators and 234 representatives voted in favor of bills implementing NAFTA, with 38 and 200 voting against, respectively. Among House Democrats, 102 voted in favor, with 156 voting against. Among House Republicans, 132 voted in favor, with 43 voting against.

7. Before him, President Reagan had substantially watered down the original proposal for protections of workers' human rights in the 1984 GSP, especially on the matter of enforcement.

on all sides. This compromise was shaped by veto politics. Unfortunately, NAFTA protections for labor backfired.

1994 to 1999

Having set a precedent by including worker protections in a PTA, Democrats hoped they had also appeased voters' fears about job security. But the new trade agreement only set into motion a profound crisis. As chapter 3 explained, the debate over NAFTA during the 1992 presidential campaign was heated and controversial. NAFTA ultimately passed by a very narrow margin of votes. Afterward, labor unions were more furious and vocal than ever, convinced that the NAALC side agreement was completely unsatisfactory and totally without teeth (Bolle 2002). Human rights advocates were equally enraged.

Some House and Senate Democrats again took up the concerns of their constituents and came out more strongly than ever in support of substantial future commitments to protecting workers' human rights and to enforcing those protections as well. The minor political shift evidenced by NAFTA's side agreement on workers' human rights was gaining momentum and placing the fair trade issue front and center. Democrats articulated again and again their intention to veto any future fast-track authority that did not protect workers' human rights and enforce those protections. This meant that once again, some group of veto players, either Democrats or Republicans, would have to compromise to make further trade integration through preferential agreements possible.

From 1994 to 2000, President Clinton was amenable to regulating labor standards and frequently requested congressional extension of fast-track authority in hopes of expanding NAFTA to include Chile and to negotiate an agreement with Singapore (Cooper 2005). But he faced a very different policymaking environment in those years, as Republicans now controlled both the House and Senate in the 104th (1995–97), the 105th (1997–99), and 106th (1999–2001) Congresses and were largely unified against regulating workers' and children's human rights in PTAs. Led by Republican majorities, Congress repeatedly refused Clinton any fast-track authority. In 1995 Democrats in both chambers supported President Clinton's proposal for fast-track authority, but Republicans rallied around an alternative policy, approved by the House Ways and Means Committee, that would delegate trade authority without any mention of workers' human rights (bill, H.R. 2371) (US House of Representatives 1995). The bill established five core negotiating objectives—none related to labor or environmental regulations—and limited the fast-track process to provisions tied directly to

those objectives. This limitation ensured that any human rights regulations would be subject to standard congressional decision making, which
allowed endless amendments, rather than to fast-track practices (Sek 2001).
The bill never reached a floor vote because enough Democrats blocked it,
so Congress failed to reach an agreement. Deadlock between parties over
labor (and environment) issues would make passage of other trade agreements nearly impossible (Destler and Balint 1999).

In 1998, with Republicans still in the majority in Congress, the House
voted overwhelmingly and strictly along party lines to deny another of
Clinton's requests to delegate trade negotiating authority (bill, H.R. 2621)
(US House of Representatives 1997). Again, a motive for defeating the bill
was the exclusion of labor and environmental standards as an objective of
future trade agreements (Sek 2001). Many Democratic opponents to trade
continued to charge that PTAs would hurt American workers (Fergusson
and Sek 2004). A Senate Finance Committee initiative for fast track one
year later again fell to the wayside. With another presidential election in
2000, the controversial issue of fast-track authority was then put aside, and
President Clinton finished his second term without ever winning fast-track
authority. Party differences over labor (and the environment) were a principal cause of this failure. Whereas the Democrats held a majority in Congress for the NAFTA vote and the Republicans were willing, although not
eager, to take on the NAALC side agreement in order to win the trade
agreement, Republicans held a congressional majority for most of Clinton's
tenure, refusing to budge on the issue of regulating workers' human rights
through trade agreements. This was a political snub that Democrats, in the
minority, could not successfully override.[8] However, this deadlock did not
last, despite the institutional hurdles.

2000

Following Congress's repeated denials of fast-track authority to President
Clinton, political circumstances prompted another shift in institutional
politics in 2000. Although the Republican-led Congress would not agree to

---

8. This narrative would seem to confirm the suspicions of scholars who suggest that
presidents under divided party government generally win less trade authority (Lohmann and
O'Halloran 1994; Milner and Rosendorff 1997). In the case of human rights, the scholars are
historically accurate: congressional Democrats with interests in regulating protections for
workers' human rights were unable to reach agreement with Republicans, who resisted standards of conduct for these rights. Interests and thus votes fell almost entirely along party
lines. However, this historical circumstance was not inevitable, as there is nothing inherent
in divided government that prevents the delegation of trade authority (Karol 2000; Mayhew
1991).

fast-track authority, several representatives from both political parties had developed interests in negotiating a PTA with Jordan and had begun to articulate these interests openly to the president. The push for an integration deal with Jordan was political; its supporters believed it would strengthen American security interests in the Middle East.

Jordan's refusal to join the American coalition in the 1990 Gulf War, coupled with its hostility toward Israel, had long been a concern for members of Congress on both sides of the aisle. When Jordan and Israel signed the Washington Declaration (1994) and subsequent peace treaty, Congress and President Clinton took immediate steps to reward the Jordanian government with new bilateral assistance and qualifying industrial zones (Ruebner 2001). Both Democrats and Republicans supported a policy of economic reward for these reforms. Following the peace accords, then House Majority Leader Richard Gephardt (D-MO) and forty-two other representatives sent President Clinton a letter advocating the negotiation of PTAs with governments that signed peace agreements with Israel. However, Congress still denied fast-track authority for these negotiations, leaving Clinton with the tough prospect of negotiating an agreement that could face multiple amendments in Congress and therefore an uncertain fate.

The political timing was not right in Jordan either. Progress stalled until 1999, when King Abdullah II took the Jordanian throne from his father and pledged his support for a trade agreement with the United States. The following year, nearly fifty members of Congress again sent President Clinton letters asking him to enter into trade negotiations with Jordan, citing market integration as a way to express American appreciation for Jordan's role in the Middle East peace process, to promote economic growth, and to enhance regional security (Bolle 2001). These requests were once more made without the delegation of fast-track authority and without any directives on regulating workers' or children's human rights, subjecting any proposed agreement to an arduous institutional process of amendment and renegotiation in Congress.

In June of 2000, President Clinton and King Abdullah II announced negotiations toward the establishment of a reciprocal free trade area (Cooper 2005). During their negotiations, congressional support for integration, although not worker protections, was strong. A bipartisan group of senators urged President Clinton to promptly conclude talks and submit a proposal for a new trade agreement. Eighteen Democrats did the same.[9] Facing overwhelming support for a trade deal, no congressional negotiating

9. For details, see Senators' Letters on Jordan FTA, Inside US Trade, August 18 2000; and Democrats' Letter on Jordan FTA, Inside US Trade, October 27, 2000.

conditions on human rights, and tough institutional hurdles to getting the agreement passed into law without fast-track authority, the Clinton administration announced it would include labor and environmental standards of conduct in its negotiations with Jordan. The administration solicited comments from private-sector organizations and citizens' associations. Remarkably, although the USTR received only three responses related to labor (Bolle 2001),[10] the final text of the agreement included the strongest language ever on protecting workers' human rights and making those standards of conduct enforceable. The agreement subjected respect for core labor principles to a robust system of dispute settlement procedures—and set them forth in the main text of the agreement, not in a side agreement as NAFTA had done (Rosen 2004).

The Clinton administration, spurred by congressional support for new trade agreements, by and large inserted these fair trade regulations single-handedly. This reflected Clinton's campaign promise to ensure that trade agreements would offer ample protections for American workers—a promise he was especially unlikely to break after organized labor's recent backlash against NAFTA.[11]

Although the Clinton administration had negotiated the Jordan agreement and Clinton signed it on October 24, 2000, the PTA was not yet approved by Congress. It came up for a vote right after Clinton left office, and institutional politics again shaped the issue of regulatory control in crucial ways.

2001 to 2002

With the Jordan agreement signed but not yet passed into law and Congress deadlocked over whether to grant fast-track authority, George W. Bush was inaugurated as the forty-third president on January 20, 2001. Market integration was one of his primary objectives. In the 107th Congress (2001–3), the Senate was split evenly along party lines, while Republicans held a majority of seats in the House. On the matter of Jordan, Senator Max Baucus (D-MT), ranking minority member on the Senate Finance

10. The Women's Edge and AFL-CIO both supported the adoption of international labor standards within the text of the new agreement, while the US Council for International Business argued that PTAs should not include labor.

11. Robert Reich had stepped down as Clinton's labor secretary in 1997. The agreement with Jordan was negotiated during Alexis M. Herman's tenure as labor secretary. At the time, an independent counsel was investigating accusations that Herman had accepted kickbacks for giving federal contracts and soliciting illegal campaign contributions for the Democratic Party. She was cleared in 2000. See Lewis (2000).

Committee, and Representative Sander Levin (D-MI), ranking member on the House Ways and Means Trade Subcommittee, had proposed bills to implement the text of the agreement Clinton had negotiated. But President Clinton's exacting regulations on the protection of workers' human rights proved controversial, even to a Congress eager to enact a PTA with Jordan for security reasons. And just as Clinton had added workers' human rights and environmental regulations into a NAFTA that his predecessor had negotiated, George W. Bush watered down Clinton's efforts on labor.

Congressional committees passed the Baucus and Levin bills only after the new Bush administration struck a side deal that appeased enough Republican veto players in Congress who wanted the agreement but opposed the regulations on human rights. To get the agreement through Congress, Catherine Novelli, assistant USTR for Europe and the Mediterranean, and Marwan Muasher, the Jordanian ambassador, exchanged identical letters promising that, in the event that a dispute developed over how to interpret the trade agreement, neither government would use the formal dispute settlement procedures to enforce the agreement in any manner that would block trade but would instead aim to resolve the disagreement through consultations and other cooperative measures (US Office of the Press Secretary 2001).[12]

Despite a failed amendment to restrict the scope of enforcement for labor and environmental regulations and a clear warning from Senator Philip Gramm (R-TX) that he would oppose any effort to use the regulations as a model for future PTAs, the House (H.R. 2603) and Senate passed bills to implement the agreement, and the PTA became law (P.L. 107-43, 2001) (Bolle 2001). The United States-Jordan Free Trade Agreement explicitly recognizes the goals of promoting "higher labor standards by building on [the United States' and Jordan's] respective international commitments and strengthening their cooperation on labor matters," and promoting "effective enforcement of their respective environmental and labor law" (preamble). Parties affirm their obligations under the ILO 1998 Declaration on Fundamental Principles and Rights at Work and its follow-up, and establish a dispute settlement procedure over labor enforcement that allows for "any appropriate and commensurate measure"—some of the strongest language in any trade agreement that addresses human rights.

Republicans' refusal to delegate fast-track authority coupled with an eagerness to accept a deal with Jordan had given former President Clinton a unique agenda-setting role that he used opportunistically to push for more

---

12. The text of both letters is available from http://www.sice.oas.org/Trade/us-jrd/usjrd .asp#Side_Letters.

enforceable trade standards protecting human rights. Now those same Republicans, with one of their own in the White House, made an unprecedented but arguably symbolic[13] exception to their opposition to worker protections to further American security interests in the Middle East. They did so with the administration's assurances that these worker regulations were as weak as possible, given what President Clinton had negotiated, and after threatening to stall the bill through endless amendments unless a deal was struck not to enforce violations of workers' or children's human rights. America had its first strong fair trade clause protecting human rights inside a PTA, but it still did not have a mandate to push for these regulations more generally. This mandate, ironically, would become law during George W. Bush's presidency, although his administration wanted very little to do with human rights or the environment. Yet to get what he wanted on trade, he had little choice.

In 2001, in an outline of his legislative agenda for international trade, Bush informed Congress he would seek to secure fast-track trade promotion authority. His intention was to negotiate a new WTO round, a Free Trade Area of the Americas, and dozens of regional and bilateral PTAs all over the world (Schott 2004a). To appease Democrats who were not eager to support the new administration's plans for more trade liberalization, the president's proposal included negotiating objectives on the protection of workers' human rights and identified a "toolbox" of labor-related actions the administration could take during negotiations (Sek 2001; Zoellick 2003). But partisan differences over the issue of labor had not faded; if anything, they had become even more entrenched. Republicans, holding a majority in the House, insisted that labor standards of conduct be excluded entirely or remain symbolic; Democrats, narrowly controlling a majority in the Senate for a short period between 2001 and 2002,[14] maintained that regulations protecting workers' and children's human rights—and enforcement provisions—must be a core objective of trade deals. Debates were again heated and split along party lines.

After nearly a decade of stalemate over fast track, and in the face of rising American priorities for market integration, the Trade Act of 2002 was

13. The exception was symbolic. The United States-Jordan Free Trade Agreement formally provides mechanisms to enforce its labor provisions. However, the exchange of letters unofficially provides agreement that these mechanisms will not be used. There is great debate as to whether this PTA's labor provisions are effectively "hard" or "soft."

14. In 2001, Senator Jim Jeffords (R-VT) left the Republican Party to become an Independent and caucused with Democrats, giving the Democrats a one-person majority in the Senate. In 2002, the Senate was evenly split again when Senator Paul Wellstone (D-MN) died.

born of bitter and persistent conflict between parties, and both parties made concessions to get the deal done (P.L.107-210) (Becker and Hanrahan 2002). In October 2001, Representative Bill Thomas (R-CA), chairman of the House Ways and Means Committee, introduced a bill to delegate trade promotion authority (H.R. 3005). Thomas had worked over the summer with several Democrats, including Representative Cal Dooley (D-CA), a leader of the New Democrats, and Representatives William J. Jefferson (D-LA) and John S. Tanner (D-TN), also members of the committee. The bill established that parties to any future PTA with the United States would agree to enforce their own domestic labor laws, not those of the ILO, and that any violations of domestic law could lead to trade-related remedies by the other party. The bill was substantially different from what several leading Democrats had wanted. The day after Thomas submitted the bill, another group of Democratic leaders, including Representatives Rangel (D-NY) and Levin (D-MI), submitted their own bill (H.R. 3019), with more comprehensive labor coverage and language supporting internationally recognized workers' human rights that would be enforceable (Sek 2003). The House Ways and Means Committee approved the first bill in October 2001, and following a great deal of debate, the House finally passed the bill (H.R. 3005) by a narrow margin in December, when Democrats held the narrow majority. A few days later, the Senate Finance Committee cleared its own version of the bill. After several amendments in the Senate, both chambers gave final approval (H.R. 3009) in July and August of 2002.

The bill, requiring substantial and reasonably enforceable protections for workers' human rights as a core feature of new trade agreements, passed the House by a single vote and the Senate by a substantial bipartisan majority (Sek 2003).[15] Human rights regulations protecting workers and child laborers had just barely become American law; they were no longer marginalized in side agreements, as they had been in NAFTA, or made on an entirely ad hoc basis, as they had been with Jordan. All future PTAs negotiated within the time limits of the Trade Act would include these regulations, whether presidents or Congress liked it or not.

The George W. Bush administration would now be legally accountable to a Congress ready to veto any agreement that did not follow the Trade Act's requirements. The law covered tariff and nontariff agreements entered into before June 30, 2007.[16] The Trade Act required American negotiators

---

15. The final compromise is based on the Senate rather than the House version of how best to adopt workers' human rights, as an effective Republican majority led the House in 2002 while the Senate was controlled by a narrow Democratic margin.

16. TPA expired in July 2007.

to "seek provisions in trade agreements under which parties to those agree-ments strive to ensure that they do not weaken or reduce the protections afforded in domestic environmental and labor laws" (Section 2102 [a][7]), "to ensure that a party to a trade agreement with the United States does not fail to effectively enforce its environmental or labor laws" (Section 2102 [b][11A]), and to "seek provisions encouraging the early identification and settlement of disputes through consultations" including "compensation if a party to a dispute under the agreement does not come into compliance with its obligations under the agreement," with the right "to impose a penalty upon a party" (Section 2102 [b]).

The US definition of "internationally recognized" worker rights was created by Congress in 1983 and is not the same as the ILO's "core" rights. During negotiations in Congress over the language of the labor regula-tion, the House version once advocated for ILO core standards of conduct while the Senate version advocated for the US definition of internationally recognized labor standards of conduct, thereby rejecting the ILO defini-tion as an infringement on American sovereignty. The Senate argument was standard. The US government ratifies ILO conventions (or human rights treaties more generally) if it is already in compliance; it does not by convention join international treaties and then change domestic laws to comply. Because the United States had not ratified many of the ILO's core conventions, a commitment to comply with ILO core standards of con-duct protecting workers' human rights was perceived by some members of Congress as an encroachment on US legal sovereignty. The final language of the Trade Act is thus a compromise in language that reflects both ILO and US definitions of workers' human rights. In part, the conflict over language reflected the legal significance of the Trade Act: it was under-stood that the definition of labor would become a precedent that, if changed for bilateral agreements, would then also need to be changed for US unilateral trade policies (like the GSP), which could pose problems for maintaining trade benefits to some key security allies (Interview record #20, 2004).

Although human rights advocates of all kinds articulated concerns about the formation of new trade agreements and the aftereffects of NAFTA on groups other than workers and children, their concerns were never em-braced by congressional decision makers, even those supportive of protect-ing workers' human rights. The new trade law calling for the adoption of "respect for worker rights and the rights of children" thus did not address other human rights.

Europe

The push to regulate human rights in Europe's diverse PTAs has been driven by the need to solve problems different from those in America and has been empowered by more decision makers with different interests, veto powers, and capacities to shape trade policy. Here, too, the policymaking process has played an important role in shaping how various preferences for human rights regulations have slowly become law.

Article 113 of the Treaty of Rome (1957)—renumbered Article 133 since the Treaty of Amsterdam (1997)—provides the legal framework for international trade and commerce policymaking in the European Community.[17] The European Community's executive body, the European Commission, is made up of independent commissioners and has the power to propose and negotiate Community trade agreements with foreign governments (Interview record #47, 2005). To this end, the Commission requests European Council authorization to open negotiations, and the Council offers the Commission directives for conducting the negotiations (Interview record #87 2007). Like the American president, the Commission therefore plays an important agenda-setting role in preferential trade policy—one that is separate from the responsibility of member states (Aggarwal and Fogarty 2004; Pollack 1997, 2003). The Council, a legislative body composed of ministers from each member state, has the power to delegate authority to negotiate a trade agreement to the Commission and to mandate directives for these negotiations. With negotiation directives in hand, various experts within the Commission negotiate new PTAs in consultation with a special committee appointed by the Council (Murphy 2000). Eventual power to implement or reject an agreement rests with the Council and sometimes also the Parliament, although agreements sometimes also require ratification by each of the member states as well, thus increasing the number of veto players that can reject a particular agreement.

Unlike those in the United States, policymaking procedures in Europe vary significantly across different types of PTAs. These PTAs include partnership and cooperation agreements such as the agreement with Georgia (1999), association agreements such as the agreement with Tunisia (1998), and economic partnership agreements such as those with ACP countries to replace trade relations under Cotonou (and formerly, Lomé)

17. Article 113 has been updated several times, although the substance of the legal authorities remains similar: 1992 Maastricht Treaty on the European Union; the 1997 Treaty of Amsterdam (which renumbered Article 113 to 133); and the 2000 Treaty of Nice.

(Miller 2004).[18] For all kinds of PTAs, the Commission is formally authorized to make recommendations to the Council by majority vote, although the Commission commonly makes these decisions by consensus (Interview record #14, 2005; Interview record #47, 2005). In America, congressional procedures for approving trade agreements vary according to whether Congress delegates fast-track trade promotion authority to the executive branch; in Europe, the procedures through which the Council issues negotiating directives to the Commission and then approves a trade agreement vary according to the legal basis of the PTA, which determines who the veto players will be (Interview record #10, 2005). This general decision-making procedure is variable in at least three important ways.

First, not all trade agreements require the same voting procedures precisely because different agreements can be negotiated under different Community laws. Some PTAs (negotiated under Article 181, for example) require support by a qualified majority in the Council to become law. Others (negotiated under Article 308 or 310) require unanimous support by all Council ministers (Interview record #10, 2005), although, for many policies, the norm is one of consensus among the ministers, despite voting procedures (Hayes-Renshaw and Wallace 1995; Lindberg 1963).[19] The same is true for so-called mixed agreements: those PTAs that are not fully covered by EC competence and therefore require approval by the Council and ratification by the member states.

Second, not all agreements are exclusive EC competence because in practice some agreements require passage by all of the member states as well as by the Council. This vastly increases the number of decision makers who can veto policy (Interview record #24, 2005; Leal-Arcas 2001). Although the Council alone has the authority to give the Commission directives for trade negotiations, whether and which member states will have a say in passing the final agreement usually influences the kind of directives

18. This book does not consider in any detail unilateral preference programs, such as the GSP, for either the United States or Europe, which offer a different kind of trade agreement.

19. Scholars disagree about the importance of the Council's formal voting procedures. Some argue that once a deal has informally been struck among the largest majority of ministers possible, subsequent legal stages can often be a formality, and voting simply ratifies the preexisting bargain. See Achen (2006). Others argue that formal voting procedures matter a great deal for veto politics. See Tsebelis and Garrett (1996, 2001). From the standpoint of experience, one member of the Commission explains that formal voting procedures do indeed play a role, shaping individual ministers' negotiating strategies within the Council during prevote bargaining, as the norm in the Council is to establish some form of consensus before voting in order to steer clear of tit-for-tat reprisals among ministers across issue areas. See Interview record #87 (2007).

the Council issues or which agreements it passes. This is because ministers are strategic policymakers who anticipate the consequences of policy failure when they make choices. In many cases, though, the Community enjoys exclusive competence in the trade policymaking process, and so it is the Council alone, without ratification by the member states, that passes a PTA into law.[20] In these cases, the Council can adopt the agreement—adoption by the European Council is equivalent to ratification by the member states—and any implementing legislation by a qualified majority vote, but it can amend the Commission's proposed text only by unanimous agreement. In theory, this right of amendment can reduce the Commission's power to set the agenda.[21]

Third, the role of the European Parliament also depends in important ways on the legal basis of the agreement being considered. The Parliament never enjoys a formal role in issuing a Community mandate to negotiate PTAs. Like the member states, however, it does sometimes play a role in the passage of agreements into law, and this role can give its members informal influence over the content of a Community agenda during international negotiations. In 1987, when the Single European Act (SEA) came into force, the EP won the right to effectively veto certain trade agreements. Ever since, in some cases[22] the Council must simply consult the Parliament before the conclusion of an agreement and the EP's opinions are noted but are nonbinding. In other cases,[23] though, the EP has the right of assent by absolute majority and enjoys a conditional power of agenda setting (Moser 1996; Pollack 1997; Tsebelis 1994, 1995; Tsebelis and Garrett 2001). By withholding its assent, the EP can block the passage of new trade agreements. Trade policymaking rules in Europe are thus complicated and vary from agreement to agreement. Knowledge of the legal basis of each PTA is essential to understanding who the key actors are and how they make decisions.[24]

20. This is the case when the legal basis of a trade agreement is Article 133, 300, or 181.

21. Once the Commission has put an issue on the agenda, it is difficult for the Council to completely ignore the issue, much in the same way congressional trade directives bind the US president. By contrast, the Council can substantially modify the Commission's initial proposal for a negotiating mandate, thereby better satisfying its own interests for policy. See Interview record #37 (2004).

22. This is the case under Article 133.

23. This is the case when agreements have strong political significance under Articles 133 and 308, have budgetary implications, or form an association.

24. I thank Pieter Jan Kuyper, principal legal adviser for external relations in the European Commission, for his invaluable help and consultation on the legal process. I also thank Lorand Bartels.

1958 to 1975

The process of including human rights-protecting regulations in external trade relations did not come easily in Europe because of demanding procedural rules, numerous policymaking veto players, and a panoply of policy interests. For a long time the Community's position on human rights had no direct or formal relationship to its trade or cooperation policy. The Council repeatedly gave the Commission negotiation directives devoid of any standards of conduct for protecting human rights, and for years the Commission never sought to include human rights on its own either. In fact, for most of the Community's early existence, human rights were neither a main nor coherent feature of internal or foreign policy.

As in the United States, human rights did not arise during the early years of European PTA regulation because few Community or European policymakers wanted them, and so few crucial veto players asked for them.[25] As chapter 3 demonstrated, a few members of the European Parliament were calling attention to human rights violations, such as murder and torture, but none enjoyed formal decision-making power over trade agreements, so their interests and opinions were not very influential at that time. Although some member states had occasionally included human rights matters in their own foreign policy, no group of ministers advocated human rights protections in Community foreign policy, let alone in PTAs. Instead, commissioners were largely focused on building Community ties with former colonies and political spheres of past or future European influence.

1975 to 1985

That lack of interest in Europe-wide human rights protections began to change with the arrival of political shocks and crises in several countries committed to trade with Europe through PTAs. In the 1970s, brutal repression broke out in Uganda, the Central African Republic, Equatorial Guinea, Liberia, and a number of other countries with which Europe was nurturing postcolonial-era political and economic ties, raising questions about the governance role of Community trade agreements. The United

25. One substantial difference between the American and European experiences is that, in the United States, some Democrats had been asking for regulations to protect workers' human rights in unilateral policies, while in Europe, policymakers had long addressed the matter of human rights in their national policies rather than through the Community's unilateral instruments. Neither, however, had mobilized strong preferences for protecting human rights in PTAs at this time.

Kingdom, reacting mainly to the outbreak of violence in Uganda under President Idi Amin, (1971–79) was among the first member states to question whether the Community could or should suspend its trade and cooperation agreements with countries as punishment for human rights atrocities. Around the same time, MEPs became democratically elected and thus accountable to voters' needs, and many repeatedly asked the Council and the Commission to take external action in support of human rights (European Parliament 1977, 1978b; Interview record #44, 2004). Their concerns came before a Commission led by Roy Jenkins, himself a member of the British Labor Party, who shared the United Kingdom's worries and began to raise questions about the governance of human rights in Europe's external relations and with respect to trade policy in Africa, the Caribbean, and the Pacific (ACP) countries in particular (Arts 2000).

The United Kingdom's concerns surfaced in a setting in which the Lomé I Convention with the ACP countries was the Community's most significant foreign trade and cooperation policy with the developing world. It was a PTA that required unanimous approval in the Council as well as ratification by all the member states (Elgstrom 2000). The agreement was negotiated by the Commission with directives from the Council, and it said nothing about protecting human rights.[26] But Lomé I was set to expire after only five years, and the process of renegotiation began almost immediately after the first convention came into force, providing an institutional window of opportunity for policymakers to change the rules.[27] Commissioner Jenkins guided the talks, which were influenced by growing public concern over Europe's trade and aid allocations to abusive countries such as Uganda, as well as by the United Kingdom's request to suspend economic privileges to Uganda. Commissioner for Development Claude Cheysson, leader of the negotiations, began to raise the issue of human rights protections in agreements with the ACP countries (Fierro 2003). On the eve of negotiations over Lomé II, Cheysson called for recognition that the "prime aim of all [Community] co-operation is to serve mankind. This implies that a man's right to live and to be respected as a person has to be recognised as a prime concern" (quoted in Fierro 2003, 47). After years of neglecting human rights, the Commission had finally taken notice of the issue, albeit informally. Identifying specific language on human rights regulations at this time proved highly controversial.

26. Most other PTAs are negotiated with the expertise of Commission Directorate General External Relations rather than Development; relations with the ACP are unique exceptions.

27. Formal negotiations at the ministerial level were officially launched on 24 July 1978, although the actual negotiating sessions had already begun in Brussels in September.

Compelled by institutional procedure to react to the Commission's proposal, the Council responded informally with one of the first cornerstones of its philosophy on the regulation of human rights in the Community's external relations. The then nine member states agreed in principle that something had to be done about Uganda and the problem Uganda represented more generally. They reached an informal agreement to include a modest reference to human rights in the preamble of the next Lomé agreement as a way to win more influence over political issues taking place inside troubled countries, but also as a way to sell the ACP trade agreement to an increasingly skeptical European public reading about the atrocities in the daily news (Garnick and Twichett 1979). In particular, the member states agreed that trade relations with the ACP countries must be founded on the principles that form the cornerstone of liberty, justice, and peace in the world as incorporated in the UN Charter and the Universal Declaration of Human Rights (UDHR) (Fierro 2003). But disagreements among ministers on the Council developed immediately over the wording of this reference because member states had different goals on enforcement. As chapter 3 explains, the United Kingdom and the Netherlands made the case for strong and enforceable human rights protections that would allow termination of PTAs such as Lomé in the event of future rights violations. Belgium and Germany agreed that human rights were of growing concern but believed that allowing suspension of PTAs was too radical. France preferred that the issues be regulated separately.

Reaching a formal Council agreement on the matter proved difficult. After the first direct election of Parliament members by universal suffrage, some members became increasingly vocal about human rights, yet they had no institutional power with which to influence the agenda. The British and Dutch governments were calling for the creation of enforceable human rights regulations in the Community's external trade relations (European Parliament 1978a, 1983, 1984a, 1985). They had some budding support from a few commissioners, who were at this time quite skeptical about implementation (*The Courier* 1979). Nonetheless, Council ministers were deeply divided on enforcement and unable to agree on language for regulation. Thus, despite some new interest in human rights, the Council repeatedly directed the Commission to negotiate new trade agreements without any specific reference to human rights protections. Thus neither Lomé II (1980) nor Lomé III (1985)[28] introduced any formal judgment about members' human rights behavior.

---

28. Lomé III set precedent with references to human dignity (Article 4), elaborated in a joint declaration in an annex to the convention, although it said nothing specifically about

1986 to 1990

Three separate events took place in the 1980s that helped to change the European approach to regulating human rights protections in trade relations. First, in 1986 the Community adopted the SEA, which took effect one year later and included the Community's first constitutional reference to human rights: the preamble recognizes the European responsibility to speak with one voice to effectively protect common interests and "in particular to display the principles of democracy and compliance with the law and with human rights" (Single European Act 1987). The SEA also changed the institutional rules of the policymaking process, granting the Parliament the right to assent by an absolute majority to certain PTAs, including association agreements such as Lomé (Rideau 1997). Until then, the Parliament had been consulted (under Article 238) only in the passage of new PTAs. Beginning in 1987, it had the authority to reject an association agreement by an absolute majority of its members, regardless of the Council's decision (Bieber 1990).[29] Thus the EP effectively became a veto player for some preferential trade agreements.

At the same time, the European Court of Justice (ECJ) recognized that the Community's common commercial policy could include provisions on development cooperation without disturbing the nature of the market agreement, thereby creating the first legal connection between Community trade and development policy (European Court of Justice 1987). The ECJ, however, plays no direct role in foreign policymaking in the European Community and is not a formal veto player on trade negotiations.[30]

---

human rights, and the provisions on human dignity were not enforceable through suspension of the agreement.

29. In practice, this majority has been possible only if the two largest political groups in the Parliament are in favor and most MEPs can be reached for a vote. Further details of the assent procedure are given in Articles 32 and 33 of the EP's Rules of Procedure. See Bieber (1990) for an excellent review.

30. Much has been written about the legal status of human rights in the European Community. See Neuwahl and Rosas (1995), Alston, Bustelo, and Heenan (1999) and in the case of the EC's external policies, Brandtner and Rosas (1998) and Bartels (2005). While the court is not a veto player on trade negotiations, the ECJ has played and still plays an extremely important role in defining the extent of the external relations powers of the European Community in relation to those of the member states. It is the ECJ that declared common commercial policy an exclusive power of the Community (Opinion 1/75); that assigned the Community exclusive external powers outside the trade policy area in all those domains where it has legislated and where that legislation would be affected or altered by member states concluding their own agreements (Case 22/70); and that denied the Community any power in external relations with respect to the conclusion of human rights agreements, including the European Convention for Human Rights and Fundamental Freedoms (Opinion 2/94), and with respect to the protection of personal data in the field of criminal law and combating

The Parliament's power to assent was granted on the eve of renegotiations for a fourth Lomé agreement, which created a politically opportune moment for the EP to exercise its new veto powers. MEPs, despite substantial disagreements over enforcing human rights rules through PTAs, lost no time in signaling their intent to use their new authority to shape Community commercial policy (Interview record #37, 2004). In exchange for parliamentary support for certain agreements, the Parliament asked the Council and Commission to make greater efforts to protect human rights through trade relations by creating enforceable standards of conduct (Interview record #31, 2005). And the MEPs meant business. In 1987, the EP postponed a trade agreement with Turkey after the politically motivated arrest of several Turkish politicians. One year later, it refused assent to an agreement with Israel, citing human rights abuses. Thus an absolute parliamentary majority held veto power over Lomé IV at a time when human rights were squarely on the agenda of MEPs, as discussed in chapter 3.

The second critical event of the 1980s was the fall of the Berlin Wall in 1989. This German milestone occurred in the context of the EP's active and repeated calls to link human rights to Europe's PTAs and, coincidentally, one month before the signing of Lomé IV. The wall's demise marked the end of the cold war and the formal period of political neutrality that had inspired Community trade relations for decades (Frisch 1997; Whiteman 1998). Facing both the challenges of a new geopolitical environment and a public upset by trade relations with brutal dictators, the Commission in 1990 proposed Europe's first human rights clause with the ACP countries, regulating standards for conduct.

---

terrorism (Case C-317/04). Sometimes the Commission uses treaty infringement procedures against member states when they overstep the limits of their external relations power. The present drafting of Article 133 (after Nice) on the scope of the Community's exclusive trade policy powers (see in particular paragraphs 5 and 6 of 133) was heavily influenced by the Court's ruling in Opinion 1/94. Case law also provides a legal basis for suspension of the EC's trade agreements. In *Portugal v. Council*, for example, the Court upheld the position that the creation of human rights trade regulations could be legally used to secure the Community's right to suspend or terminate a PTA with a trade partner that violates human rights. See European Court of Justice (1996a). Over the years, the ECJ has recognized that the pursuit of trade has human rights connotations—see Brandtner and Rosas (1999)—which may have helped legitimize the Community transformation. Moreover, some of the ECJ's more restrictive judgments concerning the Community's human rights policies in external relations have created momentum to find a legal solution through the adoption of new policies. See Fierro (2001). For example, the Court's ruling in *United Kingdom and Others v. Commission* threw into doubt the legal basis for Community funding for human rights and directly provoked the adoption of two regulations in 1999 providing a clear legal basis for the Community's human rights activities. See Alston and Weiler (1999), and Interview record #13 (2004). I again thank Pieter Jan Kuyper, principal legal adviser for external relations in the European Commission, for his input on the legal process.

Although the Parliament had no formal say in the substance of the trade negotiations with the ACP countries, its influence was certainly anticipated, thanks to its ability to veto the agreement (Clapham 1991). The Commission, led by Jacques Delors and already keen to discuss human rights, was therefore prompted to renegotiate Lomé, and the Parliament, Council, and member states were spurred to pass a fourth agreement that now included specific language on human rights (Interview record #33, 2004).[31] Article 5(1) of the new Lomé agreement with the ACP countries declared, "Respect for human rights, democratic principles and the rule of law . . . shall constitute an essential element of this convention," although no clear suspension mechanism had been developed (Council of the European Union 1991a).[32] Even though the new provisions were vague on procedures for implementation, Europe's push for regulating the protection of human rights in PTAs had begun. Protections for workers' human rights, however, were never specifically mentioned in this agreement.

Finally, and quite apart from Europe's institutional reforms or the Community's renegotiations with ACP countries, several Central and Latin American countries, such as Argentina and Chile, began the slow move toward democracy during this time, after years of brutal military-led dictatorships that murdered and disappeared thousands of people. Europe sought to foster trade and cooperation ties with the region's emerging democratic governments and made Argentina one of the first test cases for a new form of trade regulation that included human rights standards of conduct.[33]

Carlos Menem became president of Argentina the year the Berlin Wall fell and shortly after the country's troubled return to democracy. Facing a legacy of military rule, violence, and harsh economic conditions, Menem's government began negotiations for a PTA with the European Community. At Argentina's request, and to help shore up the government's commitment to democratization, Europe's 1990 Framework Trade and Economic

31. This strategic behavior has been institutionalized over time, as the Commission and Council regularly notify appropriate parliamentary committees of their progress in negotiations of an agreement. This procedure was originally introduced with no formal legal basis through an interinstitutional agreement. Bieber (1990) argues that this procedure became important after SEA since parliamentary committees that are informed about the course of negotiations can themselves make substantive proposals and signal intent.

32. Further information on these negotiations is given in chapter 5.

33. A few years earlier, in 1985, the Community had formed a cooperation agreement with various Central American countries, which affirmed countries' support for human rights and the dignity of the person (EEC-Countries Parties to the General Treaty on Central American Economic Integration [Costa Rica, El Salvador, Guatemala, Honduras, and Nicaragua] and Panama Cooperation Agreement, 1986). The human rights content, however, was neither enforceable nor included in the articles of agreement.

Co-operation Agreement with Argentina included the protection of human rights as a fundamental principle of economic cooperation (Article 1) (Council of the European Union 1990; Interview record #31, 2005).[34] The agreement was the first of its kind with a country outside the ACP, negotiated under the exclusive competence of the Community.[35] Although the Council had never issued directives asking the Commission to include regulations protecting human rights, it overcame considerable differences of opinion on enforcement to approve the agreement, formally by qualified majority. Member state ratification was not required, which created a more flexible policymaking environment with fewer veto players.

One member of the Commission who was present during the negotiations remarked in retrospect that Community support for Latin American democratization was so strong among most European policymakers that passing this seminal agreement into law was remarkably easy. There was very little resistance to the inclusion of human rights regulations in the case of Argentina, and the regulations represent one of Europe's earliest achievements on the issue outside the ACP countries, where resistance was still considerable (Interview record #87, 2007). Then again, as in the text of Lomé IV (1990), the text of the agreement with Argentina was entirely vague on enforcement. Similar trade agreements with Chile, Uruguay, and Paraguay passed under the same favorable policymaking procedures (Council of the European Union 1990b, 1990c, 1992d).

1991 to 1994

The previous chapter explained the significant impact the end of the cold war had on European policymakers' views about political neutrality in trade agreements. Despite different political interests and allegiances, many previously skeptical policymakers came to see Europe's interest in regulating human rights protections in other countries. Rather quickly, they took up the search for a coherent set of tools, including but not limited to PTAs, to shore up Europe's political influence abroad. In 1991, acting under initiative by the Commission (European Commission 1991)[36] and at the re-

34. This event offers an example of a case where another country approached the European Union and asked to create trade regulations to help lock in democratic reforms. See Pevehouse (2005).

35. To pass into law, the agreement did not require ratification by the member states of the Community.

36. The 1991 Commission communication affirmed the need to take advantage of the political momentum to regulate human rights through trade cooperation—momentum created by democratization efforts in Central and Eastern Europe, Latin American, and Africa. See Fierro (2001).

quest of the Parliament, the Council (in a nonbinding resolution taken by consensus) generalized these human rights protections to all Community trade agreements, except sectoral agreements, with developing countries (Bartels 2005; Council of the European Union 1991b; Fierro 2001; Horng 2003).[37] The Council resolution emphasized that protecting human rights was to be an explicit aim of European development policy, calling attention to "a positive approach that stimulates respect for human rights and encourages democracy" (Council of the European Union 1991b).

Although no clear or coherent legal mandate for enforcement was given, the first phase of the regulation process had taken place at the Community level and at the Commission's request (Interview record #13, 2004; Interview record #37, 2004). The call for human rights was not binding, but the Commission's 1991 communication and the Council's subsequent resolution laid the foundation for the Community's approach to the policy reforms about to take place—all despite continuing skepticism and some holdover concern among member states and MEPs over enforcing human rights trade regulations by allowing suspension of agreements.

Despite these first steps, the Community continued for several more years its ad hoc approach to regulating human rights through PTAs. The approach was further shaped by two more sets of pivotal events. As we saw in chapter 3, Yugoslavia's internal conflict, and the coup in Haiti, a Lomé agreement member, created new problems for Europe's trade policy. These crises changed some top-ranking European policymakers' outlooks on the desirability of regulating human rights through PTAs. When negotiations took place in Latin America and with the ACP countries over Lomé IV, the Community had already begun the process of trade integration in Central and Eastern Europe. Trade agreements with Yugoslavia, Hungary, Poland, and Czechoslovakia had been negotiated without any concern or commitment to human rights—these so-called Europe Agreements are mixed-competence agreements between the European Community and the member states, requiring unanimity in the Council and ratification by all member states.

But the legal precedents set in the ACP and now in Latin America, coupled with the Council's 1991 resolution and the developing crisis in Yugoslavia, ushered in a change of Community strategy (Interview record #13, 2004). Policymakers in the Commission and Council who had once resisted enforcing human rights trade regulations through PTA suspension

37. The 1991 resolution is nonbinding and sets guidelines, procedures, and priorities for improving the consistency and cohesion of EC development initiatives. http://europa.eu.int/comm/external_relations/human_rights/doc/cr28_11_91_en.htm.

provisions now feared the consequences of another situation like that in Yugoslavia or Haiti. This prompted them to create regulations to consolidate security and European influence. Voices from within all Community institutions, even among some conservatives, now began to articulate a need to redirect Europe's foreign policy strategy (Interview record #87, 2007). Trade agreements would now explicitly support human rights and democracy, thereby providing the Community with a safety valve—a means to suspend trade obligations in the case of future crises (Brandtner and Rosas 1998; Interview record #13, 2004). Thus enforcement provisions, long the main source of conflict among European policymakers, were now perceived as necessary.

At the same time, the Treaty on the European Union (TEU) (1992), also known as the Maastricht Treaty, was passed into law, modifying the many treaties that had come before it, and setting forth a distinctive vision of a European Union.[38] This passage was driven by policymakers' converging desires across Europe and throughout Community institutions to influence human rights abroad. Article 6 of the treaty declared for the first time a European commitment to the principles of liberty, democracy, and respect for human rights and fundamental freedoms and acknowledged a commitment to respect the rights guaranteed by the European Convention for the Protection of Human Rights and Fundamental Freedoms (1950). Article 6 also committed the European Union to providing itself with the means necessary to attain its objectives and carry through these policies.

The TEU's provisions on human rights provided a clearer legal basis from which to create more rules, not simply on a case by case basis, but rooted in Community law. Several policymakers involved at the time believed that if Europe was going to continue placing credible and legitimate demands on other countries to measure up to certain human rights principles and withdrawing trade privileges when crises like Haiti or Yugoslavia emerged, Europe itself needed an internal position on human rights. This reflects both the letter and the spirit of TEU Article 6 (Interview record #87, 2007; Interview record #14, 2005; Interview record #37, 2004). Until then, although the Community had become a reasonably steadfast defender of human rights at home and abroad, it lacked a consistent policy on the matter at either level, creating frequent uncertainties about its legal standing to regulate human rights through its external relations. The TEU

---

38. For scholarship on the TEU and its implications for human rights issues, see Twomey (1994) and Colvin and Noorlander (1998). For a seminal work on the EU and human rights, see Alston, Bustelo, and Heenan (1999).

provided the first institutional step in creating that foundation, yet it alone did not solve the problem of inconsistency.

In 1992, the Commission negotiated and the Council passed PTAs with Albania and the three Baltic countries. These agreements were concluded under exclusive Community competence, with the Council acting under qualified majority and without ratification by the member states. This made the policymaking process of passing these agreements considerably easier than that of many other agreements that required member states' ratification and unanimity in the Council.[39] The agreements included the most comprehensive language ever protecting human rights, allowing either party to suspend an agreement immediately and without consultation in the event of violations (Council of the European Union 1992a). These strong provisions would not likely have passed had ratification by all member states been required.[40] Thus, in only three years the Community went from PTAs with no clear implementation to agreements with instant enforcement mechanisms.

The Baltic-style agreements proved instantly controversial. Not all member states supported the principle of immediate suspension without consultation. Though they agreed that human rights were important, some member states worried that these enforcement provisions clashed with a core principle of Community legal order, established by the Vienna Convention on the Law of the Treaties (1969), which said all pacts must be respected (Fierro 2003). Anticipating the negotiation of new PTAs in the region, the Council issued a statement confirming the Community's intention to recognize human rights as an "essential element" of trade agreements with the Conference on Security and Cooperation in Europe (CSCE) (Council of the European Union 1992b). However, this declaration did not support the inclusion of the Baltic suspension mechanism, nor did it say anything about procedures for enforcement (Miller 2004).

On the same day, the Council issued negotiating directives for agreements with Bulgaria and Romania whose passage required a tough course: unanimity in the Council and ratification by all member states. Opposition from the Council all but assured that several member states would reject

39. The question of how unanimity versus qualified majority voting in the Council has shaped the policy process is a source of great debate among scholars. Some believe that the Council voting process has a clear effect on veto politics, and others point out that the Council has strong incentives to informally achieve consensus, even under qualified majority circumstances, to avoid tit-for-tat retaliation across other issue areas, although voting procedures nevertheless do shape the prevote bargaining context.

40. The motivations for the adoption of this strict enforcement clause, commonly referred to as the Baltic Clause, were a direct result of the Yugoslavia crisis. See Brandtner and Rosas (1999) and Interview record #13 (2004).

immediate trade suspension over human rights violations, so the Baltic enforcement clause was abandoned in favor of a more flexible policy. What came to be known as the "Bulgarian" clause required consultation with an offending government prior to any action and allowed suspension of an agreement only as a last resort after all other "appropriate measures" had been taken (Bartels 2005).[41]

Despite slowly converging interests, in 1993 the Community's human rights protections in PTAs were still inconsistent and ad hoc, driven in part by the shifting veto powers and voting procedures of the policymaking process. Hungary, Poland, and Czechoslovakia had secured trade agreements that said nothing about human rights. The ACP countries enjoyed trade relations that emphasized human rights rhetorically but their provisions were not yet enforceable. Human rights protection was a central element of the agreement with Argentina and its neighbors, although procedures for enforcement were never established. Trade benefits under the agreements with Bulgaria and Romania could be suspended for violations of human rights but only as a last resort and following consultations. Albania, by contrast, was a member of a PTA with the strictest procedures for enforcement to date.

1995

The turning point for Community regulations on human rights in PTAs came in 1995.[42] Responding largely to the Yugoslavian crisis and referring to Europe's new legal ability to regulate human rights under the TEU, the Commission once again took decisive action. It drafted a communication "on the inclusion of respect for democratic principles and human rights in agreements between the Community and third countries" that once again obligated Council action (European Commission 1995).[43]

41. The evidence is entirely consistent with Meunier's (2005) argument that the level of institutional unity in the European Union shapes the Community's external voice in international trade negotiations. In particular, she finds that unanimity voting strengthens the hand of EU negotiators in resisting demands for policy changes from foreign governments in multilateral negotiations but also weakens their ability to advocate policy changes. As concerns the shift in regulations, Council voting under unanimity has possibly weakened the Community's ability to advocate for strong policies of human rights enforcement in trade agreements, while majority rules may have proved more efficacious for European bargaining abroad. Clearly ratification by member states has shaped the process in important ways, making agreements harder to pass into law.

42. For analysis of the labor clause in Europe's GSP, see Tsogas (2000) as well as Bartels (2003).

43. The Commission issued a second communication in November of that year on The European Union and the External Dimension of Human Rights Policy: From Rome to

Commissioner for External Relations Hans van den Broek had informed Council President Helveg Petersen in a letter that the Commission would take up human rights "systematically" in negotiations of all future trade agreements (Fierro 2001).[44] At the same time, Austria, Finland, and Sweden became EU member states. Their new position as institutional veto players willing to protect human rights provided added momentum throughout Community institutions for a comprehensive change in Europe's external relations. The TEU, whose provisions on human rights came partly in response to the Community's ad hoc attempts at regulation through external relations, now reinforced policymakers' sense that Europe needed a more coherent framework from which to influence the politics of other countries. Policymakers from all European-level institutions were now arguing that it was paramount to create consistency between the new TEU provisions elevating the status of human rights inside the EU and any new Community regulations and policies governing external relations (Interview record #13, 2004; Interview record, #25 2004; Interview record #50, 2004). While the EP threatened to exercise its right of assent on an ad hoc basis and became more vocal on the creation of trade regulations protecting human rights, the Commission again took the initiative (Interview record #50, 2004). It drafted a communication "on the inclusion of respect for democratic principles and human rights in agreements between the Community and third countries" that provided a formal framework for Commissioner van den Broek's letter and again obligated Council action (European Commission 1995).

With the support of the new EU member states and in direct response to the Commission communication, the Council passed its first legally binding decision by consensus, mandating that future PTAs (with the exception of sectoral agreements) include a standard human rights clause with a suspension mechanism to ensure enforcement (Miller 2004). The 1995 clause appeared in various forms in the body of new agreements and

---

Maastricht and Beyond, followed by the Barcelona declaration committing all government parties at the Euro-Mediterranean Conference to "act in accordance with the United Nations Charter and the Universal Declaration of Human Rights, . . . respect human rights and fundamental freedoms and guarantee the effective legitimate exercise of such rights and freedoms, including freedom of expression, freedom of association for peaceful purposes and freedom of thought, conscience and religion, both individually and together with other members of the same group, without any discrimination on grounds of race, nationality, language, . . . [and] stress the importance of proper education in the matter of human rights and fundamental freedoms" (Barcelona Declaration 1995).

44. The letter, which was unpublished, did not clarify whether human rights would be adopted into all bilateral agreements, including sectoral agreements, or only into framework agreements.

declared that respect for fundamental human rights and democratic principles was an "essential element" of each agreement (Alston, Bustelo, and Heenan 1999; Bartels 2005). A compromise set of enforcement measures similar to those adopted in the Bulgaria agreement would be established in the event of "non-execution" (Brandtner and Rosas 1998). Europe had its first formal Community-level mandate to negotiate and enforce human rights protections through PTAs—a compromise that allowed more flexibility on enforcement than did some existing PTAs but was substantially more rigorous in its requirements than were most previous agreements. This formula was validated a short time later when the ECJ considered the case *Portugal v. Council* and recognized the legal basis of the human rights clause (European Court of Justice 1996a).[45] Europe had officially made PTAs fair by regulating standards of conduct protecting human rights. That 1995 human rights clause remains the cornerstone regulation on human rights to this day.[46]

Chapters 3 and 4 together demonstrate that fair trade policies owe their creation to core groups of policymakers, endowed with veto powers and different institutional advantages in the policymaking process, who developed interests in regulating human rights through PTAs. The development of new ideas or interests cannot alone explain, in either the United States or Europe, how or why reforms spread so quickly or why they took on the specific forms they did. Changing the rules of American and European trade agreements required more than new beliefs and preferences among policymakers. It required that these preferences emanate from people who were vested with and prepared to use their political powers to force a contentious issue onto the trade agenda. These people had to be able and willing to threaten to veto policy when they could.

Certainly, NGOs and public and private interest groups have influenced policymakers and helped to shape their beliefs, but interest group or NGO

45. Challenging a newly formed agreement with India, Portugal contested the Community's capacity to include a human rights clause in its trade agreements. The ECJ ruled that provisions concerning respect for human rights and democratic principles did not affect the character of the agreement and that Article 181 of the treaty gave an adequate legal basis for the adoption of human rights. For comments on the case see Steve Peers (1998), Case C-268/94, *Portugal versus Council* [1996] ECR I-6177 in 35 CMLR 1998, pp. 539–55. The case applies only to Article 181, however, not to Articles 133 and 300, which are also used as legal bases for the human rights clause.

46. Although this book focuses on the events leading up to the 1995 decision, several scholars examine the events that have since taken place in Europe, which build upon this foundational policy. See Alston, Bustelo, and Heenan (1999); Arts (2000); Fierro (2003); and Bartels (2005). See the time lines in the appendix for a partial history.

mobilization cannot alone claim credit for transforming PTAs. Institutional politics of decision making—over which interest groups and NGOs have little influence—have also played a role in the regulatory process by providing certain actors with veto powers and giving policymakers the ability to shape different aspects of agreements at different points in the process. The institutional process was clearly decisive in making these human rights regulations possible and shows why common explanations that look to interest groups or moral advocates for answers fall short.

The push for fair PTA trade regulations that protect human rights began almost entirely through the adoption and implementation of successive laws in the United States and Europe, culminating with the US Trade Act in 2002 and Europe's Commission Communication and Council Decision in 1995. Over time, these laws bound trade negotiators and ensured that leaders would raise the issue of protecting human rights with other governments. Yet even these laws, so crucial to the process, did not guarantee that potential trade partners would agree to the human rights regulations, particularly when so many countries around the world violently repressed or allowed the repression of human rights inside their borders. The United States and Europe would now have to convince their preferential trade partners—many of them repressive and reluctant—to get on board. This is the subject of the next chapter.

CHAPTER 5

POWER

Now that we have examined the influences that led policymakers to embrace human rights trade protections (chapter 3) and the institutional maneuvering through which they passed trade regulations (chapter 4), we arrive at the final step in the policymaking process: the dominant economic powers had to convince their trading partners to sign on. Why have so many countries—especially those with repressive and tyrannical governments—elected to join these preferential trade agreements that can punish them for their human rights abuses? And why do these same governments, most of which have rejected fair trade standards for human rights in the WTO, often accept them in PTAs? Are these governments learning over time to appreciate human rights norms? Are they responding to pressures from domestic interest groups and NGOs? Do they want to lock in policy reforms in uncertain political environments? And how much control do they have over the creation of the trade regulations designed to protect human rights?

The answer, as explained in chapter 2, is that economically weaker countries often agree to trade regulations protecting human rights because they lack the bargaining power to resist them. When the United States or Europe forces the unwelcome issue of human rights protections into international trade negotiations, countries may accept regulations they otherwise do not want in order to get what they do want, namely a trade agreement with a powerful and resource-rich United States or Europe. Indeed, developing countries are least able to turn down American or European offers for trade (Gruber 2000). Moreover, this bargaining disadvantage for developing countries was worsened when the American Congress in 2002 and the European Council and Commission in 1995 decided to require that all their trade negotiations henceforth include human rights protections (Putnam 1998).

Nevertheless, not all countries that trade with the United States and Europe are powerless or behave as such. Some are in fact successful in safeguarding their interests during international negotiations. As we shall see, countries with relatively advanced economies have been best able to resist the creation of trade regulations that protect human rights because they can afford to turn down an agreement they don't like. They are also better able to resist human rights protections when the American or European legislatures do not limit the bargaining agenda by ordering their executives to negotiate for protections.[1] This explanation of relative bargaining abilities contrasts with some scholars' suggestion that countries transitioning to democracy and suffering from political uncertainty should be eager to make these regulations, or that most trade partners should show little resistance to accepting PTA regulations protecting human rights.[2]

To demonstrate how these factors have affected trade negotiations around the world, we will examine several agreements between the United States or Europe and other countries. We will see that most other countries, even the liberal democratic governments, have been strongly opposed to PTA protections for human rights. Thus this chapter will bring full circle the explanation of how regulations protecting certain human rights for workers and children, as well as voters and citizens, were conceived and then put into PTAs all over the world. The next chapter will consider their effects on human rights policies and practices.

Case Selection

Many features of politics shape negotiations at this stage in the policy process. The cases explored in this chapter are ones that offer variations in the two most important features that influence countries' relative bargaining power. The first feature is the domestic policies of the dominant trade partner—whether or not American or European legislatures passed directives requiring human rights regulations to be negotiated, as examined in chapter 4. The second feature is market strength—whether or not the other trade partner is an advanced industrial economy, rich enough to push back on human rights standards and risk losing preferential market access and related benefits. The cases explored here, summarized in table 3,

1. These conjectures are spelled out in table 1 of chapter 2.
2. These conjectures are spelled out in table 2 of chapter 2.

TABLE 3
Case selection

	Legislative constraints			
	Say nothing about human rights		Human rights must be included	
Relative bargaining power	US	EU	US	EU
Strong	Canada (1993)	EEA (1992)	Australia (2005)	Australia (1996)
Weak	Mexico (1993)	Argentina (1990) Lomé I (1975) Lomé II (1980) Lomé III (1985) Lomé IV (1990)	Chile (2002)	Lomé IV bis (1995) Cotonou (2000)

include agreements made before and after the United States and Europe required human rights standards of conduct in their PTAs, with countries ranging from the world's poorest, such as Madagascar—whose economy relies mainly on subsistence agriculture—to its richest, including Australia, an internationally competitive advanced industrial market economy.

These cases also involve countries from different regions of the world and with various types of governments, including well-established democracies, newly transitioning countries, and long-time dictatorships, with various records of protection for or abuse of human rights. Perhaps surprisingly, not all countries that sign on to these fair preferential trade regulations are democratic or rights-protecting. Most countries that participate, in fact, are nowhere near being democratic and are guilty of considerable abuses of human rights. The United States is negotiating or has passed into law preferential trade agreements with a few democracies, including Panama, but also with many dictatorships and monarchies, such as Bahrain, Oman, and Morocco, as well as with terribly repressive countries, such as Colombia, or countries, including Thailand, where substantial abuses take place. All of these agreements or negotiations include regulations that will protect the human rights of workers and children, at least on paper. Europe, meanwhile, has negotiated and passed into law preferential trade agreements with democracies such as India, but many of its PTAs are also made with dictatorships, including Haiti, Turkmenistan, or Sudan, as well as with severe abusers of human rights, such as Sri Lanka or Zimbabwe. These agreements nevertheless include standards of conduct protecting fundamental human rights.

Trade Partners Don't Want Human Rights

While some policymakers in the United States and Europe have grown increasingly convinced of the need to make preferential trade regulations that protect human rights, almost all other countries in the world oppose the creation of fair trade standards of human rights conduct in their PTAs, even the democratic and human rights-protecting countries.

On the one hand, many countries want and need market access to the United States and Europe—either because they are poor and deprived of resources due to decolonization, country collapse, democratization, drought, war, or market competition (Organization for Economic Cooperation and Development 2005; United Nations Conference on Trade and Development 2004), or because they stand to gain political or trade advantages through such access (Whalley 1996). Now nearly every country wants to trade with the United States or Europe on a preferential basis (Schott 2004a; United Nations Conference on Trade and Development 1998). All across the developing world, these preferential agreements appear to offer countries the hope of political or economic benefits, and the poorer countries are, the more these agreements attract support. This happens despite beliefs by economists that PTAs often lead to trade diversion and thus inefficiencies, and that the WTO offers most poorer countries a more favorable bargaining environment.

Nonetheless, poor and underdeveloped countries such as Madagascar still stand to make some important economic and perhaps also political gains from a special trade relationship with the United States or Europe. These gains may include reducing poverty and redistributing resources to those most in need, as America's PTA with Nicaragua has done (Bussolo and Niimi 2006), or creating jobs and boosting exports, as America's PTA with Jordan has done (Hills 2005). In Botswana, for instance, the successive PTAs with Europe have brought large benefits that include poverty alleviation and the development of infrastructure. Moreover, Botswana's beef industry is highly dependent on the European market, and the beef protocol has enabled the country to sell beef free of tariffs, which has more than doubled profits on cattle (Botswana Press Agency 2001). In Zimbabwe, preferential trade agreements have had a considerable effect on the garment industry, which accounts for a significant percentage of the country's manufacturing employment, offering market access and investments in better equipment while at the same time easing the harmful effects of the removal of export incentives (Tekere 1999). PTAs often promise considerable benefits to richer, more advanced countries too.

On the other hand, almost no government wants its market access regulated through human rights standards of conduct either for workers and children or for voters and citizens. Most leaders and businesses value their sovereignty over their concern for protecting human rights and rarely want rules that apply political conditions to market access. Many countries stridently oppose any fair trade regulations that aim to protect human rights. Examples are easy to find. Ministers of the Association of Southeast Asian Nations (ASEAN), for instance, have

> stressed that development is an inalienable right and that the use of human rights as a conditionality for economic cooperation and development assistance is detrimental to international cooperation and could undermine an international consensus on human rights. They emphasized that the protection and promotion of human rights in the international community should take cognizance of the principles of respect for national sovereignty, territorial integrity and non-interference in the internal affairs of countries. (ASEAN 1993)

Ministers representing the thirty-four countries participating in the negotiations of the Free Trade Area of the Americas (FTAA) similarly "reject the use of labor or environmental standards for protectionist purposes. Most ministers recognized that environmental and labor issues should not be utilized as conditionalities nor subject to disciplines, the non-compliance of which can be subject to trade restrictions or sanctions" (Ministerial Declaration of Quito 2002).

American Power

Before 2002, some advanced industrial countries were able to fend off American efforts to include human rights protections in PTAs, while poorer developing countries that placed a higher premium on trade agreements had less bargaining power and so were less able to stand up to American interests. With the passage of the 2002 Trade Act, though, the United States' bargaining advantage changed. The act mandated that all subsequent trade agreements be negotiated with clear legislative directives to include some protections for workers' human rights (Interview record #53, 2005). Thus American control over the rulemaking process grew as other countries, rich and poor, were forced to accept some form of human rights regulations or lose their trade deals with the United States. The following cases illustrate the process of trade negotiations under these various degrees of bargaining power.

The North American Free Trade Agreement

In the NAFTA negotiations, the United States more easily dominated developing Mexico[3] than advanced industrial Canada,[4] and the design of NAFTA's human rights protections for workers to some degree reflects this variation.

United States Trade Representative Carla Hills came to the NAFTA bargaining table with fast-track authority from Congress that provided no clear mandate for protecting workers' human rights through PTA standards of conduct, in a climate of deep division over the issue. As chapter 4 explains, certain Democrats in Congress threatened to reject any agreement that lacked strong and enforceable protections for workers' human rights, while most Republicans in Congress and the first Bush White House threatened to oppose regulations that infringed on American sovereignty. These divisions were exacerbated by a presidential election campaign in which the issue was highly visible. The victorious Democrat, Bill Clinton, entered the White House before NAFTA was approved and aimed to make good on his campaign promise to protect workers' human rights through trade agreements (Mayer 1998).

Meanwhile, Mexico was recovering from severe economic recession in the early 1980s, and President Salinas was elected in 1988 on a platform of trade reform, so Mexico actively sought trade integration with the United States. But although Mexican labor laws were tremendously progressive on paper,[5] labor laws were rarely enforced and abuses were rampant. Millions of children under the age of fifteen were employed in Mexico, and some under the age of fourteen worked in export-oriented assembly factories that border the United States (US Department of Labor 2005). The Salinas administration was openly opposed to regulations protecting human rights in the trade agreement, which had already been negotiated with President

3. Mexico is the United States' second most important trade partner but accounted for only 9 percent of exports and 6.6 percent of imports in 1992, while the United States was and remains Mexico's most important market. Mexico continues to have a national income per capita substantially below the world average.

4. Canada and the United States are each other's most important trade partner and share roughly equal per capita incomes, more than one standard deviation above the world mean.

5. Article 123 of the Mexican Constitution is the basis for domestic labor legislation. It protects workers' right to unionize and strike and sets a range of basic labor standards. The US Constitution, by contrast, does not plainly address labor rights, although the US Supreme Court has extended constitutional interpretations of the First Amendment protecting freedom of assembly to cover related labor rights, and the US Congress passed various legislation requiring labor protections. The Canadian government chiefly protects workers' rights through a system of provincial laws, but labor rights are absent from the Constitution. See Hufbauer and Schott (2002).

George H. W. Bush. In particular, Salinas opposed any form of enforcement or the use of trade-related sanctions (Interview record #51, 2005). Ironically, the push for fair trade regulations in a NAFTA side agreement, the NAALC, did not come from the Mexican laborers who suffered exploitation. Instead it came from US opponents to preferential trade who claimed an agreement would only aggravate already bad labor practices in Mexico and from Americans seeking protection from cheap imports produced across the border (Hufbauer and Goodrich 2004).

Canada, by contrast, had only weak commercial ties to Mexico and a controversial trade agreement already in place with the United States, so it entered NAFTA negotiations reluctantly as a means to protect its own economic interests. In particular, Canada's conservative government, led by Prime Minister Brian Mulroney, was concerned that a bilateral agreement between the United States and Mexico might give Americans the advantage in attracting foreign investment and result in preferred access to the US market for Mexico (Cameron and Tomlin 2000). Although Canada did agree to pursue integration trilaterally, human rights protections for workers or children were not initially a concern. Rather, Canada wanted no interference with its own domestic system of labor legislation, in which Canadian federal law does not supersede provincial law.[6]

Formal trade negotiations between representatives of all three governments began in June 1991.[7] Faced with anti-NAFTA demonstrations, the Bush, Salinas, and Mulroney administrations negotiated over key issues, including market access, agriculture, textiles, and a range of other concerns (von Bertrab 1996). None of the three administrations wanted or pursued protections for workers' human rights. After more than a year of discussions, NAFTA negotiations came to a close, and an agreement was signed in December 1992 that included very little text on human rights (Hufbauer and Schott 2002).

President Bush, however, had signed NAFTA with the qualified support of recent president-elect Clinton, who threatened to prevent the passage of the agreement into US law without additional language on labor and the environment. Robert Reich, Clinton's secretary of labor, made it clear that Democrats in Congress would not pass NAFTA without a labor agreement. The negotiating environment had changed, and human rights protections for workers were now on the NAFTA table.

6. The federal government of Canada has jurisdiction on matters of labor for only a few sectors, affecting roughly 10 percent of the workforce; most workers are covered under various provincial legislation systems, of which there are more than ten. See Hufbauer and Schott (2005).

7. See Mayer (1998) for a first-rate analysis of the NAFTA negotiation process.

Clinton immediately set up a task force that prepared three possible approaches to the matter of workers' human rights: (1) to approve minimum standards of conduct on a narrow range of human rights with little infrastructure; (2) to create a commission with more independence and infrastructure and a mandate to inspect violations and initiate formal dialogue; and (3) to include trade sanctions or measures to punish violations. Although the Clinton administration was ambiguous about which position it would advocate when it entered negotiations on a labor side agreement, Reich was serious about enforcement and the administration's negotiating stance quickly firmed. The United States would pursue the protection of certain human rights with strong enforcement mechanisms for violations (Cameron and Tomlin 2000). With no support from Republicans or, surprisingly, organized labor unions at home, and with some Democrats in Congress taking a "wait and see" stance, the United States entered negotiations with Mexico and Canada, advocating the creation of an independent secretariat with the power to investigate citizens' complaints and to impose considerable sanctions for violations of human rights protections.

The American flip flop on the issue did not sit well with Mexico or Canada. Neither government wanted to negotiate side deals or to adopt new rules protecting workers' human rights in the trade agreement, and both were fiercely against delegation to an institution that could impose trade-related sanctions (Interview record #51, 2005). Mexico reacted defensively to what it perceived as an American power play motivated by recent election politics, and the Salinas administration set down guidelines for the new negotiations. The final accord would have to respect Mexican sovereignty; Mexico would not reopen NAFTA to introduce standards of conduct that they viewed as thinly disguised protectionism; and it would not accept commercial sanctions. Mexican Labor secretary Arsenio Farel was eager to protect Mexico's corporatist system of labor relations and rejected the creation of any independent body that could supplant domestic law (Cameron and Tomlin 2000). Motivated by similar concerns for its own system of provincial labor legislation, Canada passionately opposed trade sanctions or any violations of its sovereignty over labor issues (Mayer 1998). A fight was looming.

During several rounds of negotiations after President Clinton took office, the United States pushed for some kind of enforcement, while Mexico and Canada were unwavering in their opposition. In May, negotiations stalled as the United States put forward a proposal that featured sanctions as a condition for cooperation and Mexico circulated a draft that excluded trade sanctions but advocated reliance on nonbinding reports by the ILO.

Unwilling to compromise, Mexico and Canada broke off negotiations (Cameron and Tomlin 2000).

Subsequent rounds of talks also failed to produce concessions, with the Americans still calling for tough enforcement of internationally recognizable labor standards protecting workers' human rights and Mexico and Canada advocating existing domestic labor laws as the only basis of an agreement. As public support for NAFTA eroded in all three countries, thereby threatening to defeat the trade agreement altogether, compromise was finally reached on the NAACL (Hufbauer and Schott 2002). In order to get the deal done, Mexico would back down and agree to accept trade sanctions—albeit a milder version than the United States had originally proposed. Canada, however, would resist sanctions and would allow its own Federal Court to fine the federal government only if the Canadian government was found by the agreement's panel to have violated its own labor laws.

In September 1993, the US Congress passed NAFTA into law (P.L. 103-182, 1993), promoting eleven core labor principles in a side agreement enforced through existing domestic legislation across a tier system with different standards for different countries (Bolle 2002). All three governments agreed to pursue improvements in domestic labor standards, to enforce their own labor laws in a manner affecting trade, and not to undertake enforcement of labor law in one another's territories (Bolle 2003). No real commitment was made to ensure that countries accepted internationally recognized standards of conduct or the ILO provisions on workers' human rights.

American control over the regulatory process on human rights was thus partially limited by circumstance. A Republican leader who did not care to include labor protections had already negotiated the principal text of the agreement; any new provisions had to be covered in a side agreement; and substantial opposition to the labor agreement from Republicans, industry, and even labor unions, not to mention US trade partners, put Clinton's negotiators in a weak bargaining position. American control over the policy process was also variable in the face of two different trade partners: a weaker developing and market-dependent country with serious labor violations that threatened American workers, and an advanced industrial country that provided little threat, real or perceived, to American wages and standards. Facing no clear US law mandating inclusion of workers' rights protections in PTAs such as NAFTA, Canada and Mexico were both able to hedge. Yet, Canada could more credibly threaten to walk away, while Mexico's heightened interest in the trade agreement put it at a substantial disadvantage. The final agreement's twin provisions on labor enforcement reflect this difference in the United States' relative power over its two trade partners.

The United States-Chile Free Trade Agreement

The United States-Chile Free Trade Agreement offers a good illustration of how the US Trade Act of 2002 increased American bargaining power to insert protections for workers' and children's human rights in preferential trade regulations.

The United States had expressed interest in negotiating a trade agreement with Chile long before formal negotiations began. The first Bush administration foresaw a role for Chile in its Enterprise Initiative for the Americas—a plan to unify markets in the Western Hemisphere from Alaska to Tierra del Fuego. President Clinton envisioned Chile as the fourth member of NAFTA, although he was repeatedly denied fast-track authority by Congress to facilitate such negotiations. Nonetheless, in 2000 Clinton opened negotiations for a bilateral free trade agreement with Chile. American policymakers saw the agreement as an important initiative to support ongoing talks about the controversial Free Trade Area of the Americas (FTAA)—a PTA that could unite most of Latin America. A bilateral agreement would also encourage Chilean support for American policy, set parameters for debate on key issues such as labor, and signal American commitment to supporting market reforms in Latin America (Hornbeck 2003; Weintraub 2004). The agreement would also eliminate Canadian advantages under the Canada-Chile Free Trade Agreement (1997). After the election of President George W. Bush, Republicans offered an agreement with Chile as a compelling motivation for the passage of trade promotion authority in Congress.

Negotiations with Chile began under President Clinton, who faced a Congress profoundly divided along party lines over the link between workers' human rights and trade and a political environment characterized by two contrasting American precedents for fair trade standards protecting human rights: NAFTA and the United States-Jordan Free Trade Agreement (Rosales V 2003). Negotiations were not concluded, however, until President George W. Bush was able to use the fast-track procedures granted to his administration by the 2002 Trade Act. The new Trade Act mandated that the agreement with Chile must include protections for internationally recognized workers' and children's rights, and it required the Republican administration, largely antagonistic to the idea of protecting human rights through trade agreements at all, to seek penalties for either party in a dispute over violations (Public Law 107-210 2002).

Chile at the time was recovering from nearly twenty years of military rule by General Augusto Pinochet, and President Ricardo Lagos actively sought a bilateral trade agreement with the United States as part of a broader strategy of "open regionalism" designed to pursue liberalization and expand export markets (Hornbeck 2003).[8] Although Chile was of marginal importance to the American market—accounting for only .3 percent of US trade—the United States was Chile's largest single-country trading partner (Office of Trade and Industry Information 2005). With an average household income still far below the world average and a growth strategy that relied on export promotion, Chile had a strong interest in pursuing a trade agreement. Moreover, Lagos, the first Socialist elected president since the military coup, was not hostile to labor unions. He had promised to reform Chile's repressive, Pinochet-era labor laws, which still curtailed unions' capacity to bargain collectively and failed to provide even minimal support for unemployed workers, but he faced substantial domestic opposition to such reform (Hall 2000).

Presidents Clinton and Lagos held the first round of trade negotiations in December 2000, and the Lagos administration was ambivalent on human rights. On the one hand, Lagos was seeking domestic legislation on labor practices that had long been rejected by conservative parties in Chile's Congress. On the other hand, his administration was "horrified" by the American push for trade sanctions as a means to enforce better labor practices (Interview record #20, 2004). Negotiations lasted two years and fourteen rounds. The major controversy was over the language of dispute resolution (Fergusson and Sek 2004). In a 1997 bilateral trade agreement with Canada, Chile had adopted labor regulations in a side agreement similar to that of NAFTA, providing for monetary assessments rather than trade sanctions as a means of enforcement. Chile was now negotiating with the United States at a time when its position on enforcement was changing across administrations and by law becoming more exact. Under Clinton, the United States set a precedent with Jordan, creating an agreement that formally authorized sanctions for violations of all regulations protecting workers' human rights in the text of the contract (Boelle 2003).[9] Under George W. Bush, the 2002 Trade Act made such protections a matter of

8. This strategy included Chile's participation in regional agreements, such as the Asociación Latinoamerica de Integración (ALADI) and el Mercado Común del Sur (MERCO-SUR), as well as bilateral and extrapreferential trade agreements with the European Union, South Korea, and others.

9. It was agreed upon in an exchange of letters that these sanctions would never be implemented.

law. Enforcement in the text of the agreement was no longer optional, and Chile would have to back down or lose the deal.

The Lagos government supported domestic labor reforms in Chile but opposed trade sanctions on two grounds. It did not want Chile's sovereignty undermined by an agreement that endorsed higher standards of conduct than the government was able to support domestically, and it did not want enforcement provisions that could be used to justify protectionism (Hornbeck 2003). These concerns were especially serious in export-intensive business sectors in Chile such as the salmon industry, which feared that Alaskan salmon competitors would make use of a strong labor clause to block Chilean imports, thereby disadvantaging Chilean workers while protecting American workers in the industry (Interview record #20, 2004).[10] Chile rejected sanctions as a means of enforcing domestic standards of conduct protecting workers' human rights[11] and entered the negotiations willing to accept regulations enforceable through minimal fines but not through trade sanctions (Gresser 2001). At the same time, the United States was searching for its own template for how to implement trade promotion authority in its future agreements (Interview record #53, 2005).

Negotiations ended in 2002 when Bush signed, and the House and Senate passed into law, the trade agreement. It took effect January 1, 2004, after some delay due to the administration's irritation over Chile's refusal to support American-sponsored resolutions on Iraq in the United Nations (Fergusson and Sek 2004). The final text of the agreement reflects substantial American control over human rights protections during the negotiations and minimal compromise over the regulations that were adopted. Ensuring that Chile's domestic law protects labor principles and internationally recognized workers' human rights is a core component of the agreement. At the same time, President Lagos won a victory as well, having used bilateral negotiations to lock in labor reforms at home despite a conservative majority that had consistently blocked his efforts. He did so by credibly warning that the US Congress would reject the agreement unless domestic labor reforms were passed (Polaski 2002).

In the 2002 Trade Act, Congress left little room to maneuver around the issue of protections for workers' and children's human rights. In the margins, however, the final text of the United States-Chile agreement does

10. Fishing is one of Chile's biggest export industries. Nearly 60 percent of fish exported consist of Atlantic salmon, and the United States is Chile's principal market for fish exports (Lem 2003).
11. Chile had previously suffered US sanctions under the GSP that were suspended when General Pinochet repealed Chile's labor code and were reinstated after he was overthrown.

reflect the preference of both George W. Bush and Lagos not to include strong binding trade conditions protecting human rights. Together, both presidents negotiated an agreement with the lowest possible commitment to human rights protections, given what the Trade Act mandated. The agreement now in force requires that each party enforce its own labor laws in a manner affecting trade; it agrees neither to waive nor to derogate from domestic labor law to encourage trade or investment; it authorizes sanctions for sustained failure to enforce domestic labor law; and it caps the maximum penalty at only $15 million annually or suspension of benefits to the equivalent value (Grimmett 2003; Weintraub 2003).[12]

The United States-Australia Free Trade Agreement

The American ability to incorporate preferential trade standards protecting human rights was not limited to agreements with developing countries such as Chile. Since the 2002 Trade Act, the United States has enjoyed similar success with richer countries too. Negotiations with Australia, an advanced industrial democracy,[13] illustrate this.

The American government was equally successful in forcing human rights into its 2005 trade agreement with Australia—its first PTA with an advanced industrial economy since the agreement with Canada (1989). Because Australia had offered assistance to the United States in the wake of the September 11, 2001, attacks and was a strong supporter of American policies in Afghanistan and Iraq, President George W. Bush opened negotiations for a bilateral free trade agreement between the two countries in 2002. Lead negotiator and USTR Robert B. Zoellick had the same legally binding mandate that had shaped negotiations with Chile: to adopt language protecting children's and workers' human rights, to promote ratification and compliance with ILO conventions, and to seek penalties for either party to a dispute over violations (Public Law 107-210 2002). Although

12. In NAFTA, the failure to enforce standards for occupational safety and health, child labor, or minimum wage is subject to remedies. In the United States-Jordan agreement, violations of any labor provision are subject to "appropriate and commensurate" measures, while in agreements with Chile and Singapore, only the sustained failure by a party to the agreement to enforce its domestic labor laws in a manner affecting trade is subject to remedies. The maximum penalty in NAFTA is $20 million in the first year; there is no maximum in the Jordan agreement; and the maximum is set at $15 million annually in the agreements with Chile and Singapore. See Boelle (2003).

13. Australia is one of the less economically dependent governments with which the United States has negotiated a trade agreement, as are Singapore and Canada. Although Australia is the United States' nineteenth largest trade partner, it has a per capita income roughly equal to that of the United States and a purchasing power parity income that ranks sixteenth in the world.

most Republicans still preferred not to include workers' rights protections, the president was bound by American law to do so, and there was very little room to bargain over that issue (Interview record #53, 2005).

The Australian government, led by Prime Minister John Howard and a Liberal-National Party coalition in the House of Representatives, sought a bilateral trade agreement with the United States. Australia was a close ally under the Security Treaty between Australia, New Zealand, and the United States (ANZUS) and wanted stronger trade ties to generate economic benefits and foster improved political ties. A bilateral agreement promised to reduce significant barriers to trade and to circumvent the perceived failure of the WTO to achieve those goals in the aftermath of the failed 1999 Seattle ministerial meeting (Australian House of Representatives 2004). Human rights protections for workers were not of particular interest to Howard. He was a free-market advocate who sought to reduce the power of labor unions at home and to make compulsory unionism illegal (Vaughn and Lum 2003). Under Howard, Australia had openly supported developing countries' efforts in the WTO to stop the Americans and Europeans from imposing labor and environmental standards on the rest of the world, arguing that social issues including human rights could be used as implicit forms of trade protectionism.

While the ruling party coalition generally opposed the creation of human rights trade standards, the minority Labor Party supported rules to prevent the exploitation of child or prison labor. Senator Stephen Conroy, Labor shadow trade minister, argued that "fundamental labour standards, including the right to freely associate with and join organised labour unions, the right to collective bargaining and non-discrimination, must be respected and permitted" and that "Labour will not support any diminution of Australia's labour and environmental laws and standards" in a US trade agreement (Conroy 2004).

Beginning in November 2002, Zoellick and Australian trade minister Vaile conducted five rounds of trade negotiations that lasted more than a year. Although neither the US Republican administration nor the conservative Australian government wanted trade rules on human rights, the US Trade Act required protections for workers. The Howard government had to compromise on the issue or trade negotiations would fail. But Australia was strongly opposed (Interview record #53, 2005).

Australia wanted an agreement too much to walk away over human rights, but it stood firm on other issues in the agreement. In fact, negotiations led to substantial concessions by both governments over some very controversial aspects of integration concerning pharmaceutical access, beef imports, and investor country rules and protections (Kyl 2004).[14] Negotiations also reportedly led to some small compromises over the human rights clause (Chapter 18) that was included in the agreement but "in an attenuated form" (Australian House of Representatives 2004). The trade agreement, which is currently in force, requires the United States and Australia to enforce their respective domestic labor laws, which are generally quite good (US Senate Democratic Policy Committee 2004). The text of the labor provisions is similar to that of the United States-Chile agreement (and the United States-Singapore agreement), with some variations reflecting Australia's positive record on human rights protections. In 2004 both chambers of the US Congress passed the trade agreement by large margins.

Ironically, within the US trade advisory system, the Labor Advisory Committee (LAC) was the only group to specifically urge Congress to reject the agreement, arguing that Australia's domestic labor laws were inadequate. Committees representing industry, agriculture, the environment, and local governments were generally supportive (Office of the United States Trade Representative 2004). In the face of critiques by Teamsters Union president James Hoffa that the agreement's language "is insufficient to ensure that core labour standards will be respected in Australia" (Eccleston 2004), the law took effect on January 1, 2005.

Though Australia was led by a government strongly opposed to fair trade standards for human rights in PTAs, it is now committed to protecting workers' and children's human rights in trade-related matters and is subject to largely the same enforcement as Chile and Singapore for violations of those rights.

European Power

Before 1990, few European preferential trade agreements said anything about protecting human rights, and none enforced any protections. The Commission Communication and Council Decision of 1995 changed that and profoundly altered Europe's negotiating position vis-à-vis the rest of the world. All subsequent agreements, except sectoral ones, were required to include as "essential elements" specific provisions to protect human

14. The Australian government mobilized successfully to influence the outcome. After Bush signed the trade agreement, Australia's Labor Party, led by Mark Latham, vowed to block its passage in the Australian Senate unless two amendments were made—one on subsidized pharmaceuticals and the other on cultural property. Latham told reporters, "We're going to fight like Kilkenny cats to ensure those amendments go through," adding that he was "not in the mood for compromise" (*The CalTrade Report* 2004).

rights, enforceable through consultations. In addition, the agreements were subject to full or partial suspension in the event of violations (Bartels 2005). This legislation tied the hands of the Commission during trade negotiations with other countries that sought to avoid or water down protections for human rights. Thus countries all over the world were compelled to take on PTA human rights regulations they didn't want, although their capacity to influence the rules varied according to whether they could afford to walk away from an agreement. The following examples demonstrate the European experience of trade negotiations under varying degrees of bargaining power.

The European Economic Area

In the early years of PTAs, prior to the 1995 human rights clause, Europe paid scant attention to human rights in trade negotiations with advanced industrial countries. The Community had negotiated only a few agreements with such countries, and those did not include many human rights protections because no policymakers advocated for them. The European Economic Area (EEA) is a prime example.

Following the adoption of the Single European Act (1987) establishing the European Community's Internal Market, Commission President Jacques Delors proposed an EEA between the EC and the member states of the European Free Trade Area (EFTA)—Austria, Finland, Iceland, Liechtenstein, Norway, Sweden, and Switzerland.[15] Negotiations began in 1990 and lasted two years, leading to an agreement uniting the members of both preferential trade agreements within an internal market governed by four pillars: freedom of movement of goods, persons, services, and capital. Both sides articulated some inclination to include human rights principles in the agreement, but neither wanted to design regulations that were enforceable. Thus human rights are featured in the EEA preamble, where the member governments say they are "[c]onvinced of the contribution that a European Economic Area will bring to the construction of a Europe based on peace, democracy and human rights" (Council of the European Union 1994). Hu-

---

15. All EFTA governments are advanced industrial democracies with average national incomes substantially above the world mean, while both PTAs share relative market parity. The European Union is EFTA's main trading partner (accounting for nearly three-fourths of external trade), while EFTA is the European Union's third largest trading partner (Remøy 2005). The Swiss voted to stay out of the EEA, and Austria, Finland, and Sweden switched sides to become members of the European Union in 1995—the same year that Liechtenstein became a member. In 2004, the EEA eighteen became the EEA twenty-eight following the accession of ten new member countries to the European Union.

man rights standards of conduct are not enforceable and do not appear in the main body of the contract.

The lack of enforcement measures reflects the shared belief that human rights did not belong in trade agreements among developed countries (Fierro 2003). Although the Commission had already begun to express some interest in regulating human rights through PTAs by the time the EEA negotiations had begun, its nonbinding communication, discussed in chapter 4, concerned only the regulation of human rights in developing countries (European Commission 1991). No legislation was in place that required the Community to add a human rights clause for enforcement. In this sense, the EEA is similar to the United States-Israel agreement—no policymakers were asking for human rights regulations, so none were included.

The Framework Agreement for Trade and Economic Cooperation with Argentina

Prior to its 1995 adoption of mandatory human rights standards of conduct for trade agreements, Europe exercised substantially more control over the issue with poor trade partners than it did with rich ones because poorer governments were more easily manipulated. Nevertheless, not all agreements that opted for fair trade standards of conduct protecting human rights during this period did so at the Community's insistence. In a handful of cases, governments undergoing a transition to democracy requested PTA regulations protecting human rights as a means to lock in their commitments to reform and to demonstrate their standing among liberal countries. In these rare cases, the dominant European countries were willing to adopt measures requested by their weaker trading partners. The trade agreement with Argentina is an example.

Carlos Saul Menem was elected president of Argentina in 1989, following a period of authoritarian rule and a "Dirty War" in which thousands of Argentines disappeared—most likely were tortured and executed. His election began a fragile transition to democracy. Menem not only followed a long history of violence and repression, but he also came to power during a major economic crisis driven by hyperinflation and assumed leadership of a government characterized by rampant corruption (Zaza 2002). Menem set out to dismantle Argentina's web of protectionist trade and business practices and sought trade ties with Europe, Argentina's second largest market.

In 1990, the European Community concluded a Framework Trade and Economic Cooperation Agreement with the government of Argentina. It was an agreement that would provide the institutional structure for political cooperation in trade, economics, agriculture, and industry for years to come. The PTA was one of the first to make human rights standards a core element of the text, although it has no clear language on enforcement (European Council 1990). Article 1 provides that "cooperation ties between the Community and Argentina and this agreement in its entirety are based on respect for democratic principles and human rights, which inspire the domestic and external policies of the Community and Argentina" (Council of the European Union 1990c).[16] Argentina was a test case.[17] All the same, this agreement is exceptional because there are few like it. The vast majority of developing governments negotiating agreements with Europe or with the United States have unambiguously opposed the push for fair trade.[18] The early Lomé conventions are good illustrations of how most trade negotiations with other countries have taken place.

From Lomé I to Cotonou

The Community's relations with Africa reach back to the Treaty of Rome's annexes concerning association with developing countries (Lister 2002). Early institutional relations between the ACP and the EC were not just economic. Yaoundé I (1963) and II (1969) were designed to provide financial and political support to French-speaking Africa following decolonization (Lister 1988). Although these associations did not survive, they laid the foundation for several generations of trade agreements between the Community and the ACP countries, from the first Lomé convention in 1975, with the then forty-six ACP countries and the nine member states of the EEC, to the Cotonou agreement of 2000, with the now seventy-nine ACP countries and the then fifteen member states of the European Union.[19]

The Community negotiated the first four conventions with a group of Africa's most impoverished nations without clear legislative directives to include human rights protections (Arts 2000). The ACP, an organized

16. "Les relations de coopération entre la Communauté et l'Argentine, de même que toutes les dispositions du présent accord, se fondent sur le respect des principes démocratiques et des droits de l'homme qui inspirent les politiques internes et internationales de la Communauté et de L'Argentine."

17. There is some suggestion but no conclusive evidence that human rights were adopted in the trade agreements between the European Union and Albania (1992) for the same reason: Albania's desire to lock in political reform. See Fierro (2003).

18. The European Community negotiated similar agreements with Chile (1990) and Uruguay and Paraguay (1992).

19. Lomé II was signed with fifty-eight ACP countries, Lomé III with sixty-five ACP countries, and Lomé IV with sixty-eight. For complete text of all Lomé treaties, see http://europa.eu.int/comm/development/body/legislation/int-agree2_en.htm.

and strategic group of countries, used this flexibility to its advantage, resisting efforts by the Community or its member states to impose human
rights standards of conduct of any kind through trade agreements. But
the capacity for resistance was short lived, both because many ACP countries spiraled into severe economic turmoil and recessions in the 1980s
and 1990s, weakening their bargaining power (Whiteman 1998), and because over time the Community took on increasingly precise legislative
directives for negotiations that made the creation of human rights standards of conduct mandatory in most PTAs. Today the ACP governments
are participants in the world's most robust trade agreement with enforceable human rights standards of conduct—a regulation most members still
actively oppose.

Lomé I (1975) was negotiated after the accession of the United Kingdom
to the Community, and it was designed to include Commonwealth countries in the EEC-ACP trade cooperation program (ACP-EEC Convention
of Lomé [I] 1975). Its primary features were the provision of nonreciprocal
preferences for most exports from ACP countries to Europe and a system
to compensate losses in exports caused by fluctuation in commodity prices.
At the agreement's core was an emphasis on respect for national sovereignty and the right of each government to establish its own policies with
particular ideological, political, or economic features (Frisch 1997). Few
policymakers in either the Community or the ACP had yet articulated the
wish to make fair trade standards that would protect human rights part of
the cooperation program. ACP governments such as Uganda were accepted
into Lomé with no judgment of their human rights or other political behaviors or any requirement to reform them.

Although European policymakers were largely divided on the issue of
protecting human rights, and ACP governments were nearly uniform in
their opposition, negotiations of Lomé II (1980) opened a window of opportunity. Commissioner for development in charge of negotiations, Claude
Cheysson, was himself committed to the political neutrality of the trade
agreement, yet on the eve of discussions he declared that the Community
had made a grave error by not previously identifying protection and respect
for human beings as a core aim of Lomé I. At the request of the Dutch and
British governments, as well as MEPs directly elected for the first time,
Commissioner Cheysson raised the issue of inserting language on human
rights into the new Lomé agreement during the first ministerial meeting
(Kaminga 1989). The ACP was opposed, as representatives of the majority
of ACP governments, including Uganda, Ethiopia, and Sierra Leone, made
clear (Young-Anawaty 1980). Negotiations were thus characterized by what
one member of the European Economic and Social Committee referred to

as "a climate of confusion." Although a joint assembly eventually agreed to include mention of the Universal Declaration of Human Rights at the Community's request, ACP ministers quickly passed unilateral resolutions declaring that the Lomé conventions were principally economic in nature and that protections for human rights did not belong in the agreement (Fierro 2003).

The ACP's resistance only frustrated those in the Community who had begun to push for regulations protecting human rights in trade agreements. Commissioner Cheysson thus formally proposed the inclusion of human rights language at the opening of negotiations. However, he agreed to accept references in the preamble rather than in the text of the contract, and he decided to limit the scope of the rules to "the most fundamental rights," without any procedures for suspension. This reflected the considerable division among the then nine member states over whether human rights should be regulated or made enforceable in trade agreements at all (Fierro 2003). While the Community still confronted genuine ideological divisions over the issue, the ACP remained united in its opposition. It continued to argue that human rights protection was not an appropriate trade matter; that the United Nations and not the European Community was the proper organization to govern human rights; that political conditions for market access, such as human rights, could be unfairly employed as protectionism; and that regulating human rights would be an unwarranted intrusion in the domestic affairs of sovereign nations (Marantis 1994). Since Europe had no requirements yet for protecting human rights, the Lomé II agreement was silent on the issue (Council of the European Union 1980).[20]

Negotiations toward Lomé III (1985) were characterized by similar controversy over human rights. The Community was still divided, but support for the creation of new trade regulations was growing, as chapters 3 and 4 describe. The European Parliament had recently established a working group on human rights and passed a resolution requesting that the Commission be issued directives to include human rights in the Lomé III agreement (European Parliament 1983). To this end, Commissioner Edgard Pisani introduced the concept of a "policy dialogue"—an instrument designed to cultivate a channel of communication on cultural and social cooperation and aimed at promoting "a better understanding and greater

---

20. At the signing ceremony, however, the presidents of the European Economic Community Council and the ACP Council both made statements declaring their intent to work toward respect for human rights.

solidarity between ACP and EEC governments and peoples" (Article 114) (Buirette-Marau 1985; Fierro 2003).

This time, the ACP countries did not snub human rights as core political principles. Most had since made commitments to the African Charter of Human and Peoples' Rights (1981). Still, convinced that market agreements were not the appropriate forum in which to regulate human rights and concerned that human rights conditions would be used as tools for unfair market redistributions, the vast majority of governments remained strongly opposed to the new regulation of trade policy (Kaminga 1989). Moreover, the dialogue on human rights was contentious because many in the ACP perceived it as simply another form of backdoor conditionality (Frisch 1997).

The ACP governments continued their organized and strategic resistance to the growing push for fair PTAs, opposing even the mention of human rights, much less the creation of enforceable standards of conduct tied to market access or aid privileges. Their opposition was made easier by the Community's ongoing division over the issue and lack of a clear policy. Likewise, the Community position had become ever more sensitive to claims of double standards. Europe maintained close trade relations with apartheid South Africa while at the same time pressuring ACP governments to accept human rights trade standards of conduct. Key European member states had no intention of ending trade relations with South Africa, so the ACP's attempt to condition the human rights dialogue on reform of Community trade policy with South Africa led the Commission to back down on the adoption of strong protectionist language. Dieter Frisch, director general for the development unit in the Commission and negotiator for the Community at the time, remarked at the conclusion of difficult and complex negotiations that the ACP countries had exercised substantial bargaining power during the negotiations (Frisch 1985).

Lomé III was signed with only the vaguest reference to human rights in the preamble, reaffirming members' "faith in fundamental human rights, in the dignity and worth of the human person, [and] in the equal rights of men and women and of nations large and small" (ACP-EEC Convention of Lomé (III) 1985). The principal change of the new agreement was to shift attention from the promotion of industrial development to sustainable development on the basis of self-reliance and food security. What is more, the ACP governments successfully incorporated a joint declaration in an annex to the agreement on members' determination to end apartheid. ACP influence on the issue of regulating human rights was clear.

As chapters 3 and 4 explain, several decisive events took place before the negotiation of Lomé IV (1990). Most important, the Single European Act

(1987) gave the European Parliament new power to assent to certain trade agreements, including Lomé, by an absolute majority of members (Rideau 1997). The EP, which included many of the Community's strongest advocates for human rights, could now reject an agreement on the basis of human rights alone and actively threatened to do so (Clapham 1991). In the same year, the United Nations Declaration on the Right to Development explicitly linked the goals of development and human rights, undermining the ACP countries' argument that the UN and not the EC was the appropriate forum for governing human rights in the developing world (United Nations 1986). Additionally, the Berlin Wall fell and with it European rhetoric of political neutrality.

Although there was still no formal Community mandate to regulate the protection of human rights through preferential trade agreements, support for the regulations continued to grow internally. A parliamentary memorandum issued by the Netherlands led to the Council's first resolution on human rights in the framework of European Political Cooperation, affirming human rights as a cornerstone of Community cooperation (European Parliament 1987). Following the Council's example, the Commission again proposed the creation of human rights standards of conduct for the next Lomé trade agreement, this time advocating stronger language on respect for and enjoyment of fundamental human rights.

The ACP once more opposed the regulations, perceiving human rights language as an attack on national sovereignty and as insincere (Miller 2004). Yet the ACP countries' capacity to resist the regulatory push had weakened. The EP now offered a reasonably credible threat to refuse an agreement it didn't like by absolute majority, support from the former Soviet Union had ended, and rampant recessions were taking hold. Lomé IV was thus the Community's first trade agreement to adopt fundamental human rights in the body of the text. Article 5 declared:

> Cooperation shall be directed towards development centered on man, the main protagonist and beneficiary of development, which thus entails respect for and promotion of all human rights. . . . In this context development policy and cooperation are closely linked with the respect for and enjoyment of fundamental human rights. (ACP-EEC Convention of Lomé (VI) 1990)

Lomé IV also provided ACP governments with a formal channel to request financial resources for the promotion of human rights. The human rights clause was binding but not enforceable, since it lacked any suspension provisions in the case of violations (Korte 1990). Again, the legal content of the agreement was somewhat of a concession to the ACP governments, but it also reflected lingering uncertainties and disagreements among Community policymakers about whether or not human rights should be enforced by, or merely mentioned in, Europe's trade agreements.

The next agreement, Lomé IVbis, was negotiated in 1995 in a political environment that was very different from that of its predecessor. It followed major economic reform in the ACP, further European integration and enlargement, and the completion of the Uruguay Round. Meanwhile, the Treaty on the European Union (1992) gave the Community the capacity to incorporate political issues into its integration programs. On that basis, the Council in 1995 issued a decision mandating that human rights become "essential elements" of almost all Europe's PTAs—with substantial means of enforcement. For the first time, the Community entered negotiations with the ACP countries with a clear and binding legislative mandate for regulating human rights protections, guaranteeing the rejection of any new agreement that did not conform. European control over the regulations had intensified in relation to the ACP countries.

Although ACP resistance was still strong, its capacity to influence the design of the new agreement's human rights provisions was greatly weakened. At the Community's behest, human rights were adopted as an "essential element" of the trade agreement and, following specific consultation procedures, ACP financial benefits could for the first time be officially suspended in the event of violations. Article 5, more elaborate than other clauses of its generation, was expanded to include references to democratic principles, the consolidation of the rule of law, and good governance. The agreement's preamble now integrated references to two United Nations legal covenants on the protection of human rights (Brandtner and Rosas 1998). A new Article 366a committed violators to participation in consultations "with a view to assessing the situation in detail and, if necessary, remedying it." When consultations failed to produce a solution, or in cases of special urgency or refusal of consultations, the article allowed the Community to take "appropriate steps, including, where necessary, the partial or full suspension" of the agreement. The policy dialogue had also been transformed at the Community's request to a "greater political dialogue"—a formal channel of communication that would now embrace issues of foreign policy and security at the highest levels (ACP-EC Convention of Lomé (IVbis) 1995). Finally, the ACP countries had been offered a "take it or leave it" policy on human rights with very limited room for negotiations or compromise. Europe's growing economic strength in the face of economic and political deterioration in most ACP countries, coupled with its increasing legislative willingness to constrain the negotiation process, made all the difference.

Negotiations of the Cotonou Agreement (2000) that would replace Lomé IVbis reflected almost total Community control over the creation of regulations protecting human rights (Raffer 2001). The agreement, which offered trade benefits and aid packages for ACP governments, contained one of the most impressive European human rights clauses to date. Cotonou introduced several new areas for political dialogue and included regular reviews of members' respect for human rights. Article 9 affirmed that the protection of human rights and fundamental freedoms, including respect for social rights, democracy based on the rule of law, and transparent and accountable governance, were essential elements of the agreement. Article 96 laid out the procedures for consultations in the event of a violation of an essential element and established the conditions under which "appropriate measures" could be taken to enforce the agreement. It stated:

> The "appropriate measures" referred to in this Article are measures taken in accordance with international law, and proportional to the violation. In the selection of these measures, priority must be given to those which least disrupt the application of this agreement. It is understood that suspension would be a measure of last resort. (ACP-EC Convention of Cotonou 2003)

The succession of Lomé trade agreements thus reveals the progression of European control over regulations aimed at protecting human rights in PTAs with the ACP countries, which include some of the world's poorest and also most abusive regimes. Although inequalities have been a consistent feature of EC-ACP trade relations, Community control over the design of the human rights regulations has certainly varied over time. Often impoverished and dependent on European markets, ACP governments enjoyed considerably more influence over the regulatory process in the early stages of market cooperation. For more than a decade they were mostly successful in their resistance to regulating human rights, in part because of internal Community divisions. But that power to resist waned in the early 1990s, as the Community's many veto players grew more cohesive in their support for fair trade regulations and as many ACP countries hit economic rock bottom. By 1995 the Community had become a great deal more successful at manipulating the ACP to accept human rights standards of conduct they largely opposed in trade agreements.

Yet poor governments have not been the only foreign trade partners confronted with regulations they didn't want. Since the 1995 Council decision, rich, democratic, rights-protecting foreign governments also have been confronted with European attempts to control the trade agenda. In these cases, however, Europe has not always prevailed.

The EC-Australia Trade and Cooperation Agreement

In 1996, acting on a Commission proposal, the Council adopted negotiating directives[21] for a trade agreement with Australia, an advanced industrial country with a relatively strong market.[22] Under the guidelines of its 1995 mandate, the Community proposed making human rights an essential element of the trade agreement, including the now standard suspension mechanism and references to the United Nations Universal Declaration on Human Rights. The Australian government, however, vehemently opposed the policy, just as it would later do with America in the dispute over human rights for workers. In discussions with European trade commissioner Sir Leon Brittan, Australian foreign minister Alexander Downer reasoned that human rights conditions had no business in a trade agreement with a developed country such as Australia that already protected people. He further argued that trade agreements were not appropriate vehicles for human rights governance, that human rights issues were better dealt with through international legal structures provided by the United Nations, and that human rights standards of conduct could be used for protectionist and other unfair political purposes (European Report 1997). Downer's position was firm. "I doubt there is a country that can boast a prouder human rights record than Australia," he said. "But to have a treaty between two sides in which one can unilaterally terminate on the basis of one-sided, subjective observation is not acceptable. . . . Australia is a gutsy, up-front country" (European Report 1997). Moreover, "no other industrialised country, including the US, Japan, Canada or New Zealand, could accept the inclusion of operative human rights provisions of the type proposed by the Community in a framework co-operation agreement" (Koblanck 2003, 28).[23]

21. The agreement was made under the exclusive competence of the Community to avoid the parliamentary ratification process in France, following recent disputes with Australia over nuclear testing.

22. The European Union is Australia's main trading partner, while Australia, with an average household income far above the world mean, is in the top twenty most important trade partners for the European Union. See http://europa.eu.int/comm/trade/issues/bilateral/countries/australia/index_en.htm.

23. Reportedly there were concerns about the potential use of human rights complaints

Australia's position was nonnegotiable: it would not accept the Community's trade regulations protecting human rights, and it especially opposed procedures for enforcement, although it was not opposed to including references to human rights in the preamble or in a separate political declaration. Australia also contested the reference to the UDHR on the grounds that the agreement failed to make appropriate reference to the International Bill of Rights more broadly—specifically, two UN covenants protecting human rights (Fierro 2003). A recent ruling by the ECJ, however, had said the Community did not have the legal competence to adhere to international human rights laws;[24] only member states could be parties to such conventions. That made Community reference to binding UN human rights treaties problematic (Interview record #13, 2004).

Negotiations lasted nearly two years. Australia's uncompromising refusal to accept the Community's human rights clause now mandated by the Council led to an impasse, as the European Parliament's Subcommittee on Human Rights declared its intent to withhold assent and, in so doing, block passage of the agreement. André Soulier, the committee's chairman, made it known that "[i]f Australia wants an agreement with the EU, and if the Parliament is in favour, Australia must agree to this clause. . . . How could Australia, a democratic country par excellence, refuse? It would be a bad example to countries which might like to avoid having a human rights clause" (European Report 1997). But Australia would not concede to the Europeans. Unlike their agreement with the Americans, of substantial economic value, the European trade agreement would not have a major impact on the Australian economy. Negotiations thus collapsed, and the intended trade agreement was replaced by a less significant Joint Declaration between the Community and Australia (1997).[25] Community trade negotiations with New Zealand later failed for the same reasons and produced a similar outcome.

The lessons of Australia and New Zealand are revealing. Passing legislation that makes human rights standards mandatory in all trade agreements brings bargaining advantages for American and European negotiators, but it also brings costs, especially when negotiating agreements with advanced industrial countries that can afford to exit negotiations rather than accept a deal they do not like. As a result, very few trade agreements between the United States or Europe and developed nations today embrace human

---

regarding Australian treatment of Aborigines, as well as trade in oil acquired under the Timor Gap Treaty (European Report 1997).

24. See Opinion 2/94 on accession to the ECHR.

25. A Joint Declaration on European Union-Australia Relations was signed in Luxembourg on 26 June 1997 as a replacement. See Bull. EU 6-1997, point 1.4.103.

rights. Most of the agreements that include human rights are with countries in the developing world that face resource deprivation or credibility problems. To win valuable trade and aid packages, some of the world's worst human rights abusers have signed fair trade PTAs that protect human rights.

Power has shaped the regulation of fair preferential trade regulations in important ways. The United States and Europe are liberal bullies, pushing for more economic liberalization while at the same time forcing new regulations that protect human rights. Other countries seldom like these trade regulations, but they sign on anyway because they lack better options and need the market access. Thus developing countries are at a particular disadvantage in negotiations over trade regulations, especially since the United States and Europe passed laws in 2002 and 1995, respectively, requiring that trade negotiations cover human rights protections.

Scholars have long known that power politics shape policy outcomes, even for trade. Still, tracing the bargaining process in detail helps to explain how and why these regulations came to be. It shows again why explanations that rely only on interest groups or moral advocates for answers founder. This account of relative bargaining abilities also differs from suggestions that countries transitioning to democracy will be especially eager to make these regulations—a few are but most are not. Nor is it correct to posit that other countries will sign on to the norms and accept fair PTA regulations protecting human rights—those that sign on hardly do so for moral reasons.

Countries all over the world have participated in the process of making preferential trade agreements fair by agreeing to allow human rights into trade regulations and creating standards of conduct. Most have not wanted these regulations. Poor and underdeveloped countries have often accepted these regulations only in the face of a credible threat that American or European legislatures will reject the trade agreement unless human rights regulations are included. Today these countries are committed through trade agreements to the protection of various human rights—policies they never wanted and do not wish to implement. Yet countries that could afford to have sometimes chosen to walk away or push hard for their own interests. As we are about to see, these choices have fundamentally changed not only the nature of market integration but also the politics of human rights.

CHAPTER 6

EFFECTS

We now turn our attention to the outcomes of these preferential trade regulations protecting human rights and their impact on the politics of repression. Do these regulations actually help to protect people from harm? Do they ever stop or prevent human rights violations in other countries or prompt new policies that might help achieve that goal?

While chapters 3, 4, and 5 argue that PTA standards obligating governments to protect human rights have been made to suit a variety of political needs and circumstances, not always with the intent to stop repression, this chapter argues that the standards can help the cause of promoting human rights anyway. These agreements do not stop abuses overnight, but some may prevent abuses or encourage incremental reforms by raising costs of violations or benefits of making improvements, from either outside or inside the country. In this way, they change incentives for some perpetrators to make improvements they would otherwise avoid. Moreover, trade agreements with "hard" standards of conduct—binding obligations, precise rules, and delegation of enforcement—are sometimes more successful in encouraging reforms than are many human rights agreements with "soft" implementation measures because the latter are designed to influence governments' practices through long-term persuasion rather than more immediate coercion (Hafner-Burton 2005).[1]

---

1. These conjectures are summarized in table 1 of chapter 2.

Human Rights Agreements

To better understand how well preferential trade regulations actually protect human rights, it is helpful to explore how they differ from other regulatory tools, especially from human rights agreements such as the UN Convention Against Torture. The international human rights regime is championed by a growing number of treaties and instruments designed to protect identifiable groups, such as women and children or workers and migrants, as well as to protect all people against particular government behaviors, such as torture or violations of civil and political rights. At the heart of this regime are the UN Charter (Article 55) and seven international human rights agreements that define a set of global regulations, supported by a rich and varied set of regional HRAs in Africa, the United States, and Europe. Almost all governments in the world have ratified one or more of these instruments and thereby taken on legal commitments to abide by the norms of the agreements.[2]

Despite a substantial capacity to classify and disseminate human rights norms and establish monitoring institutions, most of these agreements were not designed to influence governments through coercion, and those that were often failed because they remained mostly soft on implementation.[3] Most HRAs supply weak or no formal enforcement mechanisms[4] to provide or disrupt valuable exchange with a target country that is violating

2. For information about the human rights legal regime, see the Office of the United Nations High Commissioner for Human Rights, http://www.ohchr.org/english/law/.

3. There is today only one major exception to this claim: the European human rights system supplies a unique set of instruments to enforce the Council of Europe's commitment to uphold HRAs. Almost all members have adopted the Convention for the Protection of Human Rights and Fundamental Freedoms into national law, obligating national courts to enforce the agreement's provisions. The European Court of Human Rights is the superior arbitrator of disputes concerning noncompliance with human rights standards under the convention, acting as a subsidiary to national enforcement in cases of failure. Europe, however, is exceptional. The vast majority of HRAs provide softer standards that are voluntary and weakly enforceable at best (Cleveland 2001a). The Organization of American States (OAS) offers the closest comparison. The OAS commission monitors observance of treaty obligations for all states committed to the American Convention on Human Rights, while its court monitors compliance under the convention for states that have also recognized the compulsory jurisdiction of the court. Yet OAS political bodies routinely fail to support or enforce the recommendations of the OAS commission or the judgments of its court, and human rights standards remain effectively soft. See Dulitzky (1999).

4. Small steps toward legal enforcement have only recently begun at the global level through the formation of the International Criminal Court (ICC), as well as at the regional level through courts such as the European and Inter-American Courts of Human Rights, and at the state level through the two International Criminal Tribunals in the former Yugoslavia and Rwanda. These institutions signal an important step toward management of human

human rights (Cottier 2002; Goodman and Jinks 2003a). They offer no material rewards in exchange for better practices, and they cannot directly punish violators by withholding valuable goods, such as aid or investment (Donnelly 1986). Instead, their greatest strength is to mobilize human rights advocates and supply countries with information and motivations to internalize new norms of appropriate behavior. The most successful agreements are those that reinforce political pressure from domestic NGOs and human rights advocates on abusive governments (Simmons 2007).

The best evidence to date supports this assessment. Studies show that regulatory influence on human rights through persuasive tactics depends on the establishment of sustainable networks of advocates among domestic and transnational actors; that persuasion happens through several stages over time; and that the inculcation of new norms among the worst abusers often requires some coercive bargaining processes, at least in the beginning, to put reforms in motion (Risse, Ropp, and Sikkink 1999). Because perpetrators have much to gain from repression, they often use repressive acts to effectively outlaw or restrict domestic human rights mobilization. And statistical studies illustrate that most countries that join HRAs do not improve many of their human rights behaviors after joining (Camp Keith 1999; Hafner-Burton and Tsutsui 2007; Hathaway 2002). Those that do tend to make modest improvements mainly when they are already in transition to democracy (Simmons 2007) or have ample civil society in place to take up their cause (Hafner-Burton and Tsutsui 2005; Neumayer 2005).

HRAs form a necessary structure of regulations, defining the standards of conduct that governments should follow. By themselves, however, they rarely create the conditions necessary for countries' swing toward better compliance with human rights because persuasion alone supplies insufficient regulatory incentives or commitment instruments to outweigh defection, at least in the short term and for most perpetrators.[5]

Preferential Trade Agreements

Consider the ways in which human rights agreements differ from preferential trade agreements. A growing number of PTAs provide member gov-

---

rights, but they nevertheless remain extremely limited in their jurisdiction and in their effectiveness to provide repressive states with the incentives to protect human rights.

5. The European case may be a unique exception to the rule. Because various European human rights instruments provide harder standards, we should expect commitment to these instruments to produce more compliant behavior.

ernments with a mandate to observe human rights, creating standards of conduct to protect workers' and children's human rights or fundamental human rights for voters and citizens more broadly. These agreements fall into two main categories. In the first category are PTAs that provide member governments with soft standards to manage their policy commitments. This type of regulation is especially common in PTAs between developing countries, although Europe has created a handful of such regulations too. On December 8, 1984, for instance, the member states of the EC and the ACP countries signed their third convention at Lomé, reaffirming their adherence to the principles of the Charter of the United Nations "and their faith in fundamental human rights, in the dignity and worth of the human person, in the equal rights of men and women and of nations large and small" (Preamble). The first annex of this agreement goes on to declare members' recognition "that every individual has the right, in his own country or in a host country, to respect for his dignity and protection by the law" (Joint Declaration on Article 4). Another example is the 1992 Framework Agreement for Cooperation between the EC and Uruguay and also the agreement with Argentina, discussed in chapter 5. These early examples of fair trade standards of conduct were vague, nonbinding, and devoid of any specific means for enforcement, although they did establish regulatory precedents that shaped later trade negotiations.[6] This type of regulation is thus similar to many human rights treaties in that both tender a set of principled ideas about appropriate behavior among a community of countries. But this class of regulations supplies few coercive mechanisms and is thus unlikely to change most repressors' human rights beliefs or practices, especially in countries run by dictators that stifle their opposition.

It is the second type of PTAs—those with hard standards of human rights conduct—that can make the most difference. Most of the agreements considered in this book—US PTAs with Mexico and Canada, Jordan, Chile, Singapore, and Australia; Europe's PTAs with Bulgaria, Kazakhstan, Laos, and now with Botswana, Cuba, Micronesia, and other ACP countries—offer some kind of hard standard of human rights conduct. The

6. Article 6 of the Common Market for Eastern and Southern Africa (COMESA) Treaty is a good example of this kind of regulation, now being made with increasing frequency outside American or European jurisdiction. It similarly articulates the "recognition, promotion and protection of human and people's rights in accordance with the provisions of the African Charter on Human and Peoples' Rights; accountability, economic justice and popular participation in development; [and] the recognition and observance of the rule of law" (Article 6[d], [e], [f], [g]). These principles are also mainly soft because the agreement provides no active mechanism to sanction or to threaten sanctions against COMESA members that do not respect these rights.

American agreement with Oman (2006) is an example. It requires that both countries respect their own laws protecting the human rights of workers, discourages them from weakening protections for workers to encourage trade or investment (Article 16.2), and ensures that violations can be brought before a tribunal for enforcement. Both countries can seek remedies in the event that abuses take place (Article 16.3). Europe's partnership and cooperation agreement with Azerbaijan, which took effect in 1999, is another example. The agreement identifies respect for human rights as an essential element of the partnership (Article 2), establishes a regular political dialogue between countries on respecting and promoting human rights (Article 5), provides technical assistance for this aim (Article 71), and allows for "appropriate measures" to be taken in the event of violations (Article 98).

These fair trade regulations protecting human rights have cooperation benefits that are in some way conditional on countries' human rights actions, and the human rights language is embedded in an enforceable incentive structure designed to provide the economic and political benefits of preferential market access. Thus perpetrators may choose to enact reforms not because of a newfound respect for human rights but in exchange for the benefits associated with the PTA—better market access or a political alliance with the West. This compliance is enforced through a direct or tacit threat to disrupt trade or aid if human rights commitments are not met and is often sweetened with promises of material rewards when compliance takes place.

Instances Where PTAs Made a Difference

States of all kinds are joining the United States and Europe in PTAs with regulations that protect human rights. These countries include institutional democracies such as Jamaica, Mauritius, Papua New Guinea, and Venezuela, and those with dictatorships such as Bahrain, Haiti, and Turkmenistan. They span human rights protectors such as Canada, Costa Rica, Cape Verde, and Vanuatu, and human rights violators such as Colombia, Côte d'Ivoire, Liberia, and Sri Lanka. Only one in three countries that signs agreements with hard standards of conduct is a democracy that is open to social groups, with strong checks on the executive's authority, competitive political participation, and binding rules that govern participation.[7] The vast majority is guilty of some abuses of human rights.[8]

---

7. For a detailed explanation of the data on democracy, see the Polity IV dataset, <http://www.cidcm.umd.edu/inscr/polity/>.

8. See the appendix for details.

In a variety of cases, hard human rights regulations appear to have made at least some difference by prompting countries to support human rights through steps they either would not otherwise have taken or would not have taken as quickly. The influence of these hard regulations shows up at a variety of stages in the policy process.

Before a PTA Becomes Law

Even before a country actually signs a PTA with the United States or Europe, the agreement's human rights regulations can exert influence. It may come during the informal or formal negotiation stages or after negotiations have taken place but before a country votes the agreement into law. Sometimes the weaker trade partner must first show a good-faith effort to enact human rights reforms. Influence at these stages in the policy process is particularly salient for countries doing preferential trade business with the United States. Democrats in Congress place a great deal of emphasis on signaling to the American public before most agreements ever come up for a vote that trade agreements will not hurt American workers. And the American Trade Act of 2002, which established human rights standards of conduct for workers and children in all future agreements within its jurisdiction, did not require trade partners to abide by international law; it required countries to enforce their own domestic labor law. Thus most countries cannot even be considered for a trade partnership with the United States unless they demonstrate that their governments have made, and will continue to make, a few meaningful domestic commitments to protecting workers' human rights.

A good example of the influence these regulations can have before they are ever put into effect is the US free trade agreement with Oman, concluded on October 13, 2005, and signed on January 19, 2006—the United States' fifth bilateral PTA in the Middle East.[9] Oman had long wanted a PTA with the United States to diversify beyond oil and gas markets because the country's oil reserves, which account for almost half of its GDP and more than half of its export revenues, could be depleted in the next few decades. The United States is Oman's third most important trade partner. Meanwhile, the PTA is apt to bring small but positive gains for the United States. From the US perspective, a PTA with Oman is valuable mostly because Oman is a strategic ally in the Middle East with a long history of

9. The US government has proposed to create a Middle-East Free Trade Area (MEFTA) with twenty member countries. Today, as part of that process, it has created PTAs with Israel (1985), Jordan (2001), Morocco (2006), and Bahrain (2006). For in-depth discussion of the Oman case, see Bolle (2006).

diplomatic and political relations with the United States and a strong supporter of its war on terrorism (Bolle 2006).

According to annual reports on human rights violations by the US State Department, analyzed carefully by scholars,[10] Oman has for a long time "severely restricted" workers' human rights. Omani laws have not allowed workers to create or belong to labor unions or to strike or to bargain collectively. And reports show that foreign workers, who make up half of the country's workforce, often toil under conditions that could almost be considered forced labor (US Department of State 2005).

Negotiations with the United States over the creation of a PTA that included hard standards of human rights conduct nudged Oman to put better domestic protections for workers' human rights into place. In 2003, Oman enacted a new labor law that extended to foreigners the country's existing protections for domestic workers. In January 2006, after the trade agreement had been negotiated but had not yet become law, the Sultanate of Oman, in a letter to the House Ways and Means Trade Subcommittee minority staff, recognized Oman's need to create better laws to protect workers' rights to bargain collectively. An accompanying letter from Oman's ambassador announced discussions with the ILO on providing technical assistance to help Oman better comply with certain ILO core standards of conduct.[11] Moreover, the Omani minister of labor made eighteen precise commitments to address forced and child labor problems and to strengthen the country's domestic laws protecting workers' human rights before 2007, in direct response to concerns being voiced by some representatives in the US Congress.[12]

In the spring of 2006, before unanimously passing a bill to implement the trade agreement, the US Senate Finance Committee drafted an advisory amendment that prohibited any trade benefits to goods made "with slave labor . . . or with the benefits of human trafficking."[13] The committee was responding to reports by the National Labor Committee that Jordan was using sweatshop labor in several production plants for merchandise being exported to the United States and that similar practices could take place in other countries that signed PTAs, including Oman (Bolle 2006).

---

10. See in particular work by David Cingranelli and David Richards and their CIRI data website for more detailed information on how these violations were measured, http://ciri.binghamton.edu/. Also see the appendix to this book.

11. The letters are dated January 4, 2006. See Bolle (2006) for details.

12. This letter is dated May 8, 2006. See Bolle (2006) for details.

13. The amendment was put forward by Senator Kent Conrad (D-ND) and supported by several committee Republicans as well, including Chairman Chuck Grassley (R-IA).

On July 8, 2006, Oman issued a royal decree revising Omani laws on workers' human rights to embrace some of the ILO's core labor standards of conduct, which Oman had for years overlooked. Now Omani workers would have the right to form and belong to labor unions, to bargain collectively, and to take part in union actions. Omani employers would also be forbidden from using forced labor of any kind, and violators could be punished. Precise punishments for violations were also set for anyone who blocked labor union activities.[14] These changes were largely the result of Oman's desire to secure a trade agreement with the United States. Many of the labor reforms would probably not have been put into effect when they were, if at all, without US insistence throughout the trade negotiations and without the 2002 Trade Act's requirements. Whether these national standards of conduct protecting workers' human rights in Oman will be meaningfully implemented or enforced still remains to be seen. Nevertheless, these laws have created a better foundation for worker protections and for further reforms.

The US free trade agreement with Chile, discussed in chapter 5, which took effect on January 1, 2004, after several years of negotiations, provides another example of how a PTA can influence a country's human rights practices and laws *before* the agreement takes effect. Chile stood to benefit greatly from a PTA with the United States because America is Chile's most important trade partner, attracting almost 20 percent of its exports (Hornbeck 2003). By eliminating tariffs on roughly 90 percent of all goods, an agreement would help the country expand exports to the United States and improve its image as a reliable free trader. For the United States, a PTA with Chile was an attractive way to further American trade interests in the region and a first step in the creation of a more valuable Free Trade Area of the Americas (FTAA) (Sullivan 2003).

The US State Department's annual reports on human rights violations reveal that Chile also has a deep history of restricting workers' human rights. When Salvador Allende was president in the early 1970s, Chile supported unions, and workers enjoyed basic human rights protections. General Augusto Pinochet came to power by military coup in 1973 and in the mid-1980s passed a Labor Code that was highly unfavorable to workers and that largely remained in place well after Chile's transition back to democracy in 1990 (Pier 1998). During Pinochet's rule, trade unions were broken up, collective bargaining agreements were destroyed, and the system of rights that had been afforded to workers was drastically undermined (US

---

14. See Qaboos bin Sa'id, Sultan of Oman. Royal Decree 74/2006. See Bolle (2006) for details.

Department of Labor 2003). The code let employers lay off workers without recourse and thereby weaken unions by firing their members, preventing effective organizing for better wages and working conditions (Sagar 2004).

After its return to democracy, Chile slowly began to revise its domestic labor laws. It also began negotiations with the United States over a PTA. Whereas Oman's trade negotiations with the United States began a process of workers' rights reforms that might never have happened otherwise, Chile's trade negotiations helped propel a process that had already begun, creating proreform incentives for Chileans opposed to improving workers' rights. In 1995, Chilean president Eduardo Frei, with the support of the Unitary Labor Central Union, had proposed a package of reforms protecting workers' human rights. But the reform package needed the legislature's approval (Pier 1998), and the conservative majority in Chile's Senate blocked it.

However, PTA negotiations with the United States required Chile to revisit workers' rights. Although the Trade Act (2002) was not yet in force when negotiations began, the NAFTA and Jordan agreements had set precedents on standards of conduct protecting workers' rights, and clearly the issue would also be central from the start in negotiations with Chile.[15] The agreement would come up for a vote after the Trade Act was in force, which meant it must include human rights standards of conduct. In 1999, Chile ratified ILO conventions protecting citizens' rights to the freedom of association and the freedom to organize and bargain collectively (US Department of Labor 2003). And in 2001, facing severe criticism from some members of America's Congress and needing to show good faith in the process of negotiations, Chile passed a new Labor Code, which had been a source of debate inside the government of Chile for many years. The new code expands protections for union members, creates a system of punishments for unfair firings, and expands laws on freedom of association and the right to organize (Sagar 2004). The USTR has emphasized that Chile reformed its laws specifically to meet the standards of conduct set forth during negotiations of the PTA (Bolle 2003).

Reports since then by the US State Department and Amnesty International show progress in Chile, but they also show that these standards of conduct protecting workers' human rights are not always being implemented or enforced. Chilean law now allows unions to conduct their business freely, and the US State Department reports that the government

---

15. A PTA with Canada was signed on December 5, 1996, in Santiago and entered into force on July 5, 1997. A side agreement, modeled after NAFTA, creates standards of conduct protecting workers' human rights.

protects this right in practice reasonably well. Yet the Labor Code does not specifically ban forced labor by children, and a recent survey by the Chilean Ministry of Labor reported that hundreds of thousands of children between the ages of five and seventeen work, and some have been working under deplorable conditions (US State Department 2007). These violations have never been remedied under the PTA.[16]

Influence early in the trade agreement process can also be found in Europe, especially in countries that have sought or are seeking to join the Community and become full-fledged European Union members.[17] Slovakia is one example. At the 1993 Copenhagen European Council, the European Community adopted a number of political criteria for accession candidates, including "Human Rights and the Protection of Minorities." Article 49 of the Treaty on the European Union established that accession must be approved by unanimous vote of the Council and an absolute majority of the Parliament, with the opinion of the Commission playing an important role. Early on, the Commission expressed the opinion that Slovakia did not yet qualify for formal negotiations, citing the government's failure to fulfill the democratic and human rights elements of the Copenhagen criteria (Bulterman 1998; Nowak 1999). Quite a few precise violations were formally articulated over several years, including recommendations for changes in national laws and policies concerning the rights of the political opposition, limitations on the power of the executive, the activities of police and secret service, and repression of Hungarian and Roma minorities (European Commission 1997).

In the subsequent discussions, the Commission cited substantial improvements in respect for civil and political rights in Slovakia, including support for civil society organizations and protection of the rights of minorities. Many of the improvements were required to be considered for accession, giving Slovakia's rulers weighty incentives and specific instructions on how to change their domestic policies. In 1999 the Commission deter-

16. As this book went to print, the United States had negotiated a trade agreement with Colombia, but that agreement had not yet passed through Congress. However, leading Democrats had declared that Congress would reject the agreement in its current form. According to Sander Levin (D–MI), who called attention to "hundreds of deaths of labor organizers and human rights activists" in Colombia, protections for workers' human rights are at the "core" of Democrats' objections. See Callan (2006). It remains to be seen whether the government of Colombia will adopt reforms in response.

17. It is important to remember that negotiations over EU membership represent the best instances of PTA influence. The European Union is a PTA in the rare form of an economic union, offering a wide range of benefits that far exceed almost all other forms of preferential trade (such as free trade agreements, customs unions, and common markets). Nevertheless, negotiations over accession to the Union provide a prime example of PTA influence at its best.

mined that Slovakia had taken the necessary steps to fulfill the basic Copenhagen political criteria, although the report identified further areas of human rights policy for reform (European Commission 1999). By 2003, the Slovakian government had ratified all the Commission's recommended human rights legal instruments, and the Commission determined that Slovakia was continuing to meet the human rights requirements of accession and taking positive steps toward improvement (European Commission 2003).

Slovakia's desire to join the European Union, the world's most developed PTA, provided strong motivation for the nation's leaders to make specific human rights reforms they might otherwise not have made and to do so sooner than expected. This provided added support to the country's own democracy movement, which actively pressured the government for reforms. The government is now fairly committed to the protections of those rights in law and in practice. The accession process, though by no means the only inspiration for Slovakia's reform, did strengthen the cause of domestic human rights advocates already championing improvements in Slovakian laws. There is no question that the content of many Slovakian reforms was directly shaped by the requests and assistance from Europe in exchange for membership in the Union.

Turkey provides another instance in which the very possibility of creating a PTA with Europe, aimed at eventual accession into the European Union, significantly influenced human rights reforms, despite continued and substantial abuses. In late 1999, at a summit in Helsinki, Finland, Europe acknowledged Turkey as a potential candidate for membership in the European Union, in spite of the country's gross and widespread human rights violations (Human Rights Watch 2000). In 2001, an Accession Partnership agreement was established to prepare Turkey for eventual accession, setting out specific priorities for reform, as well as providing the financial resources to implement those priorities. In October 2005, membership negotiations were symbolically opened, and one year later Turkey began its examination and assessment of the body of European law it will have to satisfy to become an EU member, including the political conditions set out in Copenhagen.

Europe has repeatedly specified that Turkey must establish certain standards of conduct protecting human rights before negotiations toward accession can begin, and that these standards of conduct must be implemented before an agreement could ever become law. Annual reports from the European Parliament, Council, and Commission spell out precise areas in which Turkey must improve to better protect democracy and the rule of law, to protect minorities and free speech, and to stop torture (Council of the European Union 2001; European Commission 2006b; European Parliament 2006).

Turkey has been moderately responsive to only some of these requests, initiating several reforms it might not otherwise have undertaken and making others sooner than it might have without Europe's influence. Turkey belongs to the European Convention for the Protection of Human Rights and Fundamental Freedoms and the European Convention for the Prevention of Torture and Inhuman or Degrading Treatment or Punishment, and it has accepted the compulsory jurisdiction of the European Court of Human Rights (Domke 1997). The European Commission reports that since 1999 Turkey has made several constitutional reforms and quite a few legislative reforms to better protect human rights. In September 2001, for instance, the Turkish Parliament adopted dozens of amendments to the constitution specifically to meet the requirements for EU membership, including protections of human rights. In 2005, a new penal code took effect that bans the death penalty in all circumstances, enshrines various human rights for women, and outlaws torture (Lobjakas 2004). Turkey has also made important structural reforms to strengthen the role of the judiciary, which is increasingly acting in accordance with the European Court of Human Rights. These include the implementation of several Commission recommendations. Media broadcasting is now allowed in the Kurdish language, and several university professors and authors, arrested for political activities, have been released (European Parliament 2006).

The EU accession process has without doubt prompted many of these reforms and provided support for others. Yet even with these improvements, Turkey has still not gone far enough to meet Europe's human rights requirements for joining the Union. Human rights violations are diminishing, but they still occur. Laws outlawing torture are in place, but reports of torture and ill treatment are still common (European Commission 2005b). While some political prisoners have been released, others have been arrested on charges such as "discouraging the people from military service." No monitoring system exists to oversee detention facilities, discrimination against women is still widespread, the number of Turks who seek asylum in other countries continues to be high, and politically motivated killings are still taking place (European Parliament 2006).[18]

18. Meanwhile, Europe is also aiming to exercise its influence by negotiating PTA standards of human rights conduct with countries that are never going to join the Union. For instance, a partnership and cooperation agreement with Turkmenistan was signed in 1998 but was never ratified by the European Union's member states. A few years ago, the Community resumed talks with the government of Turkmenistan on issues including human rights. In October 2006, the European Parliament voted against putting an interim trade

After a PTA Becomes Law

These examples show clear instances where PTAs with hard human rights standards of conduct have had some influence on the politics of repression before the agreements were signed or took effect. Most of these preferential trade regulations are also designed to influence behavior after they take effect by allowing one country to impose, or threaten to impose, penalties on another through consultation or dispute resolution procedures, and even to suspend parts or all of the agreement if violations take place. Europe has invoked this leverage most often, not only over countries seeking EU membership but also over countries with much lesser trade agreements and no chance of ever gaining membership in the Community. Sometimes threatening to invoke the human rights regulations and suspend the PTAs' benefits has been enough to bring about modest reforms. The case of Mauritania is one example.

On August 3, 2005, Colonel Ely Ould Mohamed Vall and his soldiers overthrew the government of Mauritania in a bloodless coup.[19] The new government did not make clear its intentions regarding a transition to democracy (N'Diaye 2006). The European Commission, on the very day of the coup, released a declaration deploring the seizure of political power by force and calling for respect for democracy and a return to lawful constitutional order in Mauritania. The Commission said it would evaluate the situation, taking into consideration the provisions of the Cotonou Agreement, to which Mauritania belonged. The agreement sets forth precise standards of conduct protecting human rights and the rule of law and calls for consultations with the violating country before punishments can be imposed. The Commission explained that the consultation procedure would provide the new Mauritanian government an opportunity to make clear through positive dialogue its position on future democratic elections and its intention to uphold commitments made by the previous government concerning good governance, reform of the justice system, and the promotion of human rights, civil liberties, and freedom of expression. The Commission maintained that the dialogue would allow the Community to determine whether it could support the country's efforts to improve compliance with the essential elements of the trade agreement,

---

agreement into effect on the basis of ongoing human rights violations. Ad hoc human rights discussions have been started between the Community and the government of Turkmenistan. See Human Rights Watch (2006a).

19. President Maouya Sidi Ahmed Taya was out of the country attending the funeral of Saudi Arabia's King Fahd.

which set forth standards of conduct protecting human rights (European Commission 2005a).

Consultations with Mauritania began on November 30, 2005, and according to the Commission were "cordial and constructive" (European Commission 2006a). Representatives from various Mauritanian political parties and civil society organizations were invited, and the new government made dozens of promises at the meeting, pledging to hold free and transparent elections at all levels of government after a transition period, guaranteeing all citizens the full enjoyment of their human rights as protected by the constitution. They also initiated a process to establish an Independent National Commission for Human Rights, implement legislation outlawing slavery, and reform the justice system. Moreover, the government promised to submit a progress report to the Commission—which it did—that laid out the many reforms it had undertaken to better comply with the human rights regulations embedded in the trade agreement (European Commission 2006a). What is more, the agreement provided for an enhanced political dialogue on human rights compliance with the EU presidency and the European Commission, which has helped to ensure that the Mauritanian government continues on the path of reform it has pledged to follow. In March 2007, Sidi Ould Cheikh Abdallahi became Mauritania's first democratically elected president since the country gained independence from France in 1960. And Europe closed the consultations procedures invoked under the PTA without ever imposing penalties.

The PTA's human rights standards do not deserve sole credit for pushing Mauritania's new military government toward protections of human rights and democracy because the government came to power with its own ideas about establishing democracy. However, the PTA standards did help the government articulate and enact specific human rights reforms, provide a time line within which those reforms would be implemented, offer aid to support the transition process—the Community claimed it would allocate future resources, in this case from the tenth European Development Fund (EDF), only after a democratically elected government was installed—and create a monitoring process to ensure that reforms were implemented. Throughout, the Community maintained the right to adjust the appropriate measures being exercised under the trade agreement in the event of either speedy reform or a breakdown in the implementation of these reforms (European Commission 2006a).

PTA standards of conduct have also been used to gain reforms that better protect human rights in Guinea-Bissau through a similarly positive process that led to improvements (Mbangu 2005).

Another case, though an unusual one, is Togo. In 1993, after a crooked election and following President Gnassingbe Eyadema's constitutional reforms that concentrated more political power in the executive branch, the Community suspended cooperation with Togo under Article 366a of the Lomé agreement. The Community was concerned about human rights abuses and the lack of democracy, although it continued to fund some social projects (Laakso, Kivimaki, and Seppanen 2007). After another flawed election in 1998, the Community reasserted its decision to suspend most cooperation with Togo under the trade agreement, and Togo was denied assistance under the eighth and ninth EDFs. Then longtime president Eyadema promised to step down for presidential elections in 2003 and to that end established an independent national electoral commission. However, he dissolved the commission before parliamentary elections took place in 2002, and one year later he ran again and won the presidency, amidst international concern over the fairness of the elections.

During negotiations with Europe over the creation of human rights preferential trade standards, Togo did not support inclusion of the regulations. In 2004, however, something unusual happened. Togo informally asked for consultations with Europe under Article 96 of the Cotonou agreement, the successor trade agreement to Lomé, which created procedures to address violations of the agreement's human rights standards of conduct. Togo did so, with the support of the ACP countries, as a means to work toward normalization of relations with Europe, even though PTA cooperation with Europe had been mostly suspended for more than a decade and Europe had not asked that more consultations take place. On March 31, 2004, the Community responded, announcing its decision to open consultations under the trade agreement because of a lack of respect for human rights, democracy, and fundamental freedoms. The consultations began a few weeks later (European Commission 2004b). Among the member states, Germany was particularly eager for consultations; France, however, was less enthusiastic (Laakso, Kivimaki, and Seppanen 2007).

To normalize relations, the Community asked Togo to work toward human rights reforms in twenty-two areas, including guaranteeing that all political parties would act freely, that legislative elections would be held, that no more extrajudicial killings or executions would take place, that torture and other inhumane treatment would be stopped, and that political prisoners would be released. To ensure that the trade dialogue would be followed by action, the Community sent country missions to Togo to investigate and monitor progress, and the government of Togo committed to report regularly to the Community on the improvements being made.

Notwithstanding continued violations of human rights and basic freedoms, this process initiated under the preferential trade agreement did have a small impact. In May 2004, the government of Togo began a political dialogue with its opposition, and also with members of civil society groups and various nonstate actors. It did not, however, meet its obligation to hold legislative elections as quickly as promised, although it did draft a new electoral code aimed at achieving better transparency and more free elections (Mbangu 2005). In June 2004, a European delegation went on a fact-finding mission to Togo and reported that the government had taken some significant measures to improve respect for human rights, although the delegation had serious concerns about the restoration of democracy. The group suggested that monitoring would be necessary for several years to come (European Commission 2004c). In November 2006, after Eyadea's son took power following his father's death, the Community decided to continue the human rights consultation process for another few years (Council of the European Union 2006).

Europe's dealings with the Côte d'Ivoire provide another example of how PTA standards of conduct protecting human rights have been used coercively to punish violators and thereby to stimulate modest reforms. This case also reveals the limitations of these standards when the country being asked to make reforms and the country responsible for enforcing those reforms both oppose the standards. In December of 1999, General Robert Guéï ousted elected president Henri Bedié in a bloodless coup. The following February, the European Commission held consultations with the new government for violating its obligation to protect human rights under the Lomé IV amended trade agreement (Article 366a). All financial commitments, apart from assistance in support of humanitarian projects, were to be suspended until successful completion of the consultations. In response to Europe's demands, the military junta pledged to respect a timetable for democratic elections and the adoption of a constitution that would guarantee separation of powers, freedom of the press, and greater transparency in decision making. The Commission, in return, agreed to provide a package of positive measures in support of these goals (Fierro 2003).

Thus Guéï took power promising to hold new democratic elections, but violence soon broke out after his newly appointed supreme court disqualified most of the opposing political candidates from taking part in the elections. In October, when political polls showed that Guéï would lose the election to the only remaining candidate, Laurent Gbagbo, Guéï disbanded the election commission and declared himself the winner. He then fled the country a few days later in the face of mounting violence and protests against him. Gbagbo was declared president, despite objections from other opposition leaders who had been excluded from the elections. Hundreds of people had been brutally killed in the process, and others had been tortured, raped, and forcibly disappeared. Yet Gbagbo took power without promising new and fair elections, without seeking accountability for the mass violations of human rights that had taken place before the elections, and without taking steps to ensure that the Côte d'Ivoire would follow the rule of law. December 2000 parliamentary elections saw further corruption and violence (Human Rights Watch 2001). Even so, consultations under the trade agreement were concluded shortly thereafter.

Under the Lomé trade agreement's sanctions for violations of human rights and the rule of law, the Community twice threatened to reopen the consultation procedure following the Côte d'Ivoire's parliamentary elections (European Parliament 2001). In January 2001, an attempted coup set Gbagbo's government on the attack against foreigners, and hundreds of people were reportedly tortured, harassed, and assaulted. One month later, the Commission opened a second round of consultations with the government under Article 366a of the trade agreement. The Côte d'Ivoire again agreed to open the political process to opposition and to investigate allegations of atrocities committed against civilians. Meanwhile, the Community initiated an intensive dialogue aimed at ensuring these commitments would be honored. It also suspended the trade agreement's benefits and pledged to finance only projects that would benefit social issues, institutions, the private sector, and democracy until reforms were fulfilled (Fierro 2003). To normalize relations under the PTA, the Community required that the Côte d'Ivoire demonstrate respect for the rule of law and for human rights and the protection of foreigners and that democratization and national reconciliation begin (Bradley 2005).

During the consultation process, in response to Europe's requests, the Côte d'Ivoire government took some measures to support free and fair elections at municipal and department levels that would probably not otherwise have been implemented. A National Reconciliation Forum was also put into place, improvements in human rights practices were made, a National Identification Office was established, and draft legislation on freedom of the press was prepared (Bradley 2005). The government also pledged to conduct three official investigations into the violence that had taken place before the presidential elections—the massacre of fifty-seven men, the murder of eighteen people whose bodies were found floating in a lagoon, and the murder of six men—and to bring the perpetrators to justice (Human Rights Watch 2001).[20] Although many human rights violations

20. These massacres were also being investigated by the United Nations.

were still taking place, and the security forces mainly responsible for the atrocities were mostly acquitted, the Community announced its intention to normalize relations with the Côte d'Ivoire on February 19, 2002.

In September 2002, rebel forces took over the northern part of the country in a failed coup attempt, and civil war broke out. The next year, after much violence, the rebels were given positions in a unity government created by the French-brokered Linas-Marcoussis Peace Accord, and Gbagbo agreed to a power-sharing arrangement aimed at keeping the country from returning to civil war. But Gbagbo did little to keep up his end of the bargain. He skirted agreed-upon procedures by appointing ministers of defense and the interior and by refusing to delegate executive powers to the prime minister and government as stipulated by the accords. Serious violations of human rights were again taking place. Journalists were executed, and security forces fired live ammunition at unarmed demonstrators in Abidjan. In 2004 the Commission again proposed that consultations be opened, this time under Article 96 of the Cotonou trade agreement, to allow a dialogue to "discover the country's intentions" on human rights violations and on credible elections (European Commission 2004a).

Despite the reforms that the Côte d'Ivoire adopted in response to European consultations under Lomé, the agreement's human rights standards of conduct have for the most part been unsuccessful at bringing about real reforms for several reasons. First, Gbagbo's government is benefiting enormously from the abuse, which allows it to maintain the power and resources necessary to rule, and these benefits have only increased since the period of civil war. Europe's offer to normalize trade relations is hardly as lucrative.

Second, Gbagbo's administration was able to ignore most of Europe's requests for reform because it had an ally inside the Community: France. By offering the Côte d'Ivoire unilateral assistance, France allowed that country to hedge against the use of harsh sanctions. To be sure, the French government has condemned the violence taking place in the Côte d'Ivoire, much as it did in Togo. According to a report by Human Rights Watch, the French claimed that in 2001 they were the first to initiate the consultation procedures under the trade agreement, which led to the temporary suspension of assistance from Europe. But members of the European Commission claim the French were unequivocally opposed to these actions (Human Rights Watch 2001). Early in 2001, while the Community moved to suspend the trade agreement's benefits to the Côte d'Ivoire, France resumed its full bilateral cooperation with the country. Meanwhile, Gbagbo himself enjoyed close ties with his nation's former colonial ruler. While the Community was putting sanctions into place, Gbagbo accepted an invitation from French president Jacques Chirac to visit France that June, and France restored its military cooperation with the Côte d'Ivoire.

These examples show clear instances where a preferential trade agreement with hard standards of conduct protecting human rights has influenced a repressive government to improve specific human rights practices before or after joining the agreement. They show various forms of influence on various actors facing different kinds of human rights problems in different regions of the world. In some places these agreements reinforce democracy and human rights movements already in action. In other places, where such movements are weak or absent, these agreements push governments to take on reforms anyway.

These examples also show that implementation of human rights regulations has been selective and political and that when influence does occur, it is modest. Often these kinds of regulations will not work at all. They can do little to influence armed opposition groups or governments under insurrection. Severely repressive leaders who reap extensive benefits from using violence will probably avoid or defect from agreements that offer only small gains or that require large-scale political change. Perpetrators who can find similar trade advantages elsewhere, without paying the price of accepting PTA regulations protecting human rights, are unlikely to join, or follow, these agreements at all. Thus, these standards of conduct cannot by themselves transform governments from serious abusers into committed protectors; they can, however, provide incentives for small, incremental changes in some policies and practices that set in motion the process of reform. When this process fails to spur change, it is because the trade agreement's human rights standards lack sufficient conceptual clarity, and because the agreement's stakeholders are not sufficiently committed to punishing violations by reducing or ceasing trade agreement benefits. The failure of the United States or Europe to enforce the human rights conditions of their agreements reduces the credibility of future threats of enforcement and weakens the agreements' ability to persuade local elites to accept improvements in human rights practices.

General Patterns of Influence

These illustrations are examples of a broader process that is taking place not just in Oman or Togo but also in a variety of other countries. This final section of the chapter sets these cases in the context of broader world experience. A more detailed explanation of the methods for analysis and the data used for this section, as well as the tools for further study, is available in the appendix. Europe is the focus here because by the year 2003—the latest for which data measuring governments' protections for workers' human rights are available—the United States had signed PTAs with workers' rights protections only with a few other countries. We look at European preferential trade agreements that protect fundamental human rights and examine their relationship to the abuse of physical integrity in particular. We also look for evidence of improvements before and after joining these agreements.

Our examination begins with the general pattern of governments' behavior, taking into account what researchers know about four types of human rights violations: the use of torture, extrajudicial killing, political imprisonment, and forced disappearances. We will use a sample of almost 190 countries for which data are available during the period 1981 to 2003 (Cingranelli and Richards 1999).[21] How do these types of human rights violations relate to whether or not a country is negotiating or belongs to a PTA with Europe that contains standards of conduct protecting human rights? In one in three instances in which countries signed such a PTA with Europe, they also improved their human rights practices during the trade negotiation process, one or two years *before* the agreement took effect. About one in two countries improved their practices one or two years *after* their trade agreement with Europe took effect.[22]

Statistics provide more systematic evidence about the relationship between these types of trade agreements and the repression of the right to physical integrity. The scale used here ranges from zero—where a government is guilty of the use of torture, extrajudicial killing, political imprisonment, and forced disappearances—to eight, where a government respects the rights to be free from all these violations of physical integrity (Cingranelli and Richards 1999). We can use these data to predict changes in countries' human rights practices from one year to the next, taking into consideration several factors: whether countries have joined a European

21. David Cingranelli and David Richards collected these data using content analysis of the annual reports published by the US State Department. The variable under examination here ranges across nine levels of observed behavior, from zero, where a government does not respect any four of these rights to personal integrity, to eight, where a government respects all four fully. Data and all coding rules and procedures are available from http://ciri.bing hamton.edu/documentation.asp. Alternative measures of the same violations, collected by Mark Gibney and by Poe and Tate (1994), are also considered in the appendix.

22. Improvement here is defined as *any* movement toward better human rights practices that registers on the measurement scale; for instance, movements from a zero to a one, as well as movements from a five to a seven are both counted as improvements. Here, 32 percent of country-years improved their respect for physical integrity rights during negotiations of the PTA, two years prior to its entry into force. The number increases to 36 percent one year before entry into force, 40 percent the year an agreement comes into effect, 47 percent one year afterwards, and 55 percent two years after the PTA has come into force.

PTA with hard human rights standards, countries' experience with democracy, the durability of their government regimes, their levels of economic development and trade, their engagement in war, their population density, and their commitments to the Convention against Torture and the Covenant on Civil and Political Rights.[23]

These analyses, the results of which are shown in the appendix, provide two further points of information. First, countries that belong to European PTAs that regulate human rights by creating hard standards of conduct are statistically more likely than countries that do not belong to improve their human rights practices over time. Second, to put this result in some perspective, countries that belong to either one or both of the two UN human rights agreements protecting people's rights to personal integrity are *not* more apt to make these improvements than countries that do not belong to these treaties—other studies show that human rights agreements work best inside democracies, especially those with a strong civil society. When it comes to pushing forward human rights reforms, European PTAs with hard human rights standards are more often associated with reforms in the short term, even if they are modest reforms, than are many human rights treaties.[24]

How much do these types of trade regulations matter? It is hard to say for certain. The statistics are crude and enable us to make only rough predictions. What, for instance, is the probability that an average country will take on human rights reforms? We calculate and compare these statistics for countries that belong to a European PTA with human rights standards and for those that do not belong. Figure 1 charts the fractional change in these two sets of probabilities across the first eight levels of human rights violations, from horrible abuses (0) to reasonable protection (7). It shows the probability that a country will make any human rights improvements *at all* after joining, even if some abuses still occur. For instance, if a country was seen to repress all categories of physical integrity rights in a given year, thus getting a 0 in that year, that country is more likely to improve its human rights practices the next year if it belongs to a PTA with Europe that has enforceable standards of human rights conduct than if it does not.[25] If a

23. The model, estimated by ordered logit, includes fixed effects for time and repression floor and ceiling dummies and calculates all statistics based on Huber/White standard errors. All variables on the right-hand side of the model are lagged by one year. Further information is available in the appendix.

24. For further information about the effects of HRAs on human rights practices, see Camp Keith (1999), Hathaway (2002), Hafner-Burton and Tsutsui (2005), Neumayer (2005), and Simmons (2007). For analysis of international war crimes tribunals, see Bass (2000). For analysis of membership behavior, see Hafner-Burton, Mansfield, and Pevehouse (2008) and Vreeland (2008).

25. Without such a PTA, we can predict the probability of reform in this sample will be about 75 percent, while with such a PTA, probability of reform will be higher, about 82 percent (82% - 75%)/75% = 9.3%.

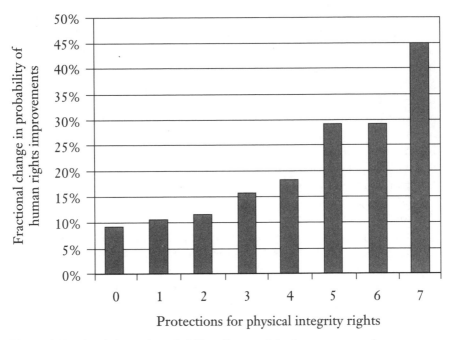

Figure 1. Fractional change in probability of human rights improvements when a country belongs to a European PTA with hard human rights standards of conduct, 1981 to 2003

country were seen to violate just one of the four types of personal integrity rights, thus getting a 7 on the physical integrity scale in that year, the chance of improvement is also greater if it belongs to a PTA with Europe that has enforceable standards of human rights conduct than if it does not. Countries that are better human rights performers before they join European PTAs with human rights standards are the ones likely to most improve after joining. Really bad human rights performers are also likely to make at least some improvements after they join a European PTA, although they are not as likely to do so as the better performers. The statistics show that countries' intention to join the European Union does not explain all of this effect and also that these improvements are not just an artifact of selective trade relationships with countries that already protect human rights.[26]

Similar statistical tests are not yet possible for the United States, though some information is available to measure countries' protections for workers'

26. Selection is accounted for with an instrumental variable model.

human rights (Cingranelli and Richards 1999).[27] As of 2003, the latest year
for which data are available, the United States had made PTAs with four
other countries, and only three of these countries were subject to any human rights standards—Canada, Mexico, and Jordan—making statistical
analysis impractical. For decades, Canada has been recorded as fully protecting workers' human rights, and NAFTA has thus had little effect on
encouraging reforms in Canada. Both Mexico and Jordan, however, have
improved their protections for workers' human rights within a few years of
belonging to PTAs with the United States. More statistical analysis on the
effects of American and European trade policies on human rights is available from Hafner-Burton 2008.

The modest but important human rights improvements examined in this
chapter shed light on the politics of implementation—a subject itself worthy of an entire book.[28] Savvy policymakers in the United States and Europe are primarily motivated by their own self-preservation to put human
rights standards into trade agreements, but these regulations can indeed
make a difference in countries guilty of abusing human rights. When the
United States or Europe uses preferential trade agreements to admonish
repressive governments for their bad practices and either promises benefits
or threatens punishment, the results can be noticeable. At the heart of this
process is something most treaties of the human rights legal regime cannot
guarantee: enough meaningful incentives and commitment instruments to
support the initial stages of compliance among perpetrators who benefit from
their acts of terror, especially in countries run by dictators.

PTAs with human rights standards of conduct are not the ideal form of
human rights governance, nor are they a replacement for global or regional
human rights laws. But policymakers did not create them for either of these
reasons. They impact human rights mainly when the countries that make
them also want to enforce them, and political will and resources to do so
are often in short supply. At the same time, the abusers that join them must
value the benefits of complying as much as, if not more, than what they
stand to lose from making reforms, and this is not always the case. Even so,
these regulations demonstrate the capacity to enforce some compliance
with human rights norms, and they have proven to be one of the more effective means available for initiating implementation of very basic human
rights in some places.

27. Data on workers' human rights and all coding rules and procedures are available
from http://ciri.binghamton.edu/documentation.asp.
28. See Bartels (2005) and Fierro (2003).

CHAPTER 7

THE FUTURE

This book examines why countries create and how they use fair preferential trade standards that protect human rights. It asks four specific questions about this process. Why did the United States and Europe begin to regulate human rights through PTAs? Why do American agreements create standards of conduct to protect workers' and children's human rights while European PTAs mainly protect fundamental human rights for voters and citizens?[1] Why do other countries, especially the ones that perpetrate human rights abuses, join these agreements that interfere with their governments' business and may have bad economic effects? And do any of these regulations change the politics of repression or help to protect people?

By looking at the evolution of human-rights-protecting trade agreements and their effects around the world, this book explores several answers. Fair preferential trade regulations protecting human rights were born from the desires of sensible policymakers to boost their own political influence, to solve trade or security problems, or to accumulate resources. The cold war and the shifting political environment that followed shaped them in important ways. They were not crafted in direct response to global norms or laws or to the desires of NGOs or labor unions. The United States and Europe have each designed these regulations differently, both because their policymakers have used them to confront different problems and because their policymaking institutions have given advantage to differ-

---

1. The Community now regulates workers' human rights through its unilateral preferential scheme, the GSP. It has also begun to include protections for workers' rights in its PTAs.

ent policymakers in different ways at various stages of the regulatory process. Most other counties that sign these agreements have no interest or intention of putting the human rights regulations into practice; they enlist because the benefits of making a PTA seem greater than the costs of taking on the human rights standards. Nonetheless, preferential trade agreements that commit members to protect human rights do in fact prevent some abuses and encourage small or gradual reforms that help to safeguard human rights.

At the same time, a variety of other explanations could be offered for the rise and success of human rights standards in trade agreements. Protectionism, for instance, has helped shape regulators' ambitions to govern human rights through PTAs and has focused some policymakers' attention on protecting workers' human rights, though it has not influenced the European experience in the same way as the American—Europe mainly regulates workers' rights in its unilateral trade schemes and human rights in its other PTAs. Protectionism is rampant. However, policymakers have almost never used the trade agreement rules protecting human rights to actually protect their workers, although some do advertise them as worker-friendly. What is more, trade unions largely dislike the regulations being made and actively protest the agreements that are currently under negotiation. Unions matter, but their demands cannot directly explain all the regulations being made.

Norms and moral advocates have also played a role. They have shaped the global discourse on human rights and created the foundation on which countries base many of their standards of conduct, although the Europeans have relied more heavily on international norms than have the Americans in this process—they sign on to more global human rights agreements and are more apt to cite them when making trade policy. But norms and their principled advocates were not the primary catalysts for fair PTAs either. Nor did they spur policymakers to use PTAs to regulate human rights. Many advocates' concerns have in fact been ignored, and most of these groups are very critical of the actual policies being adopted. NGOs have come to have influence not mainly by changing policymakers' minds but by changing their rhetoric. Since the regulations protecting human rights have been in place, though, NGOs have played a vital role in implementing the rules by helping the United States and Europe to identify the violators.

Commitment politics are also a part of this story. A few other countries such as Argentina have asked for human rights standards in trade agreements. And one country, Togo, even initiated a consultation procedure under its trade agreement for its own violations of human rights. Despite these important examples, most countries, including democratic and rights-protecting ones, have opposed the PTA regulation process from start to finish. They have resisted human rights standards in the first place and have become irritated and often uncooperative when the standards of conduct are implemented.

This process of creating and using PTA standards of human rights conduct is both relatively new and often misunderstood, with observers too eager to credit the power of NGOs and labor unions. The aim here has been to unravel the mystery behind what has happened and explore whether it affects the politics of regulation and repression—much has already been said elsewhere about the legal and economic aspects of this process.[2] This new form of human rights regulation is also telling for the politics of social justice, international relations and law, protectionism, and human rights more generally. We turn now to some of these broader implications.

Studying Social Justice

It is certainly tempting to interpret this fair trade regulation process as an achievement for human rights advocates and organizations that work tremendously hard to convince countries and their governments to better protect people. On the one hand, many advocates are calling for more attention to human rights and more fair trade. On the other hand, the United States and Europe appear to be listening—after all, they are making new rules. Yet international institutions sometimes have effects that surprise the countries that belong to them or the people who made the rules in the first place. Regulations can have unintended yet anticipated effects, such as when rules that are created to lower the inflation rate also lead to higher unemployment, an unintentional but foreseeable consequence. Or they can have unintended and surprising effects, such as when countries form a human rights agreement that they believe to be politically expedient but not legally binding, only to watch other actors in other situations use the agreement to spur policy changes (Martin and Simmons 1998).

The story presented here shows how international regulations can take on a life of their own—that is, they can shape politics in ways that the rational people who wanted, created, or joined them might never have intended. It shows how policymakers doing their best to solve important political problems of the day drafted human rights standards of conduct and inserted

---

2. See, for instance, Destler and Balint (1999), Elliot and Freeman (2003a, 2003b), and Bartels (2005).

them in PTAs mainly to win their own domestic political battles and serve their own purposes. These fair trade regulations probably would not have been created without public pressure from human rights NGOs and labor unions making principled and economic arguments; certainly the rhetoric of both groups has shaped the policy debate. But the regulations were not created simply to suit these interest groups' demands. They were designed to suit the needs of the policymakers who saw them as a way to score political victories, sometimes to appease interest groups and sometimes to solve other problems. Thus it should not be surprising that many human rights NGOs and labor unions are not at all content with the new trade regulations they would seem to have wanted.

This book also has a broader lesson to impart. Studying how social justice issues such as human rights become matters for international regulation is tricky business. Our standard methods of comparing interest groups' demands with the regulations that are made does not necessarily lead to an accurate understanding of the political process taking place or of the complexion of the resulting regulations. The United States did not adopt the Trade Act of 2002 because labor unions asked for it, and Europe did not create the Cotonou agreement because NGOs lobbied for it. Policymakers do not always want the same things that constituent interest groups are demanding, and when they appear to, it may be for different reasons that in fact end up shaping how those ideas are turned into laws. The fact that the two appear to match does not mean that one led to the other—explaining how global norms become international laws requires digging deeper into the institutional and power politics too. Policymaking institutions and relative power imbalances between countries also shape how the rules are made, and interest groups and NGOs have little influence over either.

To understand why and how these different regulations are made and enforced, researchers need to trace the process, from the source of policymakers' demand for the rules through the policymaking institutions they use to make choices, to the international negotiation process with other countries and then to implementation. This is a challenge as much for human rights research as for trade research.

Institutional Convergence

This story might appear to be a classic account of convergence—the trend of societies to become more similar by developing likeness in structures, processes, and routines (Kerr 1983)—popularized by an important strand of research in political economy on the effects of market integration (Kaufman and Segura-Ubiergo 2001; Rudra 2007). After all, both the United States and Europe began creating PTA standards of conduct protecting human rights around the same time, and both passed laws that allowed fairly standardized clauses in agreements with trade partners all over the world. This view also fits well with an important research tradition in sociology that has been applied with great success to the study of human rights (Berkovitch 1999; Goodman and Jinks 2003b; Tsutsui and Min Wotipka 2004). Several decades ago, Meyer and Rowan (1977) proposed that formal organizations tend to emerge in domains that are defined by institutional myths and that these organizations take on institutional structures to achieve "isomorphism," or sameness. They do so by incorporating rules that are legitimate and not necessarily efficient and using ceremonial evaluation criteria—for instance, relying on standardized models such as human rights norms. Some political scientists think in similar terms (Finnemore 1996).

The approach taken here cautions against concluding that ostensibly similar policies such as the American and European PTA human rights regulations are formed by similar developments and ideas or lead to similar results. On the one hand, it is true that more human rights institutions are being created and used by countries all around the world (Hafner-Burton, Mansfield, and Pevehouse 2008) and that the human rights clauses that the United States and Europe are respectively using are often practically cut and pasted from one agreement into the next. On the other hand, a snapshot of the PTA regulation process that focuses only on the similarities between American and European approaches would be misleading. There are big differences between what policymakers want and the kinds of regulations they get. And the regulations being made on both sides of the Atlantic are very different. So are the processes that led up to their creation and that drive the politics of implementation. More generally, it would be a mistake to view the growing mass of human rights institutions—the treaties, organizations, trade regulations, international courts and trials—as evidence of global convergence toward justice in either process or outcome. Despite the rhetoric, countries are not growing more alike in their respect for human rights, and the structures and processes they are developing to manage these issues are still astonishingly different. Many are weak commitments. Most cover only some small assortment of human rights or countries. Human rights abuses continue, and the sources of violations are as diverse as ever. The suggestion that we are witnessing convergence toward more and better justice is mistaken.

Protectionism

Whether it is politically justified or economically defensible, protectionism is happening in both the United States and Europe. This book does not address whether governments *should* use human rights standards of conduct in their PTAs to protect human rights. It focuses on the fact that *they are already doing it* and examines why some of them are able to do so when they cannot succeed as well in the WTO.

The effects of these PTA standards on trade, however, are unclear. Rarely have these regulations been used to limit imports on specific goods that face international competition or to raise tariffs against another country whose cheap exports threaten the livelihood of American or European workers. So far, the regulations do not seem to have a real economic effect after they are put in place at all, perhaps because they are not intended to. They may be making some economic difference before they ever come to be law, however. As this book goes to print, the United States will likely reject a trade agreement negotiated with Colombia. Democrats in Congress cite human rights abuses as one of their main objections. And the European Community has again refused to put its trade agreement with Turkmenistan into effect on the same grounds.

What is more, the protectionist standards, whether justified or not on moral, political, or some other grounds, are making it hard for the United States and Europe to negotiate with the major players such as China and India that have valuable markets and can afford to walk away from a trade deal to avoid unwanted standards of conduct. The government of India is objecting to Europe's insistence that a standard human rights and democracy clause be placed into a proposed free trade agreement, and the deal may fall apart as a result. According to India's commerce minister, the standards of conduct are "a deal-breaker" (Johnson 2007). But who really benefits from stopping these agreements? Is it better or worse for human rights? Will people in India and China and Colombia and Turkmenistan benefit or suffer? And what does that mean for Americans and Europeans?

What is happening with PTAs goes beyond just human rights. Both the United States and Europe are regulating other seemingly noneconomic issues through their preferential trade agreements too. Standards of conduct for environmental protections, for instance, are common in both American and European trade agreements. The Europeans, in fact, have become much more creative on this account, tying all sorts of issues to their new trade pacts and crafting PTAs that regulate standards of conduct on issues including corruption and even weapons of mass destruction, as they did with

Syria. These are not the only issues being discussed for trade regulation. How many political issues can countries jam into preferential trade agreements without triggering a cacophony of regulation or creating a crowding-out effect? There is a danger here, and it is not only economic: too many regulations on too many issues in too many trade agreements could result in a critical loss of focus and thereby render them essentially ineffective. International relations in general seem to be heading in this direction, to a world of too many regulations and too many institutions, where countries' loyalties are split and perpetrators of bad behavior can "forum-shop" for institutions that best allow them to get away with whatever they want (Helfer 1999).

The issue of how countries use PTAs is also evolving. We know that the United States and Europe are using PTAs to their own political ends, making human rights standards of conduct and imposing them on other countries mainly to solve their own policymakers' problems. But the fair trade process is beginning to spread, not just among countries making trade deals with the United States and Europe but also in trade agreements being made between other countries. Maybe it is not surprising that the trade agreement between Canada and Chile includes standards of conduct protecting workers' human rights, albeit weak ones. It might be more surprising, though, that the Common Market for Eastern and Southern Africa (COMESA), which includes some countries guilty of horrible human rights atrocities, or the Southern Common Market (MERCOSUR), which also has a murky record on the issue, have both placed standards of human rights conduct into their trade agreements. Many other developing countries have too. So far, most of these standards are just for show, not designed to be enforced and without strong teeth. Nonetheless, it is worth remembering that in both the United States and Europe the process of creating such regulations began that way too. Unenforceable human rights standards were established and put into PTAs without a way to implement them. Over time, though, these standards evolved into enforceable rules with clear means of implementation. The same may happen one day for some of the developing countries now wading into human rights regulations.

Human Rights

In examining how fair preferential trade standards of conduct are made, it is also important to consider the complexities of human rights: the politics surrounding them and the ways that scholars study them, governments regulate them, and policymakers use them. In the United States and Europe the policymakers involved in these new PTA regulations are trying to do what they think is best while also facing enormous political challenges that require difficult choices that rarely please everyone. Policymakers seek to address the challenges they face, which may include pleasing or assuaging their constituents, winning or keeping office, or solving a security crisis. They rarely take on regulatory battles for moral reasons alone, nor should they. This means that advocates for a particular issue are usually most successful when their cause aligns with policymakers' own interests.

That is precisely what has happened in the story told here, as American and European policymakers developed human rights standards of conduct and put them into PTAs to win more power, influence, or other resources they needed to best do their jobs. Often they used the human rights discourse along the way to justify their actions. A few have even been human rights activists, but not most. Indeed, this story suggests that the rise of a human rights discourse should be viewed with at least some skepticism because many of the people and countries now promoting that discourse may be more concerned about selling an image than fulfilling a promise to make the world a better place. Many policymakers may not actually be as invested in the human rights outcome, or the effects of the policy, as they could be or perhaps should be. And so they may be willing to trade off or sell down certain aspects of human rights to win a political compromise that seems indefensible to moral advocates and that could have harmful, and certainly unintended, effects. On the other hand, this is precisely the way most political change happens in the areas of social justice—policymakers learn that they have a stake in an issue and so adopt the cause, often for the wrong reasons.

The regulatory process at the heart of this book thus has important implications for the politics of human rights. It suggests that governments are quite successfully moving beyond standard human rights treaties and laws to a new tool—preferential trade agreements—to protect human rights. The United Nations' human rights agreements, including the regional human rights treaty systems, are no longer the only international regulations in use. Even though the PTA standards of conduct protecting human rights were not always intended to promote improvements in other countries, and their implementation is political and partial, they do clearly prompt reforms in certain situations. This means that supporters of human rights, whether scholars, NGOs, countries, or corporations, could fruitfully look beyond the international human rights regime for new ways to enact human rights norms. Many such groups are now doing just that.

China

All of this regulation is happening in a world in flux. Powerful markets are emerging in countries that do not yet wed protections for human rights to trade—not because they are less principled than the United States and Europe but because these linkages thus far create more problems than they solve and because human rights are not equally valued everywhere. China stands above the rest. In 2006, it was the world's third leading exporter, right behind the United States. It was also the third leading importer. But China's annual growth in those two measures far surpassed that of the United States and Europe, with a 27 percent increase in exports and a 20 percent increase in imports.[3] The implications for both trade and human rights are unknown and potentially huge.[4]

China has passed into law a few global human rights treaties, but it nonetheless has a terrible record on human rights protections. In 2007, Amnesty International reported:

> An increased number of lawyers and journalists were harassed, detained, and jailed. Thousands of people who pursued their faith outside officially sanctioned churches were subjected to harassment and many to detention and imprisonment. Thousands of people were sentenced to death or executed. Migrants from rural areas were deprived of basic rights. Severe repression of Uighurs in the Xinjiang Uighur Autonomous Region continued, and freedom of expression and religion continued to be severely restricted in Tibet and among Tibetans elsewhere. (Amnesty International 2007)

The great question posed by the rise of a more global China is whether its economic might and disregard for human rights will begin to undermine the West's ability to use trade agreements to improve human rights. Because of its economic strength, the United States and Europe are unlikely to convince China to sign trade agreements that protect human rights. With its market share, China has the power to say no, and the United States and Europe are not likely to try to force it to comply because the Western nations would suffer severe economic damage if China halted trade with them.

---

3. The source for these statistics is the World Trade Organization, International Trade Statistics 2007, http://www.wto.org/.
4. For an account of challenges associated with China's growth, see Perkins (2007).

The issue is not simply that China gets a free pass to abuse human rights as it pleases; it is also that China is beginning to shape American and European fair trade regulations through backdoor channels. Every time China invests in or trades with another country without imposing human rights in the deal, it weakens the ability of the United States and Europe to bully those countries into accepting regulations protecting people. This is playing out not only in Sudan but also in other countries where China is keen to step into the Western trade vacuum. If the pattern continues, the United States and Europe may lose their ability to coerce other countries into accepting trade and investment deals they can get more cheaply, without human rights standards, from countries like China. This means Western policy advocates may be lobbying for more issue linkages in trade agreements at the same time that American and European power to coerce other countries may begin to wane. Now that PTAs have proven sometimes effective and enjoy more widespread use, the challenge is to find ways to convince the biggest rights abusers, including China, to join.

The rapid spread of PTA standards of human rights conduct is a truly important event that is changing the very nature of world economic relations and globalization—and also human rights. It will probably continue into the foreseeable future, though its potential is still largely untapped. It is not, as it turns out, primarily about economics or driven by moral concerns for protecting human rights. It is mostly about politics. The regulatory shift has taken place as various policymakers, facing individual challenges, have internationalized their own political struggles. It was motivated by Americans and Europeans who sought to use PTAs to solve their policy problems: some wanted to win public support, some wanted to save people's lives, and some wanted to foster more trade or better security. And it has spread globally through pressures placed by the United States and Europe on their less fortunate trade partners. This is a story about the power of elite circles of thoughtful and influential policymakers—who are increasingly aligned in Europe and ever more deadlocked along party lines in the United States—to push their beliefs through preferential trade agreements and impose a global social agenda, maybe for all the wrong reasons, that has changed the face of economic statecraft.

APPENDIX

Statistical Analysis

The data used to analyze the European Parliament questions, discussed in chapter 3, are available upon request.

For chapter 6, I estimate the following model by ordered logit and also ordinary least squares:

$$Human\ Rights_{it} = \alpha + \beta_1\ Human\ Rights\ Floor_{it-1} + \beta_2\ Human\ Rights\ Ceiling_{it-1}$$
$$+ \beta_3\ Democracy_{it-1} + \beta_4\ Durability_{it-1} + \beta_5\ Density_{it-1} + \beta_6\ Trade_{it-1} + \beta_7\ pcGDP_{it-1}$$
$$+ \beta_8\ Civil\ War_{it-1} + \beta_9\ CAT_{it\ 1} + \beta_{10}\ CCPR_{it-1} + \beta_{11}\ Hard\ EU\ PTA_{it-1} + \delta_i + e_{it}$$

Here, *Human Rights$_{it}$* to physical integrity—government protections from torture, extrajudicial killing, political imprisonment, and forced disappearances—are measured in a sample of almost 190 countries in two different ways. The first way to measure human rights, from Cingranelli and Richards (1999), records countries' practices during the period 1981 to 2003 for which data are available.[1] This ordinal variable ranges across nine levels of observed behavior—from 0, where a government does not respect any four of these rights, to 8, where a government respects all four fully. A second way to measure human rights, collected by Steven Poe and Neil Tate

---

1. David Cingranelli and David Richards collected these data using content analysis of the annual reports published by the US State Department. Data and all coding rules and procedures are available from http://ciri.binghamton.edu/documentation.asp. I also estimate the model on *Political Terror$_{it-1}$*, an alternative coding for the same types of human rights violations.

(1994) and by Mark Gibney for the period 1976 to 2003, is used as a robustness check.

The first set of independent variables, *Human Rights Floor*$_{it-1}$ and *Human Rights Ceiling*$_{it-1}$, are binary indicators measuring whether the country was observed to be at the floor or ceiling of human rights abuses in the previous year. *Democracy*$_{it-1}$ measures countries' regime characteristics, coded by Keith Jaggers and Ted Robert Gurr. The variable takes on values ranging from 10 (most democratic) to −10 (most autocratic).[2] *Durability*$_{it-1}$ counts the number of years since a state has undergone a regime transition, defined as a movement on the *Democracy*$_{it-1}$ scale of three points or more. *Density*$_{it-1}$ measures a country's population density (per kilometer), collected by the World Bank. The measure is logged. *Civil War*$_{it-1}$ is a binary measure, available from the Correlates of War project, which indicates whether a country is at civil war (1) or not (0).[3] *Trade*$_{it-1}$ controls for the possible effects that international market transactions may have on human rights, independent from the international economic institutions. The variable, collected by the World Bank, measures the sum of a country's total exports and imports of goods and services measured as a share of gross domestic product. *pcGDP*$_{it-1}$ measures gross domestic product per capita in constant US dollars. Both measures are logged.

I also consider ratification, succession, and accession to the International Covenant on Civil and Political Rights, *CCPR*$_{it-1}$, and the Convention Against Torture, *CAT*$_{it-1}$. Both are binary variables coded 1 if a state *i* has ratified the treaty into national law in time *t*. *Hard EU PTA*$_{it-1}$ then measures countries' membership with European PTAs supplying hard standards of human rights conduct that are enforceable through sanctions, fines, or suspension of the agreement: country *i* in year *t* takes on a value of 1 if that country belongs to any PTA with the European Community that offers hard standards of human rights conduct. I coded this variable using content analysis of all PTAs made by the European Community. For each agreement, I assigned yearly values measuring membership of all countries, the explicit[4] adoption of human rights language and principles, and whether the contract specifies that the benefits can be withheld for violations of human rights. I then transformed the data into country-years and assigned a

---

2. Jaggers and Gurr construct a democracy index from five primary institutional features. For a detailed explanation of the data, see http://www.cidcm.umd.edu/inscr/polity/.

3. For complete details of the data, see http://www.correlatesofwar.org/.

4. "Explicit" here refers to those documents using the word "right" or "rights" to refer to human, worker, women, children, migrant, civil, or other rights codified by the United Nations human rights legal regime. I do not include intellectual property rights or other usages of the terms that do not refer to one of the above categories.

TABLE 4
Estimates of human rights protections, 1976 to 2003

Variables	Human rights (coding 1)	Human rights (coding 2)	Instrument model (coding 1)
Hard EU PTA$_{it-1}$	0.418 **	0.441 **	4.514***
	(0.18)	(0.164)	(1.033)
CAT$_{it-1}$	−0.007	0.128	−0.146
	(0.183)	(0.178)	(0.146)
CCPR$_{it-1}$	−0.164	−0.155	−0.332 **
	(0.2)	(0.197)	(0.120)
Human rights floor$_{it-1}$	2.409 ***	3.322 ***	1.058 ***
	(0.238)	(0.234)	(0.150)
Human rights ceiling$_{it-1}$	−2.859 ***	−4.006 ***	−2.023 ***
	(0.319)	(0.372)	(0.238)
Democracy$_{it-1}$	0.077 ***	0.067 ***	0.051 ***
	(0.014)	(0.014)	(0.009)
Durability$_{it-1}$	0.013 ***	0.014 ***	0.013 ***
	(0.003)	(0.004)	(0.002)
Trade$_{it-1}$	0.251	0.472 **	0.193
	(0.175)	(0.166)	(0.133)
pcGDP$_{it-1}$	0.261 **	0.225 **	0.268 ***
	(0.094)	(0.073)	(0.047)
Density$_{it-1}$	−0.464 ***	−0.378 ***	−0.329 ***
	(0.064)	(0.06)	(0.048)
Civil war$_{it-1}$	−1.914 ***	−2.059 ***	−1.920 ***
	(0.309)	(0.327)	(0.170)
N	2651	3271	
Wald chi2	1,061.10 ***	1114.32 ***	
Log likelihood	−4,403.63	−3002.77	2203

Note: +p≤0.1; *p≤0.05; **p≤0.01; ***p≤0.00 calculated from Huber/White standard errors. Numbers in parentheses are percentage change in odds for one unit increase.

single binary value for each outcome.[5] δ_i are fixed effects for time, and e_{it} is a stochastic error term.

The first column of table 4 reports ordered logit estimates predicting countries' protections for human rights using the first coding of human rights, collected by Cingranelli and Richards (1999), while the second column reports estimates of protections for human rights using the alterna-

5. The data are available from http://www.princeton.edu/~ehafner/. Analyses here do not include American PTAs because data on violations of workers' human rights are not yet available past 2003. However, the data set includes information on which of America's PTAs include hard standards of human rights conduct.

tive coding, collected by Poe and Tate (1994) and also Mark Gibney.[6] I report two-tailed test statistics for all parameters calculated using Huber/White standard errors adjusted for correlations of the error terms across observations within each country panel. The third column reports the results of an instrument model, estimated using two-stage least squares, with heteroskedastic and autocorrelation-consistent standard errors. I report small-sample statistics and use the number of intergovernmental organizations, $IGOs_{it-1}$ a country belongs to in a given year, as reported by the Union of International Associations,[7] as an instrument for *Hard EU PTA$_{it-1}$*—this measure predicts reasonably well whether or not a country belongs to a *Hard EU PTA$_{it-1}$* but is not well correlated with *Human Rights$_{it}$*. The Cragg-Donald test (64.47, p<0.00) shows that the instrument is identifiable, while the first-stage F statistics show that the excluded instrument is relevant.

Using the results from column 1 of table 4, I calculate the probabilities that an average country[8] that achieved a score of 0, 1, 2, 3, 4, 5, 6, or 7 on the *Human Rights$_{it}$* scale (using coding 1) will improve *at all* in the next year if they belong to a European PTA with hard human rights standards of conduct compared to if they do not belong. I chart the change in fractional risk between these two probabilities. The findings are reported in figure 1. For instance, the figure shows that countries that achieved a score of 0 for massive human rights violations have a fractional risk of about 9 percent difference. We predict that countries that do not belong to a PTA with Europe that includes hard human rights standards have a probability of making improvements from one year to the next of about 75 percent, while those in such a PTA have a probability of 82 percent. Thus, (82% - 75%)/75% = 9.3%, or about a 9 percent difference. Further statistical analysis is available from Hafner-Burton 2008.

6. The results of estimating using ordered probit and ordinary least squares are the same.

7. For more information, see http://www.uia.be/.

8. All variables in the model are held at their mean except countries' previous levels of human rights protections and their membership in hard PTAs, which are allowed to vary, and civil war, which is set to 0.

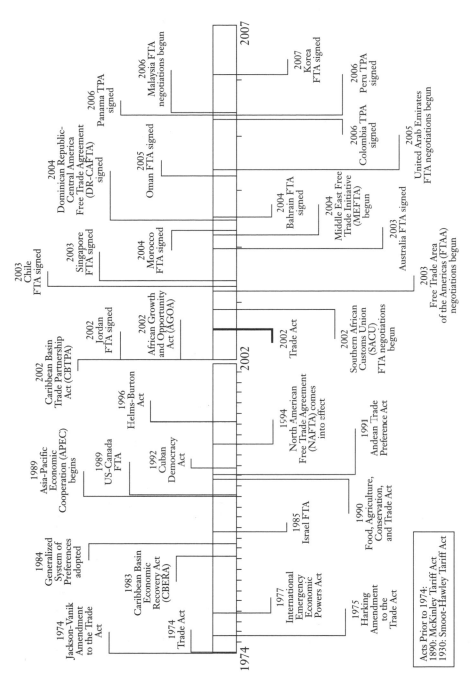

Timeline 1. Trade and human rights: US timeline, 1974–2007

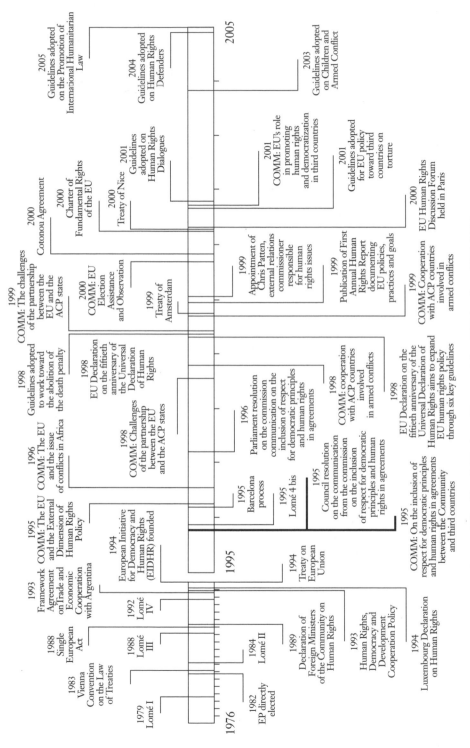

Timeline 2. Trade and human rights: EU timeline, 1976–2005

REFERENCES

Aaronson, Susan A. 2001. *Taking Trade to the Streets: The Lost History of Public Efforts to Shape Globalization*. Ann Arbor: University of Michigan Press.

Aaronson, Susan A., and Jamie M. Zimmerman. 2007. *Trade Imbalance: The Struggle to Weigh Human Rights Concerns in Trade Policymaking*. Cambridge: Cambridge University Press.

Abbott, Kenneth W., and Duncan Snidal. 2000. Hard and Soft Law in International Governance. *International Organization* 54 (3): 421–56.

Abraham, Nabeel , Janice Terry, Cheryl Rubenberg, Lisa Hajjar, and Hilary Shadroui. 1988. International Human Rights Organizations and the Palestine Question. *Middle East Report* 18 (1): 12–20.

Achen, Christopher H. 2006. Institutional Realism and Bargaining Models. In *The European Union Decides*, edited by R. Thomson, F. N. Stokman, C. Achen, and T. Konig. Cambridge: Cambridge University Press.

Ackerman, B. A., and W. T. Hassler. 1981. *Clean Coal/Dirty Air, or How the Clean Air Act Became a Multibillion-Dollar Bail-out for High Sulphur Coal Producers and What Should Be Done About It*. New Haven: Yale University Press.

ACP-EC Convention of Cotonou. 2003. 2000/483/EC: Partnership Agreement between the Members of the African, Caribbean and Pacific Group of States of the One Part, and the European Community and Its Member States, of the Other Part, Signed in Cotonou on 23 June 2000. Official Journal No. L 317, 15/12/2000, pp. 3–381.

ACP-EC Convention of Lomé (I). 1975. Official Journal No. L 025, 30/01/1976 p. 0002–167.

——. (III). 1985. Official Journal No. L 086 , 31/03/1986, p. 3.

——. (VI). 1990. Official Journal No. L 229, 17/08/1991, pp. 0228–300.

——. (IVbis). 1995. Agreement Amending the Fourth ACP-EC Convention of Lomé Signed in Mauritius on 4 November 1995. Official Journal No. L 156, 29/05/1998, pp. 03–106.

AFL-CIO. 2002. NAFTA's Seven-Year Itch: Promised Benefits Not Delivered to Workers 2002. http://www.aflcio.org/mediacenter/resources/reports.cfm.

———. 2006a. Bush Sends Oman Trade Deal to Congress. Coalition Tells Bush to Bag It. 27 June. http://blog.aflcio.org/2006/06/27/bush-sends-oman-trade-deal-to-congress-coalition-tells-bush-to-bag-it/ (accessed 11 April 2007).

———. 2006b. Time For Bold Action on Trade. 27 February. http://www.aflcio.org/aboutus/thisistheaflcio/ecouncil/ec02272006c.cfm (accessed 10 March 2007).

———. 2007a. AFL-CIO: No Trade Deal with Colombia. 16 March. http://blog.aflcio.org/2007/03/16/afl-cio-no-trade-deal-with-colombia/ (accessed 11 April 2007).

———. 2007b. Bush Administration Backpedals on Trade Statement. 18 January. http://blog.aflcio.org/2007/01/18/bush-administration-backpedals-on-trade-statement/ (accessed 11 April 2007).

———. 2007c. Lessons from NAFTA Should Stop Bad Korean Trade Deal. 28 February. http://blog.aflcio.org/2007/02/28/lessons-from-nafta-should-stop-bad-korea-trade-deal/ (accessed 11 April 2007).

Aggarwal, Vinod K., and Edward A. Fogarty, eds. 2004. *EU Trade Strategies: Between Regionalism and Globalism.* New York: Palgrave Macmillan.

ALDE. 2006. The Commission Must Insist on the Respect of Human Rights and International Labour Law. 15 November. http://www.alde.eu/ (accessed 19 April 2007).

———. 2007. ALDE Group and Human Rights. http://www.alde.eu/index.php?id=56 (accessed 19 April 2007).

Alston, Philip, Mara R. Bustelo, and James Heenan, eds. 1999. *The EU and Human Rights.* New York: Oxford University Press.

Alston, Philip, and J. H. H. Weiler. 1999. An "Even Closer Union" in Need of a Human Rights Policy: The European Union and Human Rights. In *The EU and Human Rights*, edited by P. Alston, M. R. Bustelo, and J. Heenan. Oxford: Oxford University Press.

Amnesty International. 1983. Annual Report. London.

———. 2005. Amnesty International Urges WTO Members to Respect Human Rights Obligations in Trade Negotiations in Hong Kong. http://web.amnesty.org/library/index/engior300162005 (accessed 9 December 2005).

———. 2006a. Annual Report. http://web.amnesty.org/report2006/index-eng (accessed 29 May 2007).

———. 2006b. European Union–Latin America & Caribbean Summit, Vienna, Austria—May 2006 Amnesty International's Call for Human Rights. 1 April. http://web.amnesty.org/ (accessed 12 April 2007).

———. 2007. Annual Report.

Anderson, C. A. 1989. Causal Reasoning and Belief Perseverance. In *Proceedings of the Society for Consumer Psychology*, ed. D. W. Schumann. Knoxville: University of Tennessee.

Andreoni, James, and Hal Dagger Varian. 1999. Preplay Contracting in the Prisoners Dilemma. Proceedings of the National Academy of Sciences 96:10933–38.

Arts, Karin. 2000. *Integrating Human Rights into Development Cooperation: The Case of the Lomé Convention*. The Hague: Kluwer Law International.

ASEAN (Association of Southeast Asian Nations). 1993. Joint Communiqué of the Twenty-sixth ASEAN Ministerial Meeting, Singapore, 23–24 July.

———. 1994. Joint Communiqué of the Tenth ASEAN Labour Ministers' Meeting, Singapore, 16–17 May.

Auger, Vincent. 1995. *Human Rights and Trade: The Clinton Administration and China*. Pew Case Studies in International Affairs: Georgetown University Institute.

Australian House of Representatives. 2004. US Free Trade Agreement Implementation Bill 2004. Bills Digest No. 21, Parliamentary Library 23 June.

Baehr, Peter R. 1996. *The Role of Human Rights in Foreign Policy*. London: Macmillan.

Baehr, Peter R., and Monique Castermans-Holleman, eds. 2004. *The Role of Human Rights in Foreign Policy*. 3rd ed. New York: Palgrave Macmillan.

Baier, Scott L., and Jeffrey H. Bergstrade. 2005. Do Free Trade Agreements Actually Increase Members' International Trade? Working Paper 2005-3. Federal Reserve Bank of Atlanta, Working paper series.

Balassa, Bela A. 1961. *The Theory of Economic Integration*. Homewood, Ill.: R.D. Irwin.

Baldwin, Robert E. 2003. *The Decline of US Labor Unions and the Role of Trade*. Washington, D.C.: Institute for International Economics.

Bartels, Lorand. 2003. The WTO Enabling Clause and Positive Conditionality in the European Community's GSP Program. *Journal of International Economic Law* 6:507.

———. 2005. *Human Rights Conditionality in the EU's International Agreements*. Oxford: Oxford University Press.

———. 2007. Social Issues: Labour, Environment and Human Rights. In *Bilateral and Regional Trade Agreements: Commentary, Analysis and Case Studies*, edited by S. Lester and B. Mercurio. Cambridge: Cambridge University Press.

Bass, Gary J. 2000. *Stay the Hand of Vengeance: The Politics of War Crimes Tribunals*. Princeton: Princeton University Press.

Baucus, Max. 2002. A New Trade Policy for New Democrats. Address to the Democratic Leadership Council. 12 February. http://www.ndol.org/(accessed 15 April 2007).

———. 2004. Looking Forward on Trade—The Agenda for 2005. Remarks by U.S. Senator Max Baucus to the Global Business Dialogue. 13 July. http://www.senate.gov/~finance/press/Bpress/2004press/prb071304.pdf(accessed 15 April 2007).

BBC. 2002. Euro MP 'Defects' to Tories. 6 March.http://news.bbc.co.uk/1/hi/uk_politics/1856953.stm (accessed 15 April 2007).

Becker, Geoffrey S., and Charles E. Hanrahan. 2002. Agriculture and Fast Trade or Trade Promotion Authority. Congressional Research Service Issue Brief for Congress 7 November.

Berkovitch, Nitza. 1999. *From Motherhood to Citizenship: Women's Rights and International Organization*: Baltimore: Johns Hopkins University Press.

Bhagwati, Jagdish N. 1988. *Protectionism*. Cambridge, Mass.: MIT Press.

———. 1991. *The World Trading System at Risk*. Princeton: Princeton University Press.

———. 2000. *The Wind of the Hundred Days: How Washington Mismanaged Globalization*. Cambridge, Mass.: MIT Press.

———. 2001. Free Trade and Labor. *Financial Times*, 29 August.

Bhagwati, Jagdish N., Pravin Krishna, and Arvind Panagariya. 1999. *Trading Blocs: Alternative Approaches to Analyzing Preferential Trade Agreements*. Cambridge, Mass.: MIT Press.

Bhagwati, Jagdish N., and Arvind Panagariya. 1996. Preferential Trading Areas and Multilateralism: Strangers, Friends or Foes? In *Free Trade Areas or Free Trade? The Economics of Preferential Trading*, edited by J. N. Bhagwati and A. Panagariya. Washington, D.C.: AEI Press.

Bieber, Roland. 1990. Democratic Control of European Foreign Policy. *European Journal of International Law* 48 (1/2): 148–73.

———. 2003. Free Trade Agreements with Singapore and Chile: Labor Issues. CRS Report for Congress, RS21560, 13 August.

Boli, John, and George M. Thomas. 1999. *Constructing World Culture: International Nongovernmental Organizations Since 1875*. Stanford: Stanford University Press.

Bolle, Mary Jane. 2001. US-Jordan Free Trade Agreement. Congressional Research Service Report for Congress, 25 September.

———. 2002. NAFTA Labor Side Agreement: Lessons for the Worker Rights and Fast-Track Debate. Congressional Research Service Issue Brief for Congress, 11 January.

———. 2003. Free Trade Agreements with Singapore and Chile: Labor Issues. CRS Report for Congress, RS21560, 13 August.

———. 2006. US-Oman Free Trade Agreement. CRS Report for Congress, RL33328, 10 October.

Botswana Press Agency. 2001. Botswana Benefits from Lomé Conventions. 28 August. http://www.gov.bw/cgi-bin/news.cgi?d=20010828 (accessed 15 May 2007).

Bradley, A. 2005. An ACP Perspective and Overview of Article 96 Cases. ECDPM Discussion Paper 64D, Maastricht.

Brainard, Lael, and Hal Shapiro. 2001. Policy Brief #91. Fast Track Trade Promotion Authority. http://www.brookings.edu/comm/policybriefs/pb91.htm.

Brandt, U.S., and G.T. Svendsen. 2002. Hot Air in Kyoto, Cold Air in the Hague: The Failure of Global Climate Change Negotiations. *Energy Policy* 30:1191–99.

Brandtner, Barbara, and Allan Rosas. 1998. Human Rights and the External Relations of the European Community: An Analysis of Doctrine and Practice. *European Journal of International Law* 3 (9): 468–90.

———. 1999. Trade Preferences and Human Rights. In *The EU and Human Rights*, edited by P. Alston, M. R. Bustelo, and J. Heenan. Oxford: Oxford University Press.

Brysk, Alison. 1993. From Above and Below: Social Movements, the International System, and Human Rights in Argentina. *Comparative Political Studies* 26 (3): 259–85.

Buergenthal, Thomas. 1995. *International Human Rights in a Nutshell*. Saint Paul, Minn.: West.

Buirette-Marau, P. 1985. Les Difficultés de l'Internationalisation des Droits de l'Homme à Propos de la Convention Lomé. *Revue Trimestrielle de Droit Européen* 21.

Bulterman, Mielle K. 1998. European Union Membership and Political Conditionality. In *To Baehr in Our Minds*, edited by M. K. Bulterman, A. Hendriks and J. Smith: SIM Special No. 21.Utrecht: Netherlands Institute of Human Rights, University of Utrecht.

Burma Headline News. 1996. PR Newswire December 19. http://www.ibiblio.org/obl/reg.burma/archives/199612/msg00239.html (accessed 15 April 2007).

Bussolo, Maurizio, and Yoko Niimi. 2006. Do Regional Trade Pacts Benefit the Poor? An Illustration from the Dominican Republic-Central American Free Trade Agreement in Nicaragua. World Bank Policy Research Working Paper.

Callan, Eoin. 2006. The Americas: Democrats to Throw Out Colombia Trade Accord. *Financial Times Online*. 9 June.

CalTrade Report. 2004. US, Australia FTA Hits the Wall: Australian Labor Party Blocks Final Approval of Trade Pact. 8 December.

Cameron, Maxwell A., and Brian W. Tomlin. 2000. *The Making of NAFTA: How the Deal Was Done*. Ithaca: Cornell University Press.

Camp Keith, Linda. 1999. The United Nations International Covenant on Civil and Political Rights: Does It Make a Difference in Human Rights Behavior? *Journal of Peace Research* 36 (1): 95–118.

Charnovitz, Steven. 1987. The Influence of International Labour Standards on the World Trading System: A Historical Overview. *International Labour Review* 126 (5): 565–84.

Cheysson, Claude. 1981. An Interview with Claude Cheysson. *Time*. 29 June.

Cingranelli, David L., and David L. Richards. 1999. Measuring the Level, Pattern, and Sequence of Government Respect for Physical Integrity Rights. *International Studies Quarterly* 43 (2): 407–18.

Clapham, Andrew. 1991. *The Human Rights Challenge*, vol. 1, Human Rights and the European Community: A Critical Overview. Baden-Baden: Nomos.

Cleveland, Sarah H. 2001a. Human Rights Sanctions and the World Trade Organization. In *Environment, Human Rights and International Trade*, edited by F. Francioni. Portland, Ore.: Hart Publishing.

——. 2001b. Norm Internalization and U.S. Economic Sanctions. *Yale Journal of International Law* 26:1–102.

Cohen, Michael D., James G. March, and Johan P. Olsen. 1972. A Garbage Can Model of Organizational Choice. *Administrative Science Quarterly* 17 (1): 1–25.

Colvin, Madeline, and P. Noorlander. 1998. Human Rights and Accountability after the Treaty of Amsterdam. *European Human Rights Law Review*: 191–203.

Compa, Lance, and Jeffrey S. Vogt. 2005. Labor Rights in the Generalized System of Preferences: A 20-Year Review. *Comparative Labor Law and Policy Journal* 22:199–238.

Confederation of European Business. 2006. UNICE Strategy on an EU Approach to Free Trade Agreements. 7 December. http://www.bilaterals.org/article .php3?id_article=7265 (accessed 11 April 2007).

———. 2007. Working Together for an Ambitious EU-India Trade and Investment Agreement. 17 January. http://www.bilaterals.org/article.php3?id_article=7300 (accessed 11 April 2007).

Conroy, Stephen. 2004. Trading Australia Away. An Address to the ALP Grayndler Forum by Senator Stephen Conroy, Labor Shadow Trade Minister, 13 November.

Cooper, William H. 2005. Free Trade Agreements: Impact on US Trade and Implications for US Trade Policy. Congressional Research Service Issue Brief for Congress, 12 January.

Cottier, Thomas. 2002. Trade and Human Rights: A Relationship to Discover. *Journal of International Economic Law vol. 5(1)*: 111–132.

Council of the European Union. 1976. Council Regulation (EEC) No. 199/76 of 30 January on the Conclusion of the ACP-EEC Convention of Lomé. Official Journal No. L 025, 30/01/1976. p. 0001.

———. 1980. Council Regulation (EEC) No. 3225/80 on the Conclusion of the Second ACP-EEC Convention Signed at Lomé on 31 October 1979. Official Journal No. L 347, 22/12/1980, p. 0001.

———. 1986. Third ACP-EEC Convention. Official Journal No. L 086, 31/03/1986, p. 0003.

———. 1990. Décision du Conseil Concernant la Conclusion de l'Accord-cadre de Coopération Commerciale et Économique Européenne et la République Argentine. Journal Officiel des Communautés Européennes, L 295/66 8 octobre.

———. 1991. Framework Agreement for Cooperation between the European Economic Community and the Republic of Chile. Offical Journal L 079, 26/03/1991. P.0001.

———. 1990b. Framework Agreement for Trade and Economic Cooperation between the European Economic Community and the Argentine Republic—Exchange of Letters. Official Journal No. L 295, 26/10/1990. pp. 0067–0073.

———. 1991a. Fourth ACP-EEC Convention. Official Journal No. L 229, 17/08/1991, pp. 0003–0280.

———. 1991b. European Union Council of Ministers (1991), *Resolution of the Council and of the Member States meeting in the Council on Human Rights, Democracy and Development*, 28 November 1991 [Doc. no. 10107/91] (European Commission, Brussels).

———. 1992a. Agreement between the European Economic Community and the Republic of Albania, on Trade and Commercial and Economic Cooperation. Official Journal No. L 343, 25/11/1992, pp. 0002–0009.

——. 1992b. Declaration: On Respect for Democratic Principles, Human Rights and the Principles of Market Economy. 6326/92 (Press 71G) 11 May.

——. 1992c. Framework Agreement for Cooperation between the European Economic Community and the Eastern Republic of Uruguay. Official Journal No. L 094, 08/04/1992, pp. 0002–0012.

——. 1992d. Framework Agreement for Cooperation between the European Economic Community and the Republic of Paraguay. Official Journal No. L 313, 30/10/1992, pp. 0072–0081.

——. 1994. Agreement on the European Economic Area Between the European Communities, Their Member States and the Republic of Austria, the Republic of Finland, the Republic of Iceland, the Principality of Liechtenstein, the Kingdom of Norway, the Kingdom of Sweden and the Swiss Confederation. Official Journal No. L 1/1, 3/1/1994. p. 606.

——. 2001. Council Decision: On the Principles, Priorities, Intermediate Objectives and Conditions Contained in the Accession Partnership with the Republic of Turkey. Official Journal No. L 85,24/3/2001. p. 13.

——. 2006. Council Decision Amending Decision 2004/793/EC. Official Journal No. L/2006 13/11/2006, pp.335.

Courier. 1979. No. 58 (November).

Cox, Gary. 1987. Electoral Equilibrium under Alternative Voting Institutions. *American Journal of Political Science* 31:82–108.

Currie, Duncan. 2006. Learning to Love Charlie Rangel. 17 November. http://www.american.com/archive/2006/november/charlie-rangel (accessed 14 April 2007).

De Santis, Roberta, and Claudio Vicarelli. 2006. The European Union Trade Strategy: An Empirical Evaluation of Preferential Trade Agreements' Effects on EU Import Flows. Working Paper. Presented at the Eighth Annual Conference WIIW and Universitat, 7–9 September.

DeSombre, Elizabeth. 2000. *Domestic Sources of International Environmental Policy: Industry, Environmentalists, and U.S. Power.* Cambridge, Mass.: MIT Press.

Destler, I. M. 1986. *American Trade Politics: System under Stress.* Washington, D.C.: Institute for International Business.

——. 1995. *American Trade Politics.* Washington, D.C.: Institute for International Economics.

Destler, I. M., and Peter J. Balint. 1999. *The New Politics of American Trade: Trade, Labor, and the Environment.* Washington, D.C.: Institute for International Economics.

DiCaprio, Alisa. 2005. Are Labor Provisions Protectionist? Evidence from Nine Labor-Augmented U.S. Trade Arrangements. *Comparative Labor Law and Policy Journal* 26 (1): 1–34.

Domke, Michelle D. 1997. Turkey's Human Rights Record Impedes European Integration. *The Human Rights Brief* 4 (2). http://www.wcl.american.edu/hrbrief/v4i3/index43.htm.

Donnelly, Jack. 1986. International Human Rights: A Regime Analysis. *International Organization* 40:599–642.

Dorsey, Ellen. 2000. U.S. Foreign Policy and the Human Rights Movement. In *The United States and Human Rights: Looking Inward and Outward*, edited by D. P. Forsythe. Lincoln: University of Nebraska Press.

Dowlah, Caf. 2004. *Backwaters of Global Prosperity: How Forces of Globalization and GATT/WTO Trade Regimes Contribute to the Marginalization of the World's Poorest Nations*. Westport, Conn.: Praeger.

Downs, George W., David M. Rocke, and Peter N. Barsoom. 1996. Is the Good News about Compliance Good News about Cooperation? *International Organization* 50 (3): 379–406.

Drake, Helen. 2000. *Jaques Delors: Perspectives on a European Leader*. London: Routledge.

Drezner, Daniel W. 2003. The Hidden Hand of Economic Coercion. *International Organization* 57 (3): 643–59.

———. 2006. U.S. Trade Strategy: Free versus Fair. Washington D.C. Council on Foreign Relations. http://www.cfr.org/publication/11184/.

———. 2007. *All Politics Is Global: Explaining International Regulatory Regimes*. Princeton: Princeton University Press.

Drydan, Steve. 1995. *Trade Warriors: USTR and the American Crusade for Free Trade*. New York: Oxford University Press.

Dulitzky, Ariel E. 1999. Book review of *The Inter-American Human Rights System* by Scott Davidson. *European Journal of International Law* 10 (2): 555.

Eaton, Jonathan, and Maxim Engers. 1999. Sanctions: Some Simply Analytics. *American Economic Review* 98 (2): 409–14.

Eccleston, Roy. 2004. US Unions Condemn Trade Deal. *The Australian*, 18 March.

Elgstrom, Ole. 2000. Lomé and Post-Lomé: Asymmetric Negotiations and the Impact of Norms. *European Foreign Affairs Review* 5:175–95.

Elliot, Kimberly Ann, and Richard B. Freeman. 2003a. *Can Labor Standards Improve under Globalization?* Washington, D.C.: Institute for International Economics.

———. 2003b. White Hats or Don Quixotes: Human Rights Vigilantes in the Global Economy. In *Emerging Labor Market Institutions for the 21st Century*, edited by R. B. Freeman, J. Hersch, and L. Mishel. Chicago: University of Chicago Press for the National Bureau of Economic Research.

EPP-ED. 1999. EPP Action Programme 1999–2004 (adopted by the XIII EPP Congress, 4–6 February 1999, Brussels): On the Way to the 21st Century. http://www.epp-ed.eu/Press/peve99/eve001-final_en.asp (accessed 14 April 2007).

EurActiv. 2006. Business and Trade Unions Debate Future Trade Strategy. 14 November. http://www.euractiv.com/en/trade/businesses-trade-unions-debate-future-trade-strategy/article-159649 (accessed 11 April 2007).

Eurobarometer. 1987. Relations with Third World Countries, and Energy Problems. No. 28 (November). http://www.esds.ac.uk/findingData/snDescription.asp?sn=2694.

——. 1995a. Standard Eurobaroeter 43 (Autumn). http://ec/europa.edu/public_opinion/archives/eb/eb43/eb43_en.htm.

——. 1995b. The First Year of the New European Union. No. 42 (Spring).

——. 1996. Modern Technology, Piracy on Computer Networks, and the European Common Currency. (October–November): 146.

European Commission. 1979. Ministerial Conference Opening the Negotiations of the New ACP-EEC Convention. Doc. ACP/EEC, 95-e/78.

——. 1991. Human Rights, Democracy and Development Cooperation Policy. Commission Communication to the Council and Parliament. SEC (61)91 of 25 March.

——. 1995. Communication: On the Inclusion of Respect for Democratic Principles and Human Rights in Agreements between the Community and Third Countries. COM (95)216 of 23 May.

——. 1997. Agenda 2000—Commission Opinion on Slovakia's Application for Membership in the European Union. Doc 97/20.

——. 1999. Regular Report from the Commission on Slovakia's Progress Towards Accession.

——. 2001. Communication from the Commission to the Council, the European Parliament and the Economic and Social Committee on "Promoting Core Labour Standards and Improving Social Governance in the Context of Globalisation." COM (2001) 416 final of 18 July.

——. 2003. Comprehensive Monitoring Report on Slovakia's Preparations for Membership.

——. 2004a. Communication from the Commission to the Council concerning the Opening of Consultations with Côte d'Ivoire under Article 96 of the Cotonou Agreement. COM (2004) 547 final of 10 August.

——. 2004b. Communication from the Commission to the Council concerning the Opening of Consultations with the Togolese Republic under Article 96 of the Cotonou Agreement. COM (2003) 850 final of 8 January.

——. 2004c. Togo—Commission Proposes "Roadmap" towards the Full Resumption of EU Aid. *European World*, 3 September.

——. 2005a. Communication From the Commission to the Council on the Opening of Consultations with Mauritania under Article 96 of the Cotonou Agreement. COM (2005) 546 final of 28 October.

——. 2005b. Communication from the Commission: 2005 Enlargement Strategy Paper. COM (2005) 561 final of 9 November.

——. 2006a. Proposal for a Council Decision concerning the Conclusion of Consultations with the Islamic Republic of Mauritania under Article 96 of the Revised Cotonou Agreement. Brussels, COM (2005) 166 final of 10 April.

——. 2006b. Turkey 2006 Progress Report. COM (2006) 649 final, SEC(2006) 1390 of 8 November.

European Council. 1990. Framework Agreement for Trade and Economic Cooperation between European Economic Community and the Argentina Republic. Official Journal No. L 295, 26/10/1990, pp. 0067–0073.

European Court of Justice. 1987. C-45/86 Commission v. Council, [1987] ECR 1493.

——. 1996a. Case C-149/96 Portugal v. Council [1999] ECR I-8395.

——. 1996b. Opinion 2/94 of 28 March. Accession of the Community to the European Convention for the Protection of Human Rights and Fundamental Freedoms. [1996] ECR I-1763.

European Parliament. 1977. Written Question No. 941/76 by Mr. van de Hek to the Council of the European Communities "on the human rights situation in Uganda" in Official Journal No. C 214, 7/09/1977.

——. 1978a. Report of the European Parliament on the Negotiations for a New Lomé Convention. Working Documents 1978–1979. Doc. 478/78, PE 54.5767, 1/12/1978.

——. 1978b. Written Question No. 943/77 by Mr. Adams to the Commission of the European Communities on "The Central African Empire" in Official Journal No. C 74/17. 28/3/1978.

——. 1980a. Written Question No 748/79 by Mr. Glinne to the Commission of the European Communities. Official Journal No C 80/5, 10/10/1979.

——. 1980b. Written Question No 1154/79 by Mr. Habsburg to the Commission of the European Communities. Official Journal No. C 74/43, 23/11/1979.

——. 1980c. Written Question No 1433/79 by Miss Flesch to the Council of the European Communities. Official Journal No. C 131/19, 3/1/1980.

——. 1980d. Written Question No. 1079/79 by Mr. Gendebien to the Commission of the European Communities on "Human Rights in Zaire" in Official Journal No. C 49/47, of 27/2/1980.

——. 1983. Resolution: On Human Rights in the World. Official Journal No. C 161/1, 20/6/1983.

——. 1984a. Resolution: On the Creation of a Framework for Dialogue to Foster Observance of Internally Accepted Standards of Human Rights in the European Community and Those Countries with Which It Has Close Ties. Official Journal No. C 127/126, 14/5/1984.

——. 1984b. Written Question Mrs. Emma Bonino and Mr. Marco Pannella to the Council of the European Communities. Official Journal No. C 78/19, 4/1/1984.

——. 1985. On Human Rights in the World for the Year 1984 and the Community Policy on Human Rights. Official Journal No. C 343/38, 31/12/1985.

——. 1986. Written Question No 3157/85 by Mr Gijs de Vries to the Commission of the European Communities. Official Journal No. C 290/20, 24/3/1986.

——. 1987. Memorandum: On the Action Taken in the Field of Human Rights Within the Framework of the European Political Co-operation. Drafted by the Group of the European People's Party of the European Parliament, European Centre Kirchberg, Luxembourg, 27 May.

——. 1992a. Written Question No 242/92 by Mr. Henri Saby to the Council of the European Communities. Official Journal No. C 202/43, 13/2/1992.

——. 1992b. Written Question No 1202/92 by Mr. Henri Saby to the Council of the European Communities. Official Journal No. C 247/49, 21/5/1992.

——. 1993. Written Question No. 10 by Mr. Balfe (H-0734/93).

———. 1996. Report on the Communication from the Commission on the Inclusion of Respect for Democratic Principles and Human Rights in Agreements between the Community and Third Countries. COM(95)0216—C4–0197/95. 26 June. http://www.europarl.europa.eu/.

———. 1998. News Report: Hans van den Broek Answers MEPs' Questions on Malta and Uzbekistan. 29 September. http://www.europarl.europa.eu/press/sdp/newsrp/en/1998/n980929.htm (accessed 16 April 2007).

———. 2001. European Parliament Resolution on Côte d'Ivoire. Official Journal No. C 232/357, 18/8/2001.

———. 2006. On Turkey's Progress towards Accession. Report (2006/2118(INI)) Committee on Foreign Affairs.

European Report. 1997. EU/Australia: Minister Fails to Solve Wrangle on Human Rights Clause. 1 February.

European Trade Union Confederation. 2004a. ETUC and External Relations. http://www.etuc.org/a/660?var_recherche=free+trade (accessed 11 April 2007).

———. 2004b. Observations by the European Trade Union Confederation Concerning the Communication from the Commission: The Fundamental Rights Agency. 25 October. http://ec.europa.eu/justice_home/news/consulting_public/fundamental_rights_agency/doc/contribution_etuc_en.pdf(accessed 10 March 2007).

———. 2004c. Trade Union Statement to the EU-US Summit. 25 June. http://www.etuc.org/a/656?var_recherche=%22human+rights%22 (accessed 11 April 2007).

———. 2005a. ETUC Is Very Pleased to See the European Union Opening Its Doors to Turkey but Emphasises That Turkey Must Respect Fundamental Rights. 4 October. http://www.etuc.org/a/1588?var_recherche=+%22human+rights%22+clause (accessed 11 April 2007).

———. 2005b. The WTO Conference Must Take Account of Fundamental Rights and Employment. 15 December. http://www.etuc.org/a/1877?var_recherche=%22human+rights%22(accessed 11 April 2007).

Federation of European Employers. 2007. Trade Unions across Europe. http://www.fedee.com/tradeunions.html (accessed 19 April 2007).

Fergusson, Ian F., and Lenore Sek. 2005. Trade Negotiations During the 109th Congress. Report for Congress, Congressional Research Service, 3 May.

———. 2004. Trade Negotiations in the 108th Congress. CRS Issue Brief for Congress, 6 April.

Fierro, Elena. 2001. Legal Basis and Scope of the Human Rights Clauses in EC Bilateral Agreements: Any Room for Positive Interpretation? *European Law Journal* 7 (1): 41–68.

———. 2003. *The EU's Approach to Human Rights Conditionality in Practice.* The Hague: Martinus Nijhoff Publishers.

Finnemore, Martha. 1996. *National Interests in International Society.* Ithaca: Cornell University Press.

Finnemore, Martha, and Kathryn Sikkink. 1998. International Norm Dynamics and Political Change. *International Organization* 52 (4): 887–917.

Forsythe, David P. 2000. *Human Rights in International Relations*. Cambridge: Cambridge University Press.

Franck, Thomas M. 1990. *The Power of Legitimacy among Nations*. New York: Oxford University Press.

Frank, David John, Ann Hironaka, and Evan Schofer. 2000. The Nation-State and the Natural Environment. *American Sociological Review* 65 (1): 96–116.

Frankel, Jeffrey A., Ernesto Stein, and Shang-Jin Wei. 1997. Regional Trading Blocs in the World Economic System. Washington, D.C.: Institute for International Economics.

Frieden, Jeffry A. 1992. *Debt, Development, and Democracy*. Princeton: Princeton University Press.

Frisch, Dieter. 1985. Lomé III: Living through Difficult Negotiations. *Courier*, no. 89 (January—February): 19–20.

———. 1997. The Political Dimensions of Lomé. *Courier*, no. 166.

Garnick, Laura, and Carol Cosgrove Twichett. 1979. Human Rights and a Successor to the Lomé Convention. *International Relations* 3 (6): 540–57.

Garrett, Geoffrey. 1992. International Cooperation and Institutional Choice: The European Community's Internal Market. *International Organization* 46 (2): 533–60.

Garrett, Geoffrey, and George Tsebelis. 1996. An Institutional Critique of Intergovernmentalism. *International Organization* 50:269–99.

Gillies, David. 1996. *Between Principle and Practice: Human Rights in North-South Relations*. Montreal: McGill-Queen's University Press.

Gilpin, Robert. 1981. *War and Change in World Politics*. Cambridge: Cambridge University Press.

———. 1987. *The Political Economy of International Relations*. Princeton: Princeton University Press.

Golub, Jonathan. 1999. In the Shadow of the Vote? Decision Making in the European Community. *International Organization* 53 (4): 733–64.

Gonzalez, Carlos Carnero. 1996. Report on the Communication from the Commission on the Inclusion of Respect for Democratic Principles and Human Rights in Agreements between the Community and Third Countries. COM(95)0-216—C4–0197/95. 26 June. http://www.europarl.europa.eu/ (accessed 15 April 2007).

Goodin, Robert E., ed. 1996. *The Theory of Institutional Design*. New York: Cambridge University Press.

Goodman, Peter. 2007. Democrats, White House Clash on Trade. *Washington Post*, 15 February.

Goodman, Ryan, and Derek Jinks. 2003a. Measuring the Effects of Human Rights Treaties. *European Journal of International Law* 14 (1): 171–83.

———. 2003b. Mechanisms of Social Influence and Regime Design in Human Rights Law: Toward a Sociological Theory of International Law. Working Paper.

Gowa, Joanne. 1994. *Allies, Adversaries, and International Trade*. Princeton: Princeton University Press.

Gowa, Joanne, and Soo Young Kim. 2005. An Exclusive Country Club: The Effects of the GATT on Trade, 1950–1994. *World Politics* 57 (4): 453–78.

Gresser, Edward. 2001. The U.S.-Chile Free Trade Agreement: Concrete Benefits, Strategic Value. http://www.ppionline.org/.

Grieco, Joseph. 1988. Anarchy and Limits of Cooperation: A Realist Critique of the Newest Liberal Institutionalism. *International Organization* 42:485–507.

———. 1997. Systemic Sources of Variation in Regional Institutionalization in Western Europe, East Asia, and the Americas. In *The Political Economy of Regionalism*, edited by E. D. Mansfield and H. V. Milner. New York: Columbia University Press.

Grimmett, Jeanne J. 2003. Enforcement Aspects of Labor and Environment Provisions of US Free Trade Agreements with Jordan, Singapore, and Chile: Summary and Chart. CRS General Distribution Memo 1, July.

Griswold, Daniel T. 2004. A Cause Endures: Gephardt Is Out. Is Protectionism In? *National Review*. 9 February.

Grossman, Gene M., and Elhanan Helpman. 1994. Protection for Sale. *American Economic Review* 84 (September): 833–50.

———. 1995. The Politics of Free Trade Agreements. *American Economic Review* 85:667–90.

European Election Study Group. 1996. European Election Study 1994.

Gruber, Lloyd. 2000. *Ruling the World: Power Politics and the Rise of Supranational Institutions*. Princeton: Princeton University Press.

Haas, Ernst. 1958. *The Uniting of Europe*. Stanford: Stanford University Press.

Hafner-Burton, Emilie M. 2005. Trading Human Rights: How Preferential Trade Arrangements Influence Government Repression. *International Organization* 59 (3): 593 629.

Hafner-Burton, Emilie M., Edward D. Mansfield, and Jon C. Pevehouse. 2008. Democratization and Human Rights Organizations. Unpublished manuscript.

Hafner-Burton, Emilie M., and Kiyoteru Tsutsui. 2005. Human Rights in a Globalizing World: The Paradox of Empty Promises. *American Journal of Sociology* 110 (5): 1373–1411.

———. 2007. Justice Lost! The Failure of International Human Rights Law to Matter Where Needed Most. *Journal of Peace Research* 44 (4): 407–25. Special issue, *Preventing Human Rights Abuse*, ed. Emilie M. Hafner-Burton and James Ron.

———. 2008. Marketing Justice: Trade, Aid, and Human Rights. Unpublished manuscript.

Hafner-Burton, Emilie M., Kiyoteru Tsutsui, and John W. Meyer. 2008. International Human Rights Law and the Politics of Legitimation: Repressive States and Human Rights Treaties. *International Sociology* 23 (1): 115–41.

Haggard, Stephan, and Beth A. Simmons. 1987. Theories of International Regimes. *International Organization* 41 (3): 491–517.

Hall, Kevin G. 2000. Chilean President Seeks to Overhaul Labor Laws: 6% Economic Growth Expected. *Miami Herald*. 14 March.

Hansson, Gote. 1983. *Social Clauses and International Trade*. New York: St. Martin's Press.

Hathaway, Oona A. 2002. Do Human Rights Treaties Make a Difference? *The Yale Law Journal* 111:1935–2042.

——. 2005. The Promise and Limits of the International Law of Torture. In *Foundations of International Law and Politics*, edited by O. A. Hathaway and H. H. Koh. New York: Foundation Press.

Hayes-Renshaw, F., and Helen Wallace. 1995. Executive Power in the European Union: The Functions and Limits of the Council of Ministers. *Journal of European Public Policy* 2:559–82.

Hazelzet, Hadewych. 2001. Carrots or Sticks? EU and US Reactions to Human Rights Violations (1989–2000). PhD diss., European University Institute, Florence.

Helfand, Steven M. 2000. Interest Groups and Economic Policy: Explaining the Patterns of Protection in the Brazilian Agriculture Sector. *Contemporary Economic Policy* 18 (4): 462–76.

Helfer, Laurence R. 1999. Forum Shopping for Human Rights. *University of Pennsylvania Law Review* 148 (2): 285–400.

Helfer, Laurence R., and Anne-Marie Slaughter. 1997. Toward a Theory of Effective Supranational Adjudication. *Yale Law Journal* 107:273–391.

Henderson, Conway W. 1991. Conditions Affecting the Use of Political Repression. *Journal of Conflict Resolution* 35:120–142.

Henkin, Louis. 1979. *How Nations Behave: Law and Foreign Policy*. 2d ed. New York: Columbia University Press.

Herzstein, Robert E. 1995. Labor Cooperation Agreement among Mexico, Canada, and the United States: Its Negotiation and Prospects. *US-Mexican Law Journal* 3:121–31.

Hills, Carla A. 2005. US Trade Priorities. http://www.cfr.org/ (accessed 4 May 2007).

Hinich, Melvin J., and Michael C. Munger. 1997. *Analytical Politics*. New York: Cambridge University Press.

Hirschman, Albert O. [1945] 1980. *National Power and the Structure of Foreign Trade*. Berkeley: University of California Press.

——. 1970. *Exit Voice and Loyalty: Responses to Decline in Firms, Organizations, and States*. Cambridge, Mass.: Harvard University Press.

Hix, Simon. 1999. *The Political System of the European Union*. London: Palgrave Macmillan.

Hoffman, Stanley. 1981. *Duties beyond Borders: On the Limits and Possibilities of Ethical International Politics*. Syracuse: Syracuse University Press.

Holsti, Ole. 2000. Public Opinion on Human Rights in American Foreign Policy. In *The United States and Human Rights: Looking Inward and Outward*, edited by D. P. Forsythe. Lincoln: University of Nebraska Press.

Hornbeck, J. F. 2003. The U.S.-Chile Free Trade Agreement: Economic and Trade Policy Issues. CRS Report for Congress, RL31144, 25 July.

Horng, Der-Chen. 2003. The Human Rights Clause in the European Union's External Trade and Development Agreements. *European Law Journal* 9:677–701.

Howard, Rhoda, and Jack Donnelly. 1986. Human Dignity, Human Rights, and Political Regimes. American Political Science Review 80:801–18.

Howse, Robert. 2002. Human Rights in the WTO: Whose Rights, What Humanity? Comment on Petersmann. *European Journal of International Law* 13 (3): 651–59.

Howse, Robert, and Makau Mutua. 2000. Protecting Human Rights in a Global Economy: Challenges for the World Trade Organization. International Centre for Human Rights and Democratic Development, Montreal, Quebec.

Hufbauer, Gary. 2007. Policy Council Q&A on Free Trade with Gary Hufbauer. http://policycouncil.nationaljournal.com/ (accessed 13 April 2007).

Hufbauer, Gary, Diane T. Berliner, and Kimberly Ann Elliot. 1986. *Trade Protectionism in the United States: 31 Case Studies*. Washington, D.C.: Institute for International Economics.

Hufbauer, Gary, and Jeffrey J. Schott. 2005. *NAFTA Revisited: Achievements and Challenges*. Washington, D.C.: Institute for International Economics.

Hufbauer, Gary, Jeffrey J. Schott, and Kimberly Ann Elliott. 1990. *Economic Sanctions Reconsidered*. 2nd ed. Washington, D.C.: Institute for International Economics.

Hufbauer, Gary Clyde, and Ben Goodrich. 2004. Lessons from NAFTA. In *Free Trade Agreements: US Strategies and Priorities*, edited by J. J. Schott. Washington, D.C.: Institute for International Economics.

Hufbauer, Gary Clyde, and Jeffrey J. Schott. 2002. *North American Labor under NAFTA*. Washington, D.C.: Institute for International Economics.

Human Rights Watch. 2000. Turkey: Human Rights and the European Union Accession Partnership. Report 12 (10(D)).

———. 2001. Côte D'Ivoire: The New Racism. The Political Manipulation of Ethnicity in Côte d'Ivoire. Report 13 (6[A]).

Human Rights Watch. 2002. Trade Ministers Urged to Protect Labor Rights in FTAA. 30 October. http://www.hrw.org/press/2002/10/ftaa-labor1030.htm (accessed 12 March 2007).

———. 2004. CAFTA's Weak Labor Rights Protections: Why the Present Accord Should Be Opposed. http://hrw.org/english/docs/2004/03/09/usint8099.htm (accessed 13 March 2007).

———. 2005. United States: Accept Andean Proposal to Add Non-Discrimination Provision to U.S.-Andean Free Trade Agreement: Letter to United States Trade Representative Robert Portman. 6 September. http://hrw.org/english/docs/2005/09/06/usint11670.htm (accessed 12 March 2007).

———. 2006a. EU Rejects Trade Pact With Turkmenistan Over Rights Abuses. 4 October. http://www.hrw.org/english/docs/2006/10/04/turkme14321.htm.

———. 2006b. Labor Rights and Trade: Guidance for the United States in Trade Accord Negotiations. http://hrw.org/press/2002/10/laborrights-bck.htm (accessed 12 April 2007).

Ikenberry, John G. 2001. *After Victory: Institutions, Strategic Restraint, and the Rebuilding of Order After Major Wars*. Princeton: Princeton University Press.

International Confederation of Free Trade Unions. 2004. A Trade Union Guide to Globalization. 2nd ed. http://www.icftu.org/pubs/globalisation/globguide.html (accessed 11 April 2007).

Jackson, Matthew O., and Simon Wilkie. 2005. Endogenous Games and Mechanisms: Side Payments Among Players. *Review of Economic Studies* 72 (2): 543–66.

James, Barry. 1999. Panel Condemns Conduct of European Commission. *International Herald Tribune*. 16 March.

Jepperson, Ronald, Alexander Wendt, and Peter J. Katzenstein. 1996. Norms, Identity, and Culture in National Security. In *The Culture of National Security*, ed. P. J. Katzenstein. New York: Columbia University Press.

Johnson, Jo. 2007. EU-India Trade Pact Stumbles. *Financial Times*. 4 March.

Johnston, Iain Alastair. 2001. Treating International Institutions as Social Environments. *International Studies Quarterly* 45 (4): 487–516.

Jupille, Joseph. 1999. The European Union and International Outcomes. *International Organization* 53 (2): 409–25.

Kahler, Miles, and David A. Lake. 2003. *Governance in a Global Economy: Political Authority in Transition*. Princeton: Princeton University Press.

Kaminga, Menno. 1989. Human Rights and the Lomé Conventions. *Netherlands Quarterly of Human Rights* 1: 28–35.

Karol, David. 2000. Divided Government and U.S. Trade Policy: Much Ado About Nothing? *International Organization* 54 (4): 825–44.

Katzmann, Robert A., ed. 1998. *Daniel Patrick Moynihan: The Intellectual in Public Life*. Baltimore: John Hopkins University Press.

Kaufman, Robert, and Alex Segura-Ubiergo. 2001. Globalization, Domestic Politics, and Social Spending in Latin America: A Time-Series Cross-Section Analysis, 1973–1997. *World Politics* 53 (4): 553–87.

Keck, Margaret E., and Kathryn Sikkink. 1998. *Activists beyond Borders: Advocacy Networks in International Politics*. Ithaca: Cornell University Press.

Keohane, Robert O. 1984. *After Hegemony: Cooperation and Discord in the World Political Economy*. Princeton: Princeton University Press.

———. 1989. *International Institutions and State Power : Essays in International Relations Theory*. Boulder, Colo.: Westview Press.

Kerr, Clark. 1983. *The Future of Industrial Societies: Convergence of Continuing Diversity?* Cambridge, Mass.: Harvard University Press.

Khagram, Sanjeev, James V. Riker, and Kathryn Sikkink, eds. 2002. *Restructuring World Politics: Transnational Social Movements, Networks, and Norms*. Minneapolis: University of Minnesota Press.

King, Toby. 1997. Human Rights in the Development Policy of the European Community: Towards a European World Order. *Netherlands Yearbook of International Law* XXVIII. Kluwer Law International, Netherlands.

———. 1999. Human Rights in European Foreign Policy: Success or Failure for Post-Modern Diplomacy? *European Journal of International Law* 10 (2): 313–37.

Kirkpatrick, Jeanne. 1979. Dictatorships and Double Standards. *Commentary* 68:34–45.

Knodt, Michele, and Sabastian Princen. 2003. *Understanding the European Union's External Relations.* ECPR Studies in European Political Science. London: Routledge.

Koblanck, Maria. 2003. What's in a Human Rights Clause? Its Development, Its Application, and an Insight into the Construct of a European Identity. E.MA. in *Human Rights and Democratisation*, KU Leuven June.

Koffler, Keith. 2007. Trade: Hopes Dimming for Quick Agreement on Labor Language. 30 March. http://nationaljournal.com/ (accessed 13 April 2007).

Koh, Harold Hongju. 1996–97. Why Do Nations Obey International Law? *Yale Law Journal* 106:2599–2659.

Koorney, Jonathan, and Florentin Krause. 1997. Introduction to Environmental Externality Costs. In *CRC Handbook on Energy Efficiency. Boca Raton, Fla.: CRC Press.*

Korey, William. 1998. *NGO's and the Universal Declaration of Human Rights: A Curious Grapevine.* New York: Palgrave Macmillan.

Kormenos, Barbara, Charles Lipson, and Duncan Snidal. 2001. The Rational Design of International Institutions. *International Organization* 55 (4): 761–99.

——, eds. 2004. *The Rational Design of International Institutions.* Cambridge: Cambridge University Press.

Korte, Joost. 1990. Human Rights and the Fourth ACP-EEC Convention (Lomé IV). *Netherlands Quarterly of Human Rights* 3: 292–97.

Kramer, Gerald. 1972. Sophisticated Voting over Multidimensional Choice Spaces. *Journal of Mathematical Sociology* 2:165–80.

Krasner, Stephen D., ed. 1983. *International Regimes.* Ithaca: Cornell University Press.

Krehbiel, Keith. 1998. *Pivotal Politics: A Theory of US Lawmaking.* Chicago: University of Chicago Press.

——. 2004. Pivots. Research Paper No. 1865(R) October. Stanford University.

Krueger, Alan B. 1996. Observations on International Labor Standards and Trade. National Bureau of Economic Research Working Paper 5632.

Krugman, Paul. 1991. Is Bilateralism Bad? In *International Trade and Trade Policy*, edited by E. Helpman and A. Razin. Cambridge, Mass.: MIT Press.

——. 1993. Regionalism versus Multilateralism: Analytical Notes. In *New Dimensions in Regional Integration*, edited by J. de Melo and A. Panagariya. New York: Cambridge University Press.

Kumado, Kofi. 1993. Conditionality: An Analysis of the Policy of Linking Development Aid to the Implementation of Human Rights Standards. *Review of the International Commission of Jurists* 50: 23–30.

Kupchan, Charles A. 1997. Regionalizing Europe's Security: The Case for a New Mitteleuropa. In *The Political Economy of Regionalism*, edited by E. D. Mansfield and H. V. Milner. New York: Columbia University Press.

Kuyper, Pieter Jan. 1993. Trade Sanctions, Security and Human Rights. In *The European Community's Commercial Policy after 1992: The Legal Dimension*, edited by M. Maresceau. Dordrecht, Neth.: Martinus Nijhoff.

Kyl, Jon. 2004. S.2610—The United States-Australia Free Trade Agreement Implementation Act. Legislative Notice, U.S. Senate Republican Policy Committee, 14 July.

Laakso, Liisa, Timo Kivimaki, and Maaria Seppanen. 2007. Evaluation of Coordination and Coherence in the Application of Article 96 of the Cotonou Partnership Agreement. A study commissioned by the Policy and Operations Evaluation Department, Dutch Ministry of Foreign Affairs.

Lawrence, Robert Z. 2008. *Blue-Collar Blues: Is Trade to Blame for Rising US Income Inequality?* Policy Analyses in International Economics 85. Peterson Institute for International Economics.

Leal-Arcas, Rafael. 2001. The European Community and Mixed Agreements. *European Foreign Affairs Review* 6:483–513.

Lem, Audun. 2003. Salmon. *GlobeFish*, December. http://www.globefish.org/index.php?id=2044 (accessed 4 October 2005).

Levin, Carl. 1999. Levin-Moynihan Amendment Adopted to Require Consideration of Labor Standards Before Trade Benefits Are Granted. 3 November. http://www.senate.gov/~levin/newsroom/release.cfm?id=21016 (accessed 14 April 2007).

——. 2002. Senate Fast Track Vote. 23 May. http://www.senate.gov/~levin/newsroom/release.cfm?id=211093(accessed 14 April 2007).

——. 2005. Senate Floor Statement of Senator Carl Levin on CAFTA Implementing Legislation. 30 June. http://www.senate.gov/~levin/newsroom/release.cfm?id=240042(accessed 15 April 2007).

Levin, Sander M. 2002. The FTAA: A Chance to Shape the Rules of International Trade. October. http://usinfo.state.gov/journals/ites/1002/ijee/ftaa-levin.htm (accessed 15 April 2007).

Lewis, Neil A. 2000. Labor Secretary Is Cleared in Inquiry on Kickbacks. *New York Times*, 6 April.

Lijphart, Arend. 1971. Comparative politics and Comparative Method. *The American Political Science Review* 65 (3): 682–93.

Lindberg, L. N. 1963. *The Political Dynamics of European Economic Integration*. Stanford: Stanford University Press.

Lister, Marjorie. 1988. *The European Community and the Developing World*. Avebury, UK: Aldershot.

——. 2002. European Development Policymaking: Globalization and the Post Lomé World. Paper read at University of Greenwich, UK, 9 November.

Lobjakas, Ahto. 2004. Turkey: EU Reports Pave Way for Qualified Approval of Entry Talks. *Yale Global Online*, 4 October. http://yaleglobal.yale.edu/display.article?id=4639.

Lohmann, Susanne, and Sharyn O'Halloran. 1994. Divided Government and U.S. Trade Policy: Theory and Evidence. *International Organization* 48 (4): 595–632.

Mansfield, Edward D., and Helen V. Milner. 1997. *The Political Economy of Regionalism, New Directions in World Politics*. New York: Columbia University Press.

Mansfield, Edward D., and Eric Reinhardt. Forthcoming. International Institutions and the Volatility of International Trade. *International Organization*.

Marantis, Demetrios James. 1994. Human Rights, Democracy and Development: The European Community Model. *Harvard Human Rights Journal* 7 (Spring): 1–32.

Marin, Manuel. 1993. Statement by H.E. Mr. Manuel Marin Vice President of the Commission of the European Community, Singapore, 26–28 July. http://www.aseansec.org/4462.htm (accessed 14 April 2007).

——. 1997. Address by Mr. Manuel Marin, Vice President of the European Commission, "The European Union's Mediterranean Policy," at the Nobel Institute, Oslo, 23 May. http://europa.eu/ (accessed 14 April 2007).

Martin, Lisa L. 1992. *Coercive Cooperation: Explaining Multilateral Economic Sanctions*. Princeton: Princeton University Press.

——. 1993. The Rational State Choice of Multilateralism. In *Multilateralism Matters: The Theory and Praxis of an Institutional Form*, edited by J. G. Ruggie. New York: Columbia University Press.

——. 1998. Evasive Maneuvers? Reconsidering Presidential Use of Executive Agreements. In *Strategic Politicians, Institutions, and Foreign Policy*, edited by R. M. Siverson. Ann Arbor: University of Michigan Press.

——. 2000. *Democratic Commitments : Legislatures and International Cooperation*. Princeton: Princeton University Press.

Martin, Lisa L., and Beth A. Simmons. 1998. Theories and Empirical Studies of International Institutions. *International Organization* 52 (4): 729–57.

Martin, Lisa L., and Kathryn Sikkink. 1993. US Policy and Human Rights in Argentina and Guatemala, 1973–1980. In *Double-Edged Diplomacy: International Bargaining and Domestic Politics*, edited by Peter Evans, Harold Jacobson, and Robert Putnam. Berkeley: University of California Press.

Mattli, Walter. 1999. *The Logic of Regional Integration: Europe and Beyond*. Cambridge: Cambridge University Press.

Mayer, Frederick W. 1992. Managing Domestic Differences in International Negotiations: The Strategic Use of Internal Side Payments. *International Organization* 46 (4): 793–818.

——. 1998. *Interpreting NAFTA: The Science of Art and Political Analysis*. New York: Columbia University Press.

——. 2002. Negotiating the NAFTA: Political Lessons for the FTAA. In *Greening the Americas*, edited by Carolyn L. Deere and Daniel C. Esty. Cambridge, Mass.: MIT Press.

Mayhew, David R. 1991. *Divided We Govern: Party Control, Lawmaking, and Investigations, 1946–1990*. New Haven: Yale University Press.

Mazur, Jay. 1999. Labor's New Internationalism. *Foreign Affairs* 79 (1): 79–93.

Mbangu, L. 2005. Recent Cases of Article 96 Consultations. ECDPM Discussion Paper 64C, Maastricht.

McGrane, Victoria. 2007. Trade Law Set to Expire; Agenda at Crossroads. 27 March. http://public.cq.com/docs/cqt/news110-000002479293.html (accessed 13 April 2007).

McKelvey, Richard. 1986. Covering, Dominance, and Institution-Free Properties of Social Choice. *American Political Science Review* 30:283–414.

Merriam Webster Dictionary of Law. 1996. Springfield, Mass.: Merriam-Webster, Inc.

Mertus, Julie A. 2004. *Bait and Switch: Human Rights and U.S. Foreign Policy.* London: Routledge.

Meunier, Sophie. 2000. What Single Voice? European Institutions and EU-U.S. Trade Negotiations. *International Organization* 54 (1): 103–35.

———. 2005. *Trading Voices: The European Union in International Commercial Negotiations.* Princeton: Princeton University Press.

Meyer, John W., John Boli, George M. Thomas, and Francisco O. Ramirez. 1997. World Society and the Nation-State. *American Journal of Sociology* 103:144–81.

Meyer, John W., Francisco O. Ramirez, and Yasemin Soysal. 1992. World Expansion of Mass Education, 1870–1980. *Sociology of Education* 65 (2): 128–49.

Meyer, John, and Brian Rowan. 1977. Institutionalized Organizations: Formal Structure as Myth and Ceremony. *American Journal of Sociology* 83:333–63.

Miller, Vaughne. 2004. The Human Rights Clause in the EU's External Agreements. International Affairs and Defense, House of Commons Library, Research Paper 04/33, 16 April.

Milner, Helen V. 1988. *Resisting Protectionism: Global Industries and the Politics of International Trade.* Princeton: Princeton University Press.

———. 1997. *Interests, Institutions, and Information: Domestic Politics and International Relations.* Princeton: Princeton University Press.

Milner, Helen V., and Peter B. Rosendorff. 1997. Democratic Politics and International Trade Negotiations: Elections and Divided Government as Constraints on Trade Liberalization. *Journal of Conflict Resolution* 41 (1): 117–46.

Ministerial Declaration of Quito. 2002. Seventh Meeting of Ministers of Trade of the Hemisphere. Quito, Ecuador, 1 November.

Mitchell, Neil, and James McCormick. 1988. Economic and Political Explanations of Human Rights Violations. *World Politics* 40:476–98.

Moravcsik, Andrew. 1991. Negotiating the Single European Act: National Interests and Conventional Statecraft in the European Community. *International Organization* 45 (1): 19–56.

———. 1993. Preferences and Power in the European Community: A Liberal Intergovernmentalist Approach. *Journal of Common Market Studies* 31 (4): 473–524.

———. 1997. Taking Preferences Seriously: A Liberal Theory of International Politics. *International Organization* 51 (4): 513–53.

———. 1998. *The Choice for Europe: Social Purpose and State Power From Messina to Maastricht.* Ithaca: Cornell University Press.

———. 2000. The Origins of Human Rights Regimes: Democratic Delegation in Postwar Europe. *International Organization* 54 (2): 217–52.

Moser, P. 1996. The European Parliament as a Conditional Agenda Setter: What are the Conditions? A Critique of Tsebelis. *American Political Science Review* 90:834–38.

Murphy, Anna. 2000. In the Maelstrom of Change—Article 113 Committee in the Governance of External Economic Policy. In *Administering the New Europe:*

Committee Governance in the European Union, edited by T. Christensen and E. Kirchner. Manchester, UK: Manchester University Press.

N'Diaye, Boubacar. 2006. Mauritania, August 2005: Justice and Democracy, or Just Another Coup? *African Affairs* 105:421–41.

National Foreign Trade Council. 2001. NFTC Applauds Critical Vote on Trade Promotion Authority. 6 December. http://www.nftc.org/ (accessed 11 April 2007).

——. 2002. U.S.-Morocco Free Trade Agreement Would Benefit U.S. Economic Interests. 21 November. http://www.nftc.org/ (accessed 11 April 2007).

Neumayer, Eric. 2005. Do International Human Rights Treaties Improve Respect for Human Rights? *Journal of Conflict Resolution* 49 (6): 925–53.

Neuwahl, Nanette A., and Allan Rosas, eds. 1995. *The European Union and Human Rights.* The Hague: Martinus Nijhoff.

New York Times. 1992. The 1992 Campaign; Transcript of 3d TV Debate among Bush, Clinton, and Perot. 20 October.

North, Douglass C. 1990. *Institutions, Institutional Change and Economic Performance.* New York: Cambridge University Press.

Nowak, Manfred. 1999. Human Rights "Conditionality" in Relation to, Entry to, and Full Participation in, the EU. In *The EU and Human Rights,* ed. P. Alston, M. R. Bustelo, and J. Heenan. Oxford: Oxford University Press.

Nye, Joseph. 1968. *International Regionalism.* Boston: Little, Brown, and Co.

OECD. 1996. Trade, Employment and Labor Standards, A Study of Core Workers' Rights and International Trade. COM/DEELSA/TD(96)8/FINAL. Paris: Organization for Economic Cooperation and Development.

Office of Trade and Industry Information. 2005. TradeStats Express: National Trade Data.http://tse.export.gov/NTDMap.aspx?UniqueURL=xwbxpnvk1w wdp255nzqjkor2-2005-10-3-11-20-32.

Office of the United States Trade Representative. 2004. Summary of the U.S.-Australia Free Trade Agreement. Free Trade Down Under: Expanding U.S. Manufacturing Access to a Key Market. 8 February.

Organization for Economic Co-operation and Development. 2005. Annual Report, Public Affairs Division. Paris.

Orme, William A. Jr. 1996. *Understanding NAFTA: Mexico, Free Trade, and the New North America.* 2nd ed. Austin: University of Texas Press.

Oye, Kenneth. 1979. The Domain of Choice: International Constraints and Carter Administration Foreign Policy. In *Engle Entangled: US Foreign Policy in a Complex World,* edited by Kenneth Oye, Donald Rothchild, and Robert J. Lieber. New York: Longman.

Ozden, Caglar, and Eric Reinhardt. 2005. The Perversity of Preferences: GSP and Developing Country Trade Policies, 1976–2000. *Journal of Development Economics* 78:1–21.

Payne, Rodger A. 2001. Persuasion, Frames, and Norm Construction. *European Journal of International Relations* 7 (1): 37–61.

PBS. 2002. Commanding Heights: The Battle for the World Economy. 4 April.

Peltzman, Sam. 1976. Toward a More General Theory of Regulation. *Journal of Law and Economics* 19:211.

Perkins, Dwight H. 2007. *The Challenges of China's Growth (Henry Wendt Lecture).* Washington, D.C.: AEI Press.

Perot, Ross. 1992. *United We Stand: How We Can Take Back Our Country.* New York: Hyperion Books.

Petersmann, Ernst-Ulrich. 2003. Human Rights and the Law of the World Trade Organization. *Journal of World Trade* 37:241–281.

———. 2004. The "Human Rights Approach" Advocated by the UN High Commissioner for Human Rights and by the ILO: Is It Relevant for WTO Law and Policy? *Journal of International Economic Law* 7 *(3)*: 605–28.

Pevehouse, Jon C. 2002. Democracy from the Outside-In? International Organizations and Democratization. *International Organization* 56 (3): 515–49.

———. 2005. *Democracy from Above: Regional Organizations and Democratization.* Cambridge: Cambridge University Press.

Pier, Carol. 1998. Labor Rights in Chile and NAFTA Labor Standards: Questions of Compatibility on the Eve of Free Trade. *Comparative Labor Law and Policy Journal* 19 (2): 185.

Pinelli, Cesare. 2004. Conditionality and Enlargement in Light of EU Constitutional Developments. *European Journal of Law* 10 (3): 354–62.

Poe, Steven C., and C. Neal Tate. 1994. Repression of Human Rights to Personal Integrity in the 1980s: A Global Analysis. *American Political Science Review* 88:853–900.

Polaski, Sandra. 2002. Panel III: What Role for Labor Standards in Development and Globalization. Paper read at Making Globalization Work: Expanding the Benefits of Globalization to Working Families and the Poor, Washington D.C., Carnegie Endowment for International Peace.

Pollack, Mark. 1997. Delegation, Agency, and Agenda Setting in the European Community. *International Organization* 51 (1): 99–134.

———. 2003. *The Engines of European Integration: Delegation, Agency, and Agenda Setting in the EU.* Oxford: Oxford University Press.

———. 2005. Theorizing the European Union: International Organization, Domestic Polity, or Experiment in New Governance? *Annual Review of Political Science* 8:357–98.

Porter, Roger B., Pierre Sauve, Arvind Subramanian, and Americo Beviglia Zampetti. 2002. *Efficiency, Equity, and Legitimacy: The Multilateral Trading System at the Millennium.* Washington, D.C.: Brookings Institution Press.

Powell, Walter W., and Paul J. DiMaggio, eds. 1991. *The New Institutionalism in Organizational Analysis.* Chicago: University of Chicago Press.

Price, Richard. 1998. Reversing the Gun Sights: Transnational Civil Society Targets Landmines. *International Organization* 52 (3): 613–44.

Przeworski, Adam, and Henry T. Teune. 1970. *The Logic of Comparative Social Inquiry.* Malabar, Fla.: Robert E. Krieger Publishing.

Putnam, Robert. 1998. Diplomacy and Domestic Politics: The Logic of Two-Level Games. *International Organization* 42 (3): 427–60.

Quinlan, Joseph. 2003. Drifting Apart or Growing Together? The Primacy of the Transatlantic Economy. Washington, D.C.: Center for Transatlantic Relations.

Raffer, K. 2001. Cotonou: Slowly Undoing Lomé's Concept of Partnership. European Development Policy Study Group, Discussion paper No.20.

Reich, Robert B. 1995. Highlights of the 1994 Cooperative Work Program: North American Agreement on Labor Cooperation (SuDoc L 29.2:C 77). Washington, D.C.: US Department of Labor, International Labor Affairs Bureau, National Administrative Office.

Reinhardt, Erik. 2005. The Perversity of Preferences: GSP and Developing Country Trade Policies, 1976–2000. *Journal of Development Economics* 78(1): 1–21.

Remøy, Sebastian. 2005. EFTA and the EEC-EFTA Secretariat, EEA Coordination Unit. http://66.102.9.104/search?q=cache:DeoFTRldc30J:europa.eu.int/comm/external_relations/euromed/etn/9mtg_0405/a3_remoy_enpefta.pdf+EU+EFTA+trade&hl=en&client=firefox-a (accessed 10 October 2005).

Ricardo, David. [1817] 1996. *On the Principles of Political Economy and Taxation.* London: Prometheus Books.

Rideau, Joël. 1997. Le Rôle de l'Union Européenne en Matière de Protection des Droits de L'homme. *Recueil des Cours* 265:9–480.

Risse, Thomas, and Stephen C. Ropp. 1999. International Human Rights Norms and Domestic Change: Conclusions. In *The Power of Human Rights: International Human Rights Norms and Domestic Change*, edited by T. Risse, S. C. Ropp, and K. Sikkink. Cambridge: Cambridge University Press.

Risse, Thomas, Stephen C. Ropp, and Kathryn Sikkink, eds. 1999. *The Power of Human Rights: International Norms and Domestic Change.* Cambridge: Cambridge University Press.

Risse-Kappen, Thomas. 1994. Ideas Do Not Float Freely: Transnational Coalitions, Domestic Structures, and the End of the Cold War. *International Organization* 48 (2): 185–214.

Rogowski, Ronald. 1989. *Commerce and Coalitions: How Trade Affects Domestic Political Alignments.* Princeton: Princeton University Press.

Rosales, Osvaldo V. 2003. Chile-U.S. Free Trade Agreement: Lessons and Best Practices. Paper presented to the American Chamber of Commerce, Washington, D.C., 28 April.

Rose, Andrew K. 2003. Do We Really Know that the WTO Increases Trade? *American Economic Review* 94 (1): 98–114.

Rosen, Howard. 2004. Free Trade Agreements as Foreign Policy Tools: The US-Israel and US-Jordan FTAs. In *Free Trade Agreements: US Strategies and Priorities*, edited by J. J. Schott. Washington, D.C.: Institute for International Economics.

Rudra, Nita. 2007. Welfare States in Developing Countries: Unique or Universal? *Journal of Politics* 69 (2): 378–96.

Ruebner, Joshua. 2001. United States-Israel Free Trade Area: Jordanian-Israeli Qualifying Industrial Zones. Congressional Research Service Report for Congress, RS20529, 29 March.

Ruggie, John Gerard. 1998. *Constructing the World Polity: Essays on International Institutionalization*. New York: Routledge.

Ruggiero, Renato. 2004. Comment. In *Free Trade Agreements: US Strategies and Priorities*, edited by J. J. Schott. Washington, D.C.: Institute for International Economics.

Rutherford, Malcolm. 1994. *Institutions in Economics: The Old and the New Institutionalisms*. New York: Cambridge University Press.

Sagar, Jay V. 2004. The Labor and Environment Chapters of the United States-Chile Free Trade Agreement: An Improvement Over the Weak Enforcement Provisions of the NAFTA Side Agreements on Labor and the Environment? *Arizona Journal of International and Comparative Law* 21 (3): 913–49.

Sandholtz, Wayne, and Alec Stone Sweet. 1998. *European Integration and Supranational Governance*. Oxford: Oxford University Press.

Schelling, Thomas C. 1960. *Strategy of Conflict*. Cambridge, Mass.: Harvard University Press.

Schott, Jeffrey J. 2004a. Free Trade Agreements: Boon or Bane of the World Trading System? In *Free Trade Agreements: US Strategies and Priorities*, edited by J. J. Schott. Washington, D.C.: Institute for International Economics.

———, ed. 2004b. *Free Trade Agreements: US Strategies and Priorities*. Washington, D.C.: Institute for International Economics.

Schwitzgebel, Eric. 1999. Gradual Belief Change in Children. *Human Development* 42:283–96.

Sek, Lenore. 2001. IB10084: Fast-Track Authority for Trade Agreements (Trade Promotion Authority): Background and Developments in the 107th Congress. Congressional Research Service Issue Brief for Congress, 14 May.

———. 2003. Trade Promotion Authority (Fast-Track Authority for Trade Agreements): Background and Developments in the 107th Congress. Report for Congress, Congressional Research Service, 2 April

Shepsle, Kenneth A., and Barry R. Weingast. 1981. Structure-Induced Equilibrium and Legislative Choice. *Public Choice* 37:503–19.

Sikkink, Kathryn. 2004. *Mixed Signals: U.S. Human Rights Policy and Latin America*. Ithaca: Cornell University Press.

Sikkink, Kathryn, and Jackie Smith. 2002. Infrastructures for Change: Transnational Organizations, 1953–93. In *Restructuring World Politics: Transnational Social Movements, Networks, and Norms*, edited by S. Khagram, J. V. Riker and K. Sikkink. Minneapolis: University of Minnesota Press.

Simmons, Beth. 2007. Human Rights: Theorizing Treaty Commitment: Unpublished manuscript.

Single European Act. 1987. Official Journal NO. L 169, 29/6/1987.

Slaughter, Anne-Marie. 1995. International Law in a World of Liberal States. *The European Journal of International Law* 6:139–70.

———. 2004. *A New World Order.* Princeton: Princeton University Press.

Slusher, M.P., and C.A. Anderson. 1996. Using Causal Persuasive Arguments to Change Beliefs and Teach New Information: The Mediating Role of Explanation Availability and Evaluation Bias in the Acceptance of Knowledge. *Journal of Educational Psychology* 88:110–22.

Smith, Carolyn C. 2006. Trade Promotion Authority and Fast Track Negotiating Authority for Trade Agreements: Major Votes. CRS Report for Congress, RS21004, 29 September.

Smith, Jackie, Charles Chatfield, and Ron Pagnucco. 1997. *International Social Movements and Global Politics: Solidarity beyond the State.* Syracuse: Syracuse University Press.

Smits, René J.H. 1980. The Second Lomé Convention: An Assessment with Special Reference to Human Rights. *Legal Issues of European Integration* 2:47–74.

Stavridis, Stelios. 1991. Foreign Policy and Democratic Principles: The Case of European Political Co-operation. PhD diss., London School of Economics.

Stein, Arthur A. 1980. The Politics of Linkage. *World Politics* 33(1): 62–81.

Steiner, Henry J., and Philip Alston. 1996. *International Human Rights in Context: Law, Politics, Morals, Text and Materials.* Oxford: Clarendon Press.

Stigler, George J. 1971. The Economic Theory of Regulation. *Bell Journal of Economics and Management Science* 2:3–21.

Sullivan, Mark P. 2003. Chile: Political and Economic Conditions and US Relations. CRS Report for Congress, RL30035, 5 August.

Sweeney, John. 2005. Statement by AFL-CIO President John Sweeney on CAFTA Passage in House. 28 July. http://www.aflcio.org/mediacenter/prsptm/pr07282005.cfm (accessed 10 March 2007).

Swindler, Ann. 1986. Culture in Action. *American Sociological Review* 51 (April): 271–86.

Tapper, Jake. 1999. Bill Bradley: Al Gore's Debate Coach. *Salon*, 10 November. http://www.salon.com/news/feature/1999/11/10/bradley/index.html (accessed 15 April 2007).

Targ, Nicholas. 1987. Trading in Workers' Rights. *Multinational Monitor* 8 (2). http://multinationalmonitor.org/hyper/issues/1987/02/targ.html.

Tarrow, Sidney. 2005. *The New Transnational Activism.* Cambridge: Cambridge University Press.

Tekere, Moses. 1999. Expiry of Lomé IV: Challenges for Zimbabwe's Garment Export Industry. http://www.tradescentre.org.zw/publications/issue2.html (accessed 15 May 2007).

Testas, Abdelazis. 2002. The Advantages of an Intra-Maghrib Free Trade Area: Quantitative Estimates of the Static and Dynamic Output and Welfare Effects. *Journal of North African Studies* 7 (1): 99–108.

Thomas, George M., John W. Meyer, Francisco O. Ramirez, and John Boli, eds. 1987. *Institutional Structure: Constituting State, Society, and Individual.* Newbury Park, Calif.: Sage.

Thomson, Robert, Frans N. Stokman, Christopher Achen, and Thomas Konig, eds. 2006. *The European Union Decides*. Cambridge: Cambridge University Press.

Thorbecke, Willem. 1997. Explaining House Voting on the North American Free Trade Agreement. *Public Choice* 92:231–42.

Tomz, Michael, Judith Goldstein, and Douglas Rivers. 2007. Do We Really Know that the WTO Increases Trade? *American Economic Review* 97 (5): 2005–2018.

Trubek, David M., Jim Mosher, and Jeffrey S. Rothstein. 2000. Transnationalism in the Regulation of Labor Relations: International Regimes and Transnational Advocacy Networks. *Law & Social Inquiry* 25 (4): 1187–1211.

Tsebelis, George. 1994. The Power of the European Parliament as a Conditional Agenda Setter. *American Political Science Review* 88 (1): 128–42.

———. 1995. Decision Making in Political Systems: Veto Players in Presidentialism, Parliamentarism, Multicameralism and Multipartyism. *British Journal of Political Science* 25 (2): 289–325.

———. 2000. Veto Players and Institutional Analysis. *Governance* 13 (4): 441–74.

———. 2002. *Veto Players: How Political Institutions Work*. Princeton: Princeton University Press.

Tsebelis, George, and Geoffrey Garrett. 1996. Agenda Setting Power, Power Indices, and Decision Making in the European Union. *International Review of Law and Economics* 16:345–61.

———. 2001. The Institutional Foundations of Intergovernmentalism and Supranationalism in the European Union. *International Organization* 55 (2): 357–90.

Tsogas, George. 2000. Labour Standards in the Generalized System of Preferences of the European Union and the United States. *European Journal of Industrial Relations* 6(3): 349–70.

Tsutsui, Kiyoteru, and Christine Min Wotipka. 2004. Global Civil Society and the International Human Rights Movement: Citizen Participation in Human Rights International Nongovernmental Organizations. *Social Forces* 83 (2): 587–620.

Twomey, Patrick. 1994. The European Union: Three Pillars without a Human Rights Foundation. In *Legal Issues of the Maastricht Treaty*, edited by D. O'Keeffe and P. Twomey. London: Chancery Law Publishing.

United Nations. 1986. Declaration on the Right to Development Adopted by General Assembly Resolution 41/128. 4 December.

United Nations Conference on Trade and Development. 1998. The Least Developed Countries Report: Trade, Investment, and the Multilateral Trading System. Geneva.

———. 2004. The Least Developed Countries Report: Linking International Trade with Poverty Reduction. Geneva.

US Bureau of Labor Statistics. 2007a. Facts about Missouri Manufacturing. February. www.nam.org/s_nam/bin.asp?CID=202163&DID=233516&DOC=FILE.PDF (accessed 15 April 2007).

———. 2007b. Facts about Montana Manufacturing. February. www.nam.org/s_nam/bin.asp?CID=202163&DID=233517&DOC=FILE.PDF (accessed 15 April 2007).

US Chamber of Commerce. 2000. U.S. Chamber Welcomes U.S.—Jordan Free Trade Agreement but Opposes Non-Trade Provisions. 25 October. http://www .uschamber.com/press/releases/2000/october/00–185.htm (accessed 11 April 2007).

——. 2004. NAFTA at 10: Gauging the Agreement's Impact on the US Economy, Manufacturing, and Jobs. January. http://www.uschamber.com/issues/index/in ternational/nafta.htm (accessed 11 April 2007).

US Congressional Budget Office. 2003. The Pros and Cons of Pursuing Free-Trade Agreements. http://www.cbo.gov/showdoc.cfm?index=4458&sequence=0 (accessed 5 March 2007).

US Council for International Business. 2001. USCIB Applauds House Passage of Trade Promotion Authority Bill. 7 December. http://www.uscib.org/index .asp?documentID=1910 (accessed 11 April 2007).

——. 2007. Labor and Employment. http://www.uscib.org/index.asp?document ID=825 (accessed 11 April 2007).

US Department of Labor. 2003. Labor Rights Report: Chile. www.dol.gov/ilab/ media/reports/usfta/HR2738ChileLaborRights.pdf (accessed 2 June 2007).

——. 2005. Mexico Bureau of International Labor Affairs. http://www.dol.gov/ ilab/media/reports/iclp/sweat/mexico.htm#1 (accessed 29 September 2005).

US Department of State. 2005. Country Reports on Human Rights Practices—2004. Bureau of Democracy, Human Rights, and Labor.

——. 2007. Country Reports on Human Rights Practices. Bureau of Democracy, Human Rights, and Labor.

US House of Representatives. 1995. To Provide Trade Agreements Authority to the President. H.R. 2371.

——. 1997. To Extend Trade Authorities Procedures with Respect to Reciprocal Trade Agreements, and for Other Purposes. H.R. 2621.

US International Trade Commission. 1998. Overview and Analysis of Current U.S. Unilateral Economic Sanctions.

US Office of the Press Secretary. 1993. Remarks by President Clinton, President Bush, President Carter, President Ford, and Vice President Gore in Signing of Nafta Side Agreements. 14 September. http://www.ibiblio.org/pub/archives/ whitehouse-papers/1993/Sep/Remarks-by-Clinton-and-Former-Presidents-on-NAFTA (accessed 19 April 2007).

——. 2001. Overview: US-Jordan Free Trade Agreement (FTA). Press Release, 28 September.

——. 2002. President Calls on Senate to Pass Trade Promotion Authority: Remarks by the President on Trade Promotion Authority. 4 April. http://www .whitehouse.gov/news/releases/2002/04/20020404-4.html (accessed 13 April 2007).

US Senate. 1999. Senate Concurrent Resolution 1—Expressing Congressional Support for the International Labor Organization's Declaration on Fundamental Principles and Rights at Work. 19 January. http://thomas.loc.gov/cgi-bin/ query/z?r106:S19JA9-0065 (accessed 20 April 2007).

US Senate Democratic Policy Committee. 2004. S. 2610, the United States—Australia Free Trade Agreement Implementation Act. Legislative Notice, Chairman Byron L. Dorgan, 14 July.

Vaughan, Martin. 2007. Balance of Payments—Trade Limbo. 12 April. http://nationaljournal.com/ (accessed 13 March 2007).

Vaughn, Bruce, and Thomas Lum. 2003. Australia: Background and U.S. Relations. CrS Issue Brief for Congress RS21358, 4 August.

Viner, Jacob. 1950. *The Customs Union Issue*. New York: Carnegie Endowment for International Peace.

Vogel, David. 2005. *The Market for Virtue*. Washington, D.C.: Brookings Institution Press.

von Bertrab, Hermann. 1996. Negotiating NAFTA, A Mexican Envoy's Account. Center for Strategic and International Studies, Washington Papers.

Vreeland, James R. 2008. Political Institutions and Human Rights: Why Dictatorships Enter into the United Nations Convention against Torture. *International Organization* 62 (1): 65–101.

Wallace, Helen, William Wallace, and Mark Pollack. 2005. *Policy-Making in the European Union*. New York: Oxford University Press.

Waltz, Kenneth N. 1979. *Theory of International Politics*. New York: McGraw-Hill.

Weimer, David L., ed. 1995. *Institutional Design*. Boston: Kluwer Academic Publishers.

Weintraub, Sidney. 2003. Lessons from the Chile and Singapore Free Trade Agreements. In *Free Trade Agreements: US Strategies and Priorities*, edited by J. J. Schott. Washington, D.C.: Institute for International Economics.

———. 2004. Lessons from the Chile and Singapore Free Trade Agreements. In *Free Trade Agreements: US Strategies and Priorities*, edited by J. J. Schott. Washington, D.C: Institute for International Economics.

Weiss, Thomas George, and Leon Gordenker. 1996. *NGOs, the UN, and Global Governance*. Lynne Rienner.

Whalley, John. 1996. Why Do Countries Seek Regional Trade Agreements? NBER Working Paper 5552.

Whiteman, Kaye. 1998. Africa, the ACP and Europe: The Lessons of 25 Years. *Development Policy Review* 16:29–37.

Williamson, Oliver E. 1975. *Markets and Hierarchies: Analysis and Antitrust Implications*. New York: Free Press.

Wiseberg, Laurie S. 1992. Human Rights Nongovernmental Organizations. In *Human Rights in the World Community: Issues and Action*, edited by Richard Pierre Claude and Burns H. Weston. Philadelphia: University of Pennsylvania Press.

World Trade Organization. 1996. First Ministerial Declaration. December.

Yandle, Bruce. 1983. Bootleggers and Baptists: The Education of a Regulatory Economist. *Regulation* 7 (3): 12.

———. 1999. Bootleggers and Baptists in Retrospect. *Regulation* 22 (2): 5–7.

Young-Anawaty, Amy. 1980. Human Rights and the ACP-EEC Lomé II Convention. *New York University Journal of International Law and Politics* 1 (13): 63–98.

Zaza, Yanqui J. 2002. Privatization and Deregulation, or No Aid: Poor Countries Dilemma. *The Perspective* (Atlanta, Ga.), 30 December.

Zoellick, Robert B. 2003. The U.S. Free Trade Agenda. Speech before the Senate Committee on Finance, Washington, D.C.

INDEX

Abdallahi, Sidi Ould Cheikh, 155
Abdullah II (King of Jordan), 92
Acculturation. *See* Cultural issues
ACP. *See* African, Caribbean, and Pacific
    countries
Afghanistan, 127
AFL-CIO. *See* American Federation of
    Labor and Congress of Industrial
    Organizations
Africa, 73, 132
African, Caribbean, and Pacific countries
    (ACP): Cotonou agreements and, 2, 7, 51,
    138; economic issues of, 133; European
    Community and, 132, 138–139; European
    labor unions and, 58; European Parlia-
    ment and, 79; European trade policies
    and, 102, 103; formation of, 71; human
    rights and, 73, 78, 105–106, 132–134, 135,
    136–138; Lomé conventions and, 1, 51,
    136–137; policy dialogue and, 134–135;
    turmoil in, 73; United Nations and, 136.
    See also Europe, specific trade agree-
    ments; Lomé conventions; individual
    countries
African Charter of Human and People's
    Rights (1981), 135, 145n
Agriculture and agricultural issues, 61
Ahtisaari, Martti, 79
Albania, 132n17
ALDE. *See* Alliance of Liberals and
    Democrats for Europe
Allende, Salvador, 149
Alliance of Liberals and Democrats for
    Europe (ALDE), 80, 81

American Convention on Human Rights,
    143n3
American Federation of Labor and
    Congress of Industrial Organizations
    (AFL CIO), 57–58
Amin, Idi, 72, 101–102
Amnesty International, 42, 54, 55, 150,
    173
Andriessen, Frans, 75
Apartheid, 135
Argentina, 106–107, 131. *See also* Europe,
    specific trade agreements
ASEAN. *See* Association for Southeast
    Asian Nations
Association for Southeast Asian Nations
    (ASEAN), 119
Australia, 117, 127, 128, 139nn22–23. *See
    also* Europe, specific trade agreements;
    United States, specific trade agreements
Australia, New Zealand, United States
    Security Treaty (ANZUS; 1951), 128
Austria, 79, 112, 130

Bahrain, 146
Balfe, Richard, 80
Baltic Clause, 110–111
Baucus, Max (D-MT), 67, 93–94
Bedié, Henri, 157
Belgium, 78, 80, 103
Berlin Wall, fall of (Germany), 55, 76, 105,
    136
Bootlegger-Baptist theory, 14–15, 20,
    25–26, 30, 43–44, 48, 66
Bosnia, 73, 76

Bradley, William W. ("Bill"; D-NJ), 63–64, 68

Brittan, Leon, 139

Brown, Jerry, 63

Bulgarian clause, 111

Burma, 74

Bush, George H.W., 62, 65, 86, 87, 88, 89, 120–121

Bush (George H.W.) administration, 120, 121, 124

Bush, George W.: agenda for international trade, 65–66, 93, 95; human rights measures and, 81, 94, 95; US-Australia Free Trade Agreement and, 127; US-Chile Free Trade Agreement and, 124, 126–127. See also Trade Act of 2002

Bush (George W.) administration, 65, 94, 95, 96, 124–125, 126

Business issues, 59–60, 63, 68, 69

Callaghan, James, 77

Canada, 89, 120, 122–124, 146, 171. See also North American Free Trade Agreement; United States, specific trade agreements

Canada-Chile Free Trade Agreement, 124, 125

Cape Verde, 146

Capital punishment, 86, 153

Carlsson, Ingvar, 79

Carter, Jimmy, 52

Central African Empire, 101

Chamber of Commerce (US), 59

Cheysson, Claude, 71–73, 78, 102, 133, 134

Chicago Council on Foreign Relations, 55

Chile, 90, 106, 124, 125, 126, 149–151, 171. See also Europe, specific trade agreements; United States, specific trade agreements

China, 64, 67, 81, 170, 173–174

Chirac, Jacques, 159–160

Christian Democratic Party, 75, 78, 81

Clinton, William J. ("Bill"): fast-track authority and, 91–92, 94; human and workers' rights issues, 63–65, 89, 90, 94–95; NAFTA and, 64–65, 68n, 89, 90, 120, 121, 122, 124; US-Chile Free Trade Agreement, 124, 125; US-Jordan Free Trade Agreement, 92, 94, 125

Clinton (William J.) administration, 68, 92–93, 122

Cold war: end of, 5, 15, 26, 73, 74, 78, 83, 105; globalization and, 54, 57; human rights issues and, 26, 43, 50, 71, 82, 83, 165; trade agreements and, 61

Colombia, 146. See also United States, specific trade agreements

COMESA. See Common Market for Eastern and Southern Africa

Commission Communications (European Commission; 1991, 1995), 18, 85, 108, 111, 112, 114, 129, 131

Common Market for Eastern and Southern Africa (COMESA), 145n, 171

Communism, 70–71

Confederation of European Business, 59, 60

Conference on Security and Cooperation in Europe (CSCE), 110

Congress (US), 85–86, 88. See also Legislative branch; Political issues

Conroy, Stephen, 128

Conservative Party, 77, 81

Constitutions, 85, 153, 120n5

Convention for the Protection of Human Rights and Fundamental Freedoms. See European Convention for the Protection of Human Rights and Fundamental Freedoms

Copenhagen European Council (1993), 151–152

Costa Rica, 146

Côte d'Ivoire, 146, 157–160

Cotonou agreements (2000, 2003), 2, 7–8, 51, 98–99, 132, 138, 154, 156

Council Decision (European Council; 1995), 52n14, 85, 114, 129, 139

Croatia, 80–81

CSCE. See Conference on Security and Cooperation in Europe

Cultural issues, 41

Declaration on Fundamental Principles and Rights at Work (ILO; 1998), 94

Declaration on the Right to Development (UN; 1987), 136

Delors, Jacques, 71–72, 73–74, 75, 106, 130

Democracy and democracies: externalities and interest groups, 37–38; human rights issues of, 44; policymaking and, 24; PTAs with hard standards and, 146; regional organizations and, 44

Democratic Party (Europe), 80

Democratic Party (US): Colombia trade agreements and, 151n16, 170; human and workers' rights and, 62, 63, 64, 65, 66, 68, 147; NAFTA and, 70, 86–89, 90, 91, 120, 121, 122; trade agreements and, 62. See also Political issues

Denmark, 71, 74

Developing countries: fair trade issues and, 6n7, 37, 44–45; human rights regulations and, 12–13, 17, 21, 37, 43–44, 115, 119, 171; Lomé I Convention and, 102; power politics and, 25, 115–116; trade agreements and, 15, 17, 21, 35, 107–108, 131, 132, 141. *See also* World Trade Organization; individual countries

de Vries, Gijs M., 80

Dominican Republic-Central America Free Trade Agreement (DR-CAFTA), 58, 66, 70

Dooley, Calvin ("Cal"; D-CA), 96

Downer, Alexander, 139

DR-CAFTA. *See* Dominican Republic-Central America Free Trade Agreement

Dunn, Newton, 81

Eastern Europe, 71, 108

EC. *See* European Community

ECJ. *See* European Court of Justice

Economic issues: acceptance of agreements, 32; employment and jobs, 38, 39–40, 66; enforceable PTA standards, 33; externalities, 37; regulations protecting human rights, 23; wealth redistribution, 38. *See also* Trade issues

EDF. *See* European Development Fund

EEA. *See* European Economic Area

EFTA. *See* European Free Trade Area

Egypt, 80–81

Elections: 1992, 62–64, 88–89, 90, 120; 2000, 65, 91

Employment and jobs. *See* Economic issues

Enforcement: Bush, George W. and, 65, 81; EC and, 78–79; in the European Economic Area, 130–131; in the European human rights system, 143n3; of human rights agreements, 32–33, 143–144; of human rights trade measures, 35, 81–82, 83, 95, 96, 107, 108–109, 110–111, 112–113; legal enforcement, 143n4; of Mexican labor laws, 120; by the Organization of American States, 143n3; in preferential trade agreements, 21–22, 60; violation of agreement terms, 8

Enforcement, specific agreements: ACP-EC Convention of Lomé, 77–78, 137; Canada-Chile Free Trade Agreement, 125; Cotonou agreements, 154, 156; EC-Azerbaijan agreement, 146; Lomé conventions, 158; NAFTA, 122–123, 127n12; US-Australia Free Trade Agreement, 127; US-Chile Free Trade Agreement, 124, 125, 126, 127n12; US-Jordan Free Trade Agreement, 127n12; US-Oman Free Trade Agreement, 146, 149; US-Singapore Free Trade Agreement, 127n12

Enterprise Initiative for the Americas (US; 1990), 124

Environmental issues, 37n, 119, 170

EP. *See* European Parliament

EPC. *See* European Political Co-operation

EPP-ED. *See* European Democrats in the European Parliament

Equatorial Guinea, 101

Ethiopia, 133

ETUC. *See* European Trade Union Confederation

EU. *See* European Union

Eurobarometer, 56

Europe: business issues in, 59–60; export subsidies of, 61; foreign policies of, 75; former colonies of, 71, 132; human rights issues in, 39, 50–52, 82–83, 98, 134, 141, 143n3, 161–163; labor unions in, 57, 58; legislation and legislatures in, 77; preferential trade agreements of, 5, 39, 43, 151–153, 161–163; public support for human rights in, 56; standards of conduct in, 8. *See also* Eastern Europe; European Community; European Union; individual countries

Europe, fair trade agreements: human rights issues in, 1, 8, 9, 51, 60, 82, 98–114, 117, 129–130, 138; negotiations for, 98, 130; policymaker preferences and, 71–83, 107; policymaking procedures and, 98–100; regulatory focus of, 13; trade unions and, 58; workers' rights issues in, 10n12

Europe, specific trade agreements (A-L): ACP countries, 58, 77–78, 98, 105–106, 108, 111, 132–133, 135, 137–138, 145; Albania, 110, 111, 132n17; Algeria, 1, 51; Argentina, 8, 51, 106–107, 111, 131–132, 145, 166; Australia, 139–141; Azerbaijan, 146; Baltic countries, 110; Bangladesh, 2; Botswana, 118, 145; Bulgaria, 8, 110, 111, 113, 145; Burma, 74; Chad, 1; Chile, 107, 132n18; Côte d'Ivoire, 157–160; Cotonou Agreement, 138; Cuba, 145; Czechoslovakia, 108, 111; Ethiopia, 80; Georgia, 98; Haiti, 76, 117; Hungary, 108, 111; Iceland, 51; India, 117, 170; Iraq, 2; Israel, 8, 80, 105; Jordan, 39; Kazakhstan, 2, 8, 39, 145; Laos, 145; Latin America and Caribbean countries, 55, 108; Liberia, 1

Europe, specific trade agreements (M-Z): Macao, 8; Macedonia, 8; Mauritania, 154; Micronesia, 145; Morocco, 8; Norway, 51; Paraguay, 8, 107, 132n18; Poland, 108, 111; Romania, 110, 111; Solomon Islands, 1; South Africa, 2, 135; Sri Lanka, 117; Sudan, 117; Syria, 1, 51, 170–171; Togo, 156, 166; Tunisia, 98; Turkey, 58, 105; Turkmenistan, 117, 170; Uganda, 72; Uruguay, 107, 132n18, 145; Uzbekistan, 77; Vietnam, 8; Yugoslavia, 76, 108; WTO, 58; Zimbabwe, 117, 118. *See also* Cotonou agreements; European Economic Area; Lomé conventions

Europe Agreements, 108

European Commission: agenda of, 71, 72, 98; human rights issues and, 73, 74–76, 77, 79, 80, 81, 85, 98–114, 133–134, 136; Internal Market of, 130; Mauritania and, 154–155; powers of, 98; trade agreements and, 17, 51–52, 74, 98–114. *See also* Commission Communications; European Community; European Council

European Community (EC): Côte d'Ivoire and, 157, 1588; Cotonou Convention and, 51; countries joining, 71; criteria for accession candidates, 151; European Union and, 50n8; foreign policy of, 109; human rights and trade agreements in, 17, 50, 51, 72, 74, 98–114, 133, 135, 136–141; Latin America and, 107; Togo and, 156. *See also* African, Caribbean, and Pacific countries; Cotonou agreements; European Commission; European Council; European Parliament; Lomé conventions; individual countries

European Convention for the Protection of Human Rights and Fundamental Freedoms (European Convention on Human Rights; 1950), 44, 50, 109, 143n3, 153

European Convention for the Prevention of Torture and Inhuman or Degrading Treatment or Punishment (1987), 153

European Council: accession candidates and, 151; human rights issues and trade agreements, 52, 76, 77, 79, 80, 98–114, 137, 143n3; voting in, 110n39. *See also* Council Decision

European Court of Human Rights, 143nn3–4, 153

European Court of Justice (ECJ), 104, 113, 140

European Democrats in the European Parliament (EPP-ED), 81–82

European Development Fund (EDF), 8, 155, 156

European Economic Area (EEA), 130–131

European Economic Community, 134

European Free Trade Area (EFTA), 130

European Parliament (EP): election of members, 102, 103; human rights issues and, 51, 52, 56, 79–82, 102, 103, 105, 107–108, 112, 133, 134, 136; political issues and, 79–82; role of, 100, 101; trade agreements and, 51, 52, 73, 98, 104, 105, 106, 108, 140

European Political Co-operation (EPC; 1970), 51, 136

European Trade Union Confederation (ETUC), 57, 58, 74

European Union (EU): as a democracy, 17; European Community and, 50n8, 109; human rights issues and, 109, 112; labor unions in, 57n25; market share of, 16n14; membership in, 151, 152; as a PTA, 151n17; trade agreements and, 16n15; voting in, 111n41; workers' human rights and, 10n12. *See also* Europe; European Community; Treaty on the European Union; individual countries

Executive branch, 26–28, 32, 36, 84. *See also* Presidents

Eyadema, Gnassingbe, 156, 157

Farel, Arsenio, 122

Fast track procedures. *See* United States, fair trade agreements

Finland, 79, 112, 130

Flesch, Colette, 80

Framework agreements. *See* Europe, fair trade agreements; Europe, specific trade agreements

Framework Trade and Economic Co-operation Agreement (Argentina-Europe; 1990), 106–107

Framework Understanding on Trade and Investment (Mexico-US; 1987), 61–62

France, 56, 71, 73, 78, 79, 103, 156, 159–160

Free Trade Area of the Americas (FTAA), 95, 119, 124, 149

Frei, Eduardo, 150

Fresco, the, 71

Frisch, Dieter, 135

FTAA. *See* Free Trade Area of the Americas

Gbagbo, Laurent, 157–158, 159–160
General Agreement on Tariffs and Trade
  (GATT; 1947), 23n1, 49, 59–60, 61, 62, 78
Generalized System of Preferences (GSP;
  UK, US), 8, 39, 49–50, 52, 78, 79
Gephardt, Richard (D-MO), 69, 88, 92
Germany, 56, 74, 78, 103, 156. *See also*
  Berlin Wall
Giscard d'Estaing, Valéry, 78
Glinne, Ernest, 80
Globalization: competition and, 69;
  externalities of, 37; global human rights
  regime, 43; human rights issues and,
  40–41, 46, 53, 57, 60; interest groups and,
  2, 12; NGOs and, 54; unions and, 57
Goold, William, 69
Gramm, Philip (R-TX), 94
Group of the European People's Party, 81
GSP. *See* Generalized System of Preferences
GSP Renewal Act (US; 1984), 62, 68–69
Guéï, Robert, 157
Guinea-Bissau, 155
Gulf War (1990), 92

Habsburg-Lothringen, Karl, 81
Haiti, 76, 78, 82, 108, 146
Harking Amendment (US; 1975), 49
Havana charter (1948), 23n1
Helsinki summit (1999), 152
Hills, Carla, 9, 62, 120
Hoffa, James, 129
Howard, John, 128
HRAs (human rights agreements). *See*
  Human and workers' rights
Human and workers' rights: accession to
  the EU and, 151, 152–153; coercion and
  persuasion and, 33–34; as a foreign policy
  goal, 55–56; global norms of, 2, 40–41,
  46, 53, 169; human rights agreements
  and laws, 33, 35, 143–144, 145–146;
  human rights entrepreneurs, 40–41;
  international and regional agreements
  on, 53, 143–144; legislation and
  regulations, 49–52; NAFTA and, 64,
  88–91; norms and advocates, 40–43;
  political issues and, 2, 5, 116, 160; public
  support for, 55–56; reforms of, 32–35,
  144; repression and, 144, 160; slave and
  sweatshop labor, 148, 151; standards of,
  8, 10n12, 21; timelines of, 179–180; trade
  and, 2, 5, 21, 35, 38, 39; trading partners'
  views of human rights, 118–119; US and
  European approaches to, 10, 13, 16–17,
  24, 39, 131, 169; violations of, 33, 50. *See*

  also Enforcement; Preferential trade
  agreements
Human and workers' rights, specific
  countries: Chile, 149–151; Colombia,
  151n16; Côte d'Ivoire, 157–160; Europe,
  70–83, 98–114, 166; Mauritania, 154–155;
  Oman, 147–149; Slovakia, 151–152; Togo,
  156–157; Turkey, 152–153; US, 61–70, 71,
  76, 86–97
Human rights organizations, 43
Human Rights Watch, 42, 54, 55, 159

ICC. *See* International Criminal Court
Iceland, 130
ICFTU. *See* International Confederation of
  Free Trade Unions
ILO. *See* International Labor Organisation
India, 58, 59–60, 170
Institutions, 13–14, 26–30, 168–169. *See also*
  Policies and policymaking; Political
  issues
Inter-American Court of Human Rights,
  143n4
Interest groups: economic policies and,
  37–38; human rights advocates, 144, 166;
  norms and advocates, 40–43; preferential
  trade agreements and, 24, 113–114;
  regulatory demands of, 13; trade
  protection and, 11–12. *See also* Labor
  issues
International Bill of Human Rights (1976),
  6, 140
International Confederation of Free Trade
  Unions (ICFTU), 57
International Criminal Court (ICC), 143n4
International Development and Food
  Assistance Act (US; 1978), 49
International Labor Organisation (ILO):
  conventions of, 9n, 53, 150; core rights of,
  97; human and workers' rights and, 43,
  60, 70; labor standards and, 6n7, 10n12,
  53n18, 68, 94, 97, 127; unilateral
  incentives program, 9n; US and
  European ratification and, 54, 97
International organizations (IOs), 26, 41,
  42, 44, 48
International Socialist Party, 80
International Trade Organization (ITO), 23
IOs. *See* International organizations
Iraq, 127
Ireland, 71, 79
Israel, 1, 50 , 92. *See also* United States,
  specific trade agreements
ITO. *See* International Trade Organization

Jackson, Jesse, 63
Jackson-Vanik Amendment (US; 1974), 49
Jamaica, 146
Jefferson, William J. (D-LA), 96
Jenkins, Roy, 102
Johnson (Lyndon B.) administration, 67
Joint Declaration on European Union-
    Australia Relations (1997), 140
Jordan, 92, 148. *See also* United States,
    specific trade agreements

Kantor, Mickey, 64
Kennedy (John F.) administration, 67
Korea. *See* South Korea

Labor Advisory Committee (LAC; US), 129
Labor issues: free trade, 59, 64; human and
    workers' rights and, 3, 5, 38–39, 40, 55,
    56, 64, 82, 87–88, 93, 96–97, 119; labor
    competition, 63n30; NAFTA, 63, 64, 90,
    91, 122; prison labor, 49; protectionism,
    11; slave and sweatshop labor, 148, 151;
    specific union views, 57–59, 166; trade
    advisory committee system, 57n26; trade
    agreements and, 46, 58, 87–88, 167–168
Labor issues, specific countries: Australia,
    128; Canada, 121; Chile, 149–151;
    Europe, 39, 57n25, 58–59, 79; Oman,
    147–149, 150; US, 97
Labor parties (UK, Australia), 77, 79, 102,
    128
LAC. *See* Labor Advisory Committee
Lagos, Ricardo, 125, 126–127
Lagos (Ricardo) administration, 125–126
Latin America, 107, 124
Legislative branch, 26–28, 32, 36, 84. *See
    also* Congress
Levin, Carl (D-MI), 66, 67–68
Levin, Sander (D-MI), 70, 93–94, 96
Liberal Democratic parties (Europe), 80
Liberal-National Party (Australia), 128
Liberal parties (Europe), 80
Liberia, 101, 146
Liechtenstein, 130
Linas-Marcoussis Peace Accord (2003), 159
Lobbies and lobbyists. *See* Interest groups
Lomé conventions (Europe): ACP countries
    and, 51, 102; enforcement under, 158; the
    "Fresco" and, 71; human rights and, 73,
    76, 78, 80, 81, 103, 106, 132, 133–134–139;
    Lomé I (1975), 1, 72, 102, 132, 133; Lomé
    II (1980), 72, 80, 81, 102, 103, 132n19,
    133–134; Lomé III (1985), 80, 103,
    132n19, 134–135, 145; Lomé IV (1990),
    105, 106, 107, 108, 132n19, 136–137, 157;
    Lomébis (1995), 137; Togo and, 156; trade
    negotiations and, 132
Lubbers, Ruud, 78

Maastricht Treaty. *See* Treaty on the
    European Union
Madagascar, 117, 118
Major, John, 77
Marín, Manuel, 74
Mauritania, 154–155
Mauritius, 146
McKinley Tariff Act (US; 1890), 49
MEFTA. *See* Middle-East Free Trade Area
Members of Parliament (MEPs). *See*
    European Parliament
Menem, Carlos Saul, 106, 131
MEPs (Members of Parliament). *See*
    European Parliament
MERCOSUR (Mercado Commún del Sur).
    See Southern Common Market
Methods: analysis of PTAs, 18–22; case
    selection, 116–117; statistical analysis,
    175–178
Mexico, 61–62, 87, 88, 89, 120–121,
    122–124. *See also* North American Free
    Trade Agreement
Meyer, John, 169
Michigan, 66
Middle-East Free Trade Area (MEFTA),
    147n
Missouri, 69
Montana, 67
Moral entrepreneurs, 12, 13
Moral norms and activism: human rights
    regulations and, 26, 35, 48, 53, 60, 81, 82,
    83; political factors of, 20, 22, 24, 25–26,
    83; preferential trade agreements and,
    166; rise and spread of, 12; US labor
    union case against free trade, 58
Moravcsik, Andrew, 44
Moynihan, Daniel Patrick (D-NY), 63–64,
    67–68
Muasher, Marwan, 94
Mulroney, Brian, 121
Mulroney (Brian) administration, 121
Multilateral trade negotiations, 6n7, 8–9

NAALC. *See* North American Agreement
    on Labor Cooperation
NAFTA. *See* North American Free Trade
    Agreement
National Foreign Trade Council (NFTC),
    59, 60

National Trade Union Confederations
(EC), 57
Netherlands, 71, 74, 77, 78, 79, 103, 133, 136
Network of European World Shops, 54
New Zealand, 140
NFTC. *See* National Foreign Trade
Council
NGOs. *See* Nongovernmental organizations
Nongovernmental organizations (NGOs):
enforcement issues and, 144; globalization and, 54; human rights issues and, 2, 5, 12, 25, 40–42, 43, 48, 54–55, 166; trade agreements and, 42, 43, 54, 55, 113–114, 167–168
North American Agreement on Labor
Cooperation (NAALC; 1994), 52, 89, 90, 91, 121, 123
North American Free Trade Agreement
(NAFTA; 1992): concerns about, 55, 57, 66, 67, 88; enforcement issues in, 122–124, 127n12; human and workers' rights and, 88–91, 94, 120–124; negotiations for, 62–65, 68; political issues of, 86–91; support for, 59; U.S. dominance in, 120
Norway, 130
Novelli, Catherine, 94

OAS. *See* Organization of American States
Oil, 62
Oman, 147 149
Organization for Economic Cooperation
and Development (OECD), 34n15
Organization of American States (OAS),
143n3
Owen, David, 72

Papua New Guinea, 146
Party of European Socialists (PES), 79
Pease, Donald J. (D-OH), 69
Penalties and sanctions. *See* Enforcement
Perot, Ross, 62–63
PES. *See* Party of European Socialists
Petersen, Helveg, 112
Pevehouse, Jon, 44
Pinochet, Augusto, 125, 149
Pisani, Edgard, 134
Poland, 72
Policies and policymaking: agenda setting
and negotiations, 26–27; businesses and, 59; collective decision making, 20; domestic policymaking rules, 24–26; domestic politics and, 26–30, 48;

European policies and policymakers, 61, 70–82, 98–114; executive branch and legislatures, 26–28, 32, 36, 84; fair trade regulations, 14; human rights entrepreneurs and, 41; human rights policymakers, 61–83; human-rights-protecting trade agreements and, 14–15, 24, 25–26, 48, 86; NGOs and, 26; political factors in, 24, 25–26, 168, 172; preferential trade agreements and, 147–160; regulatory preferences and, 14; structure of domestic policymaking and, 15; US policies and policymakers, 61–70, 85–97
Policy dialogue, 134–135
Political issues: business role in policymaking, 59; domestic politics, 26–30; European trade policies, 70–83, 107–108; human and workers' rights, 2, 16, 20, 25, 44, 75, 82–83, 95, 172; international regulations and, 167–168; moral persuasion, 20, 22, 24, 25–26; NAFTA, 62–65, 66, 67, 86–91; power politics, 20–21, 25; preferential trade agreements, 16, 21, 24, 43, 91–93, 114, 166–168, 172, 174; protectionism, 62; repression, 5, 25, 35, 50, 144; trade, 5, 61–70; US trade policies, 61–70, 71. *See also* individual political parties
Portugal, 79, 113n45
Portugal v. Council (ECJ; 1996), 113
Power: agenda-setting and negotiation powers, 26–27, 32; of developing countries, 115–116; of executives and legislatures, 26–28, 32, 36, 84, 85–86; institutional design and change and, 13–14; market-power inequalities, 31–32; negotiating bullies, 141, 174; power politics, 20–21, 31–32, 141; power sharing, 28; relative economic power, 32, 36; trade policies and, 30–32, 36; U.S. power in rulemaking processes, 119–129
Preferential trade agreements (PTAs):
advanced industrial countries and, 140–141; categories of, 144–146; with democracies and dictatorships, 117; developing countries and, 15, 17, 35, 44–45, 141; changes in regulations, 49–52, 170; credible commitment and, 43–45, 46; economic issues of, 11, 16, 37–38, 170; effects of, 3, 6, 8–9, 35, 118, 142–164, 166, 172, 174; environmental issues of, 170; goals and growth in, 5–6, 165; human rights and, 4, 6, 8, 9, 16, 21,

Preferential (*cont.*)
  23, 25, 35, 39, 41–45, 60, 61, 64–65, 82,
    89, 96, 116, 117, 141, 144–145, 166, 172;
    internalization of externalities and, 37;
    NGOs and, 54–55; norms and moral
    advocates, 40–43, 45–46; policymaking
    and policy process of, 26–27, 61–83,
    147–160, 171–172; political issues and, 16,
    21, 24, 25, 43–44, 165, 170–172, 174;
    protectionism and, 37–40, 45; role of
    executives and legislatures in, 26–28, 84;
    soft and hard standards of, 145–146;
    specific agreements, 5n; trade policy
    outcomes, 24–47; trading partners' views
    of human rights in, 118–119. *See also*
    Lomé conventions; Regulations; Europe,
    fair trade agreements; North American
    Free Trade Agreement; United States,
    fair trade agreements
Preferential trade agreements (PTAs),
    European and US: European businesses
    and, 59–60; European policymakers and,
    61, 70–83, 98–114; US and European
    agreements, 10, 13, 16–17, 24, 39, 43,
    49–52, 102, 129, 165–166, 169, 171; US
    policymakers and, 61–70, 76, 83, 91–97,
    113, 147. *See also* Europe, specific trade
    agreements; United States, specific trade
    agreements
Presidents (US), 85–86, 87. *See also*
    Executive branch
Protectionism. *See* Trade issues
PTAs. *See* Preferential trade agreements

Rangel, Charles (D-NY), 70, 96
Reagan, Ronald, 62, 86, 89n7
Reagan (Ronald) administration, 61–62,
    87n
Regional organizations, 44. *See also*
    International organizations
Regulations: costs and adverse effects of, 23,
    35; changes in global trade regulations,
    1–3; development of, 11–14; effectiveness
    of, 5, 11, 35; enforcement of, 32–33, 35;
    institutions and, 26–30, 36; interests of
    policymakers and, 14; legislation and
    regulations, 49–52, 60; preferences and,
    25–26; repression and, 35, 50. *See also*
    Human and workers' rights; Labor issues
Reich, Robert, 64, 121, 122
Repression. *See* Political issues
Republican Party (US): human and
    workers' rights issues and, 66, 86–97;
    NAFTA and, 62, 86, 87, 89, 90, 91–92,

    120, 122; US-Australia Free Trade Agree-
    ment, 128; US-Chile Free Trade
    Agreement, 124. *See also* Political issues
Rowan, Brian, 169
Russia, 80–81
Rwanda, 143n4

Saby, Henri, 80
Salinas de Gortari, Carlos, 62, 120–121
Salinas de Gortari (Carlos) administration,
    120, 121, 122
SEA. *See* Single European Act
Seattle (WA), 10n12, 128
Security issues, 8, 76, 82–83, 109
September 11, 2001, 127
Serra, Jaime, 62
Sierra Leone, 133
Singapore, 90. *See also* United States,
    specific trade agreements
Single European Act (SEA; 1987), 73, 100,
    104, 130, 135–136
Slovakia, 151–152
Smoot-Hawley Tariff Act (US; 1930), 49
Social Democratic parties, 79
Socialist parties, 75, 78, 79, 80
Social justice, 167–168
Soulier, André, 140
Southern Common Market (Mercado
    Commún del Sur; MERCOSUR), 171
South Korea, 58
Sovereignty: human rights issues and, 43,
    78, 86, 119; labor standards of conduct
    and, 97; Lomé conventions and, 133, 134,
    136; NAFTA and, 122; political issues
    and, 120; US-Chile trade agreement and,
    126
Soviet Union, 49, 71
Sri Lanka, 146. *See also* Europe, specific
    trade agreements
State, Department of (US), 86, 149, 150–151
Sudan, 80–81
Sweden, 74, 79, 112, 130
Switzerland, 130

Tanner, John S. (D-TN), 96
TEU. *See* Treaty on the European Union
Thatcher, Margaret, 77
Thomas, William ("Bill"; R-CA), 96
Timelines, 179–180
Times Mirror Co., 56
Togo, 156–157
TPA. *See* Trade promotion authority
Trade Act (US; 1974), 49, 57n26, 85
Trade Act of 2002 (US): fast-track

procedures and, 124; human rights protections and, 9, 20–21, 52n14, 96–97, 114, 124, 125, 126, 127, 128, 147, 149, 150; political issues of, 95–96; PTAs under, 18
Trade and Tariffs Act (1974, 1984 amendment), 87
Trade issues: China, 173–174; free trade, 59, 60, 64; international trade, 39; most favored nation trading status, 64; negotiations of trade agreements, 28–29; protectionism, 11–12, 37–40, 59–60, 119, 128, 166, 170–171; rules of trade, 13; timelines of, 179–180; trade policy outcomes, 24–47, 170; trade standards, 21; US trade deficit, 69. See also Europe, fair trade agreements; Preferential trade agreements; United States, fair trade agreements
Trade promotion authority (TPA; 2002), 59, 60, 66, 67, 70
Treaty of Amsterdam (1997), 98
Treaty of Rome (1957), 98, 132
Treaty on the European Union (TEU; Maastricht Treaty; 1992), 76–77, 83, 109–110, 111, 112, 137, 151
Tsongas, Paul, 63
Turkey, 80–81, 152–
Turkmenistan, 146, 153n

UDHR. See Universal Declaration on Human Rights
Uganda, 72, 73, 78, 101–102, 103, 133. See also Europe, specific trade agreements
UK. See United Kingdom
UN. See United Nations
UNICE (Union of Industrial and Employers' Confederations of Europe). See Confederation of European Business
Unilateral preference schemes, 9n
Union of Industrial and Employers' Confederations of Europe (UNICE). See Confederation of European Business
Unitary Labor Central Union (Chile), 150
United Kingdom (UK), 56, 71, 73, 77, 101–103, 133
United Nations (UN): charter of, 53, 55, 103, 143, 145; Convention Against Torture, 143; Declaration on the Right to Development, 136; human rights regulations and, 43, 140, 162, 172; Iraq and, 126. See also Universal Declaration of Human Rights
United States (US): business issues in, 59; as a democracy, 17; foreign policies of,

49–50, 55; human and workers' rights and, 49–50, 82–83, 96, 141, 163–164; Iraq and, 126; labor unions in, 57; public support for human rights in, 55–56
United States, fair trade agreements: changes in, 1, 50; congressional and presidential responsibilities for, 85–86; with democracies and dictatorships, 117; economic issues of, 39; "fast track" authority and procedures, 85–86, 87–88, 90, 91, 94–95, 99, 120; human rights issues in, 1, 6–7, 39, 43, 82–83, 86–97, 163–164; labor unions and, 39; market share and, 16n14; policymaker preferences and, 61–70; policymaking procedures and, 85–97, 99; political issues in, 43; power in rulemaking processes, 119–129; preferential trade agreements of, 5, 16–17, 39, 43; regulatory focus of, 13; standards of conduct in, 8
United States, specific trade agreements (A–K): Australia, 1, 7, 127–129, 140, 145; Bahrain, 1, 7, 117; Canada, 1, 7, 50, 62, 86, 120nn4–5, 121, 145, 164; Chile, 1, 7, 59, 70, 124–127, 145, 149–151; Colombia, 7, 58, 117, 151n16, 170; Costa Rica, 7; Dominican Republic, 7; El Salvador, 7; Honduras, 7; Israel, 1, 50, 62, 64, 86, 92, 131; Jordan, 7, 9, 39, 52, 59, 60, 65, 92–95, 118, 125, 127n12, 145, 164; Kazakhstan, 39
United States, specific trade agreements (M–U): Malaysia, 7; Mexico, 7, 87, 120, 145, 164; Morocco, 1, 7, 59, 70, 117; Nicaragua, 7, 118; Oman, 7, 58, 70, 117, 146, 147–148, 150; Panama, 7; Peru, 7; Republic of Korea, 7; Singapore, 1, 7, 59, 70, 127n12, 145; South Africa, 7; South Korea, 58, 59; Swaziland, 7; Thailand, 7, 117; United Arab Emirates, 7. See also Free Trade Area of the Americas; North American Free Trade Agreement
United States Trade Representative (USTR), 62, 64, 93, 150. See also Hills, Carla
Universal Declaration of Human Rights (UDHR; UN; 1948), 53, 103, 134, 139, 140
Uruguay Trade Round, 61, 137
US. See United States
USBIC. See US Business and Industry Council
US Business and Industry Council (USBIC), 59n

US Chamber of Commerce, 59, 60
USCIB. *See* US Council for International
Business
US Council for International Business
(USCIB), 59, 60
USTR. *See* United States Trade Representative
Uzbekistan, 77

Vaile, Mark, 128
Val Duchesse process, 74
Vall, Ely Ould Mohamed, 154
van Agt, Andreas, 78
van den Broek, Hans, 75, 77, 112
van Miert, Karl, 80
Vanuatu, 146
Venezuela, 146
Veto power and players: Europe, 98, 99,
101, 104, 106, 107, 110n39, 112, 138; fair
trade policies and, 113, 114; United
States, 15, 84, 87, 88, 89, 90, 94
Vienna Convention on the Law of the
Treaties (1969), 110
Vienna Declaration and Program of Action
(UN; 1993), 10n12

Voting and voters: collective decision
making and, 20; in the European
Council, 99n19; regulations and, 24–25;
views of protection of human rights,
55–56; voting rules, 15
Vranitzky, Franz, 79

Washington Declaration (Jordan-Israel;
1994), 92
Western countries, 6n7, 8, 12. *See also*
individual countries
World Trade Organization (WTO): Bush,
George W. and, 95; Cotonou waiver
from, 7n9; creation of, 49, 61; developing
countries and, 21; European businesses
and, 59–60; European trade agreements
and, 58; human and workers' rights issues
and, 6, 21, 23, 78; PTAs and, 118; Seattle
(WA) 1999 meetings, 10n12, 128

Yandle, Bruce, 58–59
Yaoundé I and II (1963, 1969), 132
Yugoslavia, 76, 78, 82, 108, 111, 143n4

Zoellick, Robert B., 127, 128